T0301505

Managing Virtual Teams

Managing Virtual Teams

Silvester Ivanaj

Associate Professor, ICN Business School, Nancy–Metz and Member of CEREFIGE, France

Claire Bozon

Procurement Manager, Brasserie de Champigneulles, Nancy, France

Edward Elgar
PUBLISHING

Cheltenham, UK • Northampton, MA, USA

© Silvester Ivanaj and Claire Bozon 2016

All rights reserved. No part of this publication may be reproduced, stored in a retrieval system or transmitted in any form or by any means, electronic, mechanical or photocopying, recording, or otherwise without the prior permission of the publisher.

Published by
Edward Elgar Publishing Limited
The Lypiatts
15 Lansdown Road
Cheltenham
Glos GL50 2JA
UK

Edward Elgar Publishing, Inc.
William Pratt House
9 Dewey Court
Northampton
Massachusetts 01060
USA

A catalogue record for this book
is available from the British Library

Library of Congress Control Number: 2016938583

This book is available electronically in the **Elgar**online
Business subject collection
DOI 10.4337/9781785369278

ISBN 978 1 78536 926 1 (cased)
ISBN 978 1 78536 927 8 (eBook)

Typeset by Servis Filmsetting Ltd, Stockport, Cheshire

Printed and bound in Great Britain by
TJ International Ltd, Padstow, Cornwall

Contents

PART V   CASE STUDIES

Figures

Tables

Foreword

The rapid pace of globalization and the development of a variety of information and communication technologies (ICTs) have led to a proliferation of new organizational and work arrangements that seek to leverage the potential of resources, technologies, and talent from the far corners of the globe. Virtual teaming is an important component of these new work arrangements, and is now used by a majority of large organizations as well as by small- and medium-sized enterprises (SMEs).

Mature organizations use virtual teaming as a means to connect operations spread across distance and time zones. Small- and medium-sized enterprises are able to increase their reach through virtual teaming. Despite an increase in the prevalence of virtual teaming, there remains considerable uncertainty about how to make virtual teams work effectively and efficiently. Whereas the promise of virtual teams is great, they also create new challenges for employees, managers, and organizations, which can undermine their effectiveness. Indeed, organizations are often surprised by the complexity and nuances involved in managing virtual teams well. How can organizations leverage the benefits and mitigate the challenges of virtual teaming?

This book *Managing Virtual Teams* explores the critical elements that must be considered in managing virtual teams in organizations—from the structural, managerial, and process points of view. Based on solid research and encompassing a wide coverage of the research and managerial literature on virtual teams, the book provides an indepth look at the nature of virtual teams and the factors that enable their success. It lays out in clear detail the key characteristics of virtual teams and traces their emergence within organizations and the research literature. Delving into the critical inputs necessary for setting up virtual teams for success, the book elaborates on the organizational arrangements and team characteristics that facilitate the functioning and effectiveness of virtual teams. It further discusses key processes—socio-emotional, technological, and managerial—that must be actively managed within virtual teams.

Finally, the book examines key affective and performance outcomes in virtual teams, along with ways to assess and monitor them. Throughout, the authors illustrate their points with case studies and anecdotes of issues confronted by virtual team members and managers. Furthermore, they present compelling primary data on the scope of the literature on virtual teams along with the issues that the literature has highlighted.

Based on scholarly research and analysis of a wide range of managerial and organizational experiences *Managing Virtual Teams* makes a valuable contribution with clear practical guidelines—both to researchers interested in learning about virtual teams, and to managers and organizations dealing with the challenges of managing virtual teams.

Luis Martins
Austin McCombs School of Business, University of Texas, USA

Preface

When we had the chance to discuss matters with virtual team members or virtual team managers, very often we noticed that they miss some information on virtual team processes or underestimate its importance. Consequently, a feeling of frustration emerged rapidly when they have to work virtually. The idea of this book came from that observation and the wish to consolidate the theoretical knowledge on virtual team management along with practical recommendations to virtual team managers.

Our book differentiates from the prior books written on the topic by its methodology and the exhaustive bibliography dealing with virtual teams. Additionally, we complete each chapter with guidelines for managerial practice, easily usable by practitioners for a comprehensive understanding and affording concrete applications. We thus provide researchers, practitioners and any individual linked to virtual teaming with a comprehensive and updated global knowledge on virtual team management. We started writing the book a decade after Martins et al.'s, 2004: 'inputs/process/ outputs model'.

Based on that model, we augmented and improved the matrix by identifying the attributes of virtual teams (input), the essential factors to keep virtual teams functioning (processes) and the outcomes of those teams (outputs). The book suggests different ways to transform those factors into performing processes, which is longer and more complex to reach with virtual teams than with co-located teams. We went through two phases to gather our data. First, we scanned the research publications on the topic. Second, we considered prior books on virtual teams written by academics and practitioners. Only articles reviewed through double-blind-peer-review, and therefore recognized by the research community, were selected in the review of findings; thus considered as reliable. We used science mapping associated with the co-word analysis method to go through a series of conceptual or semantic maps called clusters. These clusters are generated by various statistical classification methods to analyse a set of selected words. These semantic maps are formed from classes or groups of words that have strong links to each other, and that may account for the cognitive structure of the field by indicating areas and subareas of research.

Research findings converge to the same conclusion: practising and working within a virtual team or within a virtual team network becomes more commonplace but it is not a spontaneous way of working. Virtual teams concern nearly all individuals working today, in a business context or not, with higher or lower levels of complexity and degrees of virtuality.

About two decades ago, virtual teams became an attractive domain for academic researchers who identified this new way of working as different from conventional team management mainly because of the distance dimension and new technologies. Technologies have been a key element in the research approach which has since moved to more complex inputs and mechanisms due to dispersion and distance.

Thanks to academic research, empirical studies and expanding practices, the different stakeholders increased their understanding and application of virtual team processes. As demonstrated in the book, virtual team leaders and their organizations need to analyse virtual team inputs and assess the virtuality of the team. Guidelines at the end of each chapter can be a helpful framework for virtual team analysis. This investigation helps the virtual team manager to determine the appropriate processes and the leadership style/s to be used, and more specifically the requested preparation and learning structures to achieve optimal, efficient virtual teaming. It involves various relevant factors, some perhaps less technical and more oriented to socio-emotional or managerial processes as well as performance management within a virtual context.

We note that virtual teaming as such continuously evolves which is one of virtuality's characteristics, thus requesting regular adaptation to the environments where it operates in order to fit in those environments, as well as to the concerned organization's strategy. Essential levers need to be identified to foster team and individual satisfaction recognized as key triggers to performance, especially difficult to set up and manage at distance. Thus, seen as efficient conveyors of performance, virtual teams have become the support of strategic orientations, and competitive advantages through cost reductions, work mobility or work distribution towards various international local opportunities, staffing and talent resources. Virtual teams and the global context enables the organization to find the right person with the requested critical knowledge and able to share it within a virtual environment, as long as the virtuality challenges are mastered within the organization.

However, generalization about virtual teaming is not possible due to the broad spectrum of diversities. For example, dealing with the younger generation and, therefore, with new characteristics and different expectations, differs from those conveyed by the conventional workforce. This possible gap may be stressed or caused by multicultural diversity, new opportunities and necessities. Research should consider changes in economies and see the influence of emerging countries, and the constraints on virtual team management. Would they bring new ways of working and thinking, together with unexpected new methods of management, opening the era of 'post-globalization'? How can emerging practices and already established methods match together in a constructive, productive and sustainable evolution? Technology development might partially answer this question. On a micro level, we can already see the evolution of contacts that become more and more distant or virtual. This is the case of service providers and customers, where companies try though to give a sense of 'reality' to virtual relationships. E-learning and massive open online courses (MOOC) enable students to join prestigious courses without being penalized by the requested high costs or travel distance. It gives access to a wider spectrum of students as long as they have adequate Internet connection capability and equipment. Virtual teaming seems likely to develop even more in the future and, therefore, the awareness of its processes and challenges can contribute to higher efficiency and satisfaction.

To present the theory and the key points (complete with guidelines for managerial practices) and render the book easily usable by practitioners requiring a comprehensive understanding and concrete applications, we have organized the book in to 11 core chapters, illustrative case studies and a comprehensive references section.

Professor Silvester Ivanaj and Claire Bozon

Acknowledgements—Part V, Chapter 12 Case studies

We would like to acknowledge the people who have been very helpful in illustrating the book with their written personal, concrete and professional experience in regards to virtual teams for our book's Part V Case studies. We warmly thank them for their contribution, time, application and enthusiasm.

Pierre Rosius, human resources director at Thomson Reuters, kindly agreed to share his experience of virtual teams. Thomson Reuters has implemented a new strategy and a new operating model in their Sales function. Pierre Rosius analyses the evolution of that organization and the impact of virtual teaming in an international context from a human resources point of view. He highlights the virtual teaming challenges and the consequences in Thomson Reuter's process.

Kim Poldner experienced an enthusiastic approach for virtual teaming through her online engagement in Eco Fashion World and a small dispersed team. Cultural differences, the difficulties to be 'all connected' whilst sharing a common goal at a distance, computer-mediated communication and the requisite team cohesion levels are some of the real barriers faced by Kim. She underlines the main considerations faced in a small virtual team, which is very instructive in comparison to larger international company structures.

Frederic Reiser realized as a virtual team member that virtual teaming requires adapted processes, especially when virtual teams are implemented together with organizational restructuring. Working process, new structure and adequate behaviours confronted with cultural diversity may foster unexpected results and may endanger the success of a strategy. Therefore, effective preparation for virtual teaming should not be underestimated.

Chloé Guerin Gosselin, a student in teaching history and geography, has chosen an e-learning programme offered by the University of Quebec at Trois-Rivières. Based on her experience, Chloé presents the advantages and challenges of virtual classrooms, virtual teamwork and online courses. She emphasizes that e-learning requires adapted behaviours and pedagogy techniques; in order to ensure effective and optimal teaching and learning outcomes.

Professor Silvester Ivanaj and Claire Bozon

PART I

What are virtual teams all about?

1 Evolutionary definition of virtual teams

1.1 INTRODUCTION

Relatively new literature mentions the concept of virtual teams or virtual management when they emerged around the 1990s. The notion of the concept linked to virtuality and virtual organizations might be interpreted in various forms. In order to clarify the definition of virtual teams, we review the existing academic definitions given to 'virtual teams'. One global definition for 'virtual team' has been suggested, even though there is not yet a widely accepted definition in the research community due to various interpretations of virtuality.

The definitions have evolved during the past two decades, from the initial focus of researchers on virtual teams up to wider consideration integrating today's knowledge and evolution of virtual teaming. Definitions started with gradual approaches to virtuality then began to include a deeper knowledge and understanding of the characteristics, the processes and the challenges arising from virtual teams. Researchers very often compared virtual teams to conventional teams. Then they looked for the differences that existed between virtual teams and co-located teams, and finally they introduced the specific-to-virtual-team dimensions. These dimensions combine the strategy, infrastructure, characteristics and management context of multinationals or any organizations operating in a virtual mode.

They have finally come to the notion of 'virtuality degree' characterizing a team and its level of dispersion which can be temporal, spatial, cultural or organizational. As research progresses, critical factors appear more clearly and can be identified and recognized. Therefore, a more standardized definition can be given.

1.2 WHAT DOES 'VIRTUAL' MEAN?

Virtual organizations, virtual teams, virtual work, virtual space . . . . A common definition explains that 'virtual' is related to something: 'having

the essence or the effect but not the appearance or the form of . . .'
(Dictionary, 2009); and 'not physically existing as such but made by software to appear to do so' (Dictionaries, 2012).

The word 'virtual' takes various meanings when attached to different
words. 'Virtual organization' describes disparate conditions for organizations that outsource key components of their production (Robert et al.,
1999). Related to teams and according to Jarvenpaa et al. (1998) 'virtual'
defines teams created with members issued from different locations to
solve problems. They have the appearance of teams but team members are
not operating physically in the same location. In parallel, 'virtual work'
determinates work done from home, from satellite offices, on the road, or
from hotels (Davenport and Pearlson, 1998).

These diverse descriptions refer to one common point: the close relationship of 'virtual' with distance and computer technology (Chudoba
et al., 2005). In the case of virtual teams, 'virtual' illustrates the way these
teams interact and highlights virtuality as one of the main team characteristics (Griffith and Neale, 2001). Martins and Schilpzand (2011), who
analysed the degree of virtuality within global virtual teams, introduce
the notion of 'team-ness, virtual-ness and global-ness'. The purpose of
these terms is to emphasize the evolution of the 'virtual team' definition
around key factors. These factors refer to the challenge in creating an
effective team mindset and efficient teamwork, while coping with distance
and diversity. They imply the introduction of technology. They also refer
to the importance of virtual team processes when defining a virtual team,
thus enlarging the focus on conventional team attributes towards virtuality
characteristics.

Semantics evolves too and becomes more precise. Virtual could be
replaced by 'digital'. However, the term 'digital' is reserved to a system
in which the information is recorded or sent out electronically, involving the creation of computer-based representations of physical phe-
nomena (Bailey et al., 2012). Digitization operates as a facilitator over
distance and separation between people. 'Digital' is more dedicated to
the equipment based on computer technology, such as digital camera
or digital boards for instance (Dictionary, 2000, 2012b; Dictionaries,
2012). Whereas, 'virtual' is mainly used for activities or organizations that
imitate their real equivalents and occur when physical objects, processes
and/or people operate through digitization. 'Digital team' is very rarely
used and we found this term almost nonexistent in research literature.
Consequently, we keep then the general term 'virtual team' to designate
the teams in question.

The designation of virtual activities or organizations is often preceded
by the letter 'e' or 'cyber' such as 'e-commerce', 'e-business', 'e-learning',

'e-team' or 'cyber space'. It points out the link between virtuality and the electronic technology again as these activities cannot be operated without the support of computers, software and the Internet. The evolution of the semantics and the vocabulary are still going on in the field of virtual teams which explains that the expressions are not yet totally concretely designated and may still change in the future according to the proper change of virtual teams and their context.

1.3 WHAT IS A TEAM?

In the research papers, the definition of a team very often refers to the one suggested by Katzenbach and Smith (1992). For them, a team is: 'a small group of people with complementary skills who are committed to a common purpose, performance goals and approach for which they hold themselves mutually accountable'. They differentiate the terms 'team' and 'group' because the sense of both terms differs in regards to the way that team and group operate. A group is a collection of individuals gathered for independent tasks that will be consolidated in a final outcome. A group may not constitute a team and does not focus on the coordination of its members at the same level as a team does. The authors point out the key components for an effective team, which include independent or interdependent tasks. A team includes team members, team organization and common objectives. Team members bring their individual competencies such as experience, skills and behaviour in order to contribute and develop the competencies of the whole team. Because they operate with a richness of diverse expertise, virtual teams are the appropriate way to deal with interdependent tasks within a complex context. The organization of the team might differ according to the context, activities, objectives, and management system within which the team functions. Teams can be functional or departmental, cross-functional, and self-managed or led by a manager. No matter the form of organization, the individual and mutual accountability with the team is one of the most critical elements to be considered for a virtual team. Accountability and membership are of great importance in the performance of the team. They also contribute to the synergy of the team and to the coordinated efforts towards common goals. They directly influence the process of a team in regards to the way the team members will work together.

1.4 A COMBINED DEFINITION FOR 'VIRTUAL TEAM'

1.4.1 Semantic and Evolutionary Context

Researchers are not all using the same term to identify virtual teams. It seems to depend on the dimension they consider. Either they refer to a group of individuals working together or to a whole entity set up in a more or less complex context. Therefore, various designations appear such as 'virtual group' or 'virtual organization' (Dubinskas and Hargreaves, 1993; Glückler and Schrott, 2007); 'cross-national teams' (Cogburn and Levinson, 2003); 'distributed working team', 'distributed work team' or 'dispersed team', 'geographically distributed teams' (Hinds and Mortensen, 2005); 'remote project teams' (Larbi and Springfield, 2004); 'distributed remote teamwork' (Davidson, 2013); 'cross-cultural virtual team' (Anawati and Craig, 2006; Breitenöder, 2009); 'global virtual team' (Martins and Schilpzand, 2011); 'corporate' or 'global corporate virtual team' (Grosse, 2010); 'far-flung' teams (Watson-Manheim et al., 2012); 'e-teams', 'cyber teams' or 'online teams' (DuFrene and Lehman, 2010); and 'nomadic teams' (Ko et al., 2011). The most frequent name that appears in academic literature is 'global virtual teams' according to Connaughton and Shuffler (2007). The terms frequently associated to virtual teams are 'transnational', 'cross-cultural', 'multicultural', 'intercultural' and 'multinational'. In addition, a rather new expression has emerged to designate the work operated under virtual conditions such as 'virtual teaming'. Among scholars, 'virtuality' or 'virtual-ness' (Martins et al., 2004) has also become a rather common term to describe the virtual context and all the connected characteristics of that context. The definitions of virtual teams have evolved along with the researchers' investigations and their findings which have become more and more focused on the concept. The first definitions mainly addressed the concept of virtual teams in contrast to conventional and co-located or traditional face-to-face teams. Team members of co-located teams work in close proximity, geographical, temporal or cultural. Therefore, they easily use informal communication to interact, more specifically for daily interaction and usual visual cues. Most of the time, they are located in the same place, and share common practices and processes. A virtual team is 'an evolutionary form of a network organization' (Miles and Snow, 1986). It is a group of people who can be separated by space, time, and organizations, and work closely together supported by information and communication technologies (ICTs) (Davidow and Malone, 1992; Jarvenpaa and Ives, 1994; Johnson et al., 2001; Martins and Schilpzand, 2011). Mohrman

(1999) defines virtual teams as 'groups of individuals in different location or business units or companies', 'located in two or more countries' (Martins and Schilpzand, 2011). This definition concerns 'global virtual teams' because virtual team members do not need to be separated by a great distance. They could work in the same building but belong to different divisions of the same corporation and share common activities operated in a virtual team. Usually, this type of virtual team tends to be a cross-functional team, gathering various experts for a common goal. Virtual team members are identified as those 'who share the accountability of a product, service or collective functions or tasks, interdependent in carrying out their accountabilities and thus must work collaboratively to accomplish them' (Mohrman, 1999). Virtual teams are commonly defined as work teams that are 'created, simulated, or carried on by means of a computer or computer network' (Dictionary, 2000). Information and communication technologies are always associated to 'virtual teams'. The community of researchers recognizes that technology is one of the major enablers and drivers of these types of teams. Today, the existence of pure face-to-face teams is rare due to the invasive presence of technology within the business environment. The support of technology aims to increase team productivity, access to information and communication (Arnison and Miller, 2002). 'Virtual teams are teams whose members use technology to varying degrees in working across locational, temporal, and relational boundaries to accomplish an interdependent task' (Martins et al., 2004). The definitions include the idea of a team members' network supported by ICTs for interdependent tasks (Edwards and Wilson, 2004). The definitions then took into account the notion of dispersion, accountability, and collaboration (Dubé and Paré, 2001). Virtual teams are described as an essential element in companies' internal and external environments; dealing with different time zones supported by computer-mediated communication. As the understanding of virtual teams becomes more precise, critical issues linked to diversity boundaries and interdependent tasks were addressed. It led researchers to identify virtual teams as 'global virtual teams' in the same way the business environment evolves into a global context. In our book, we retain 'virtual team' or 'global virtual team' with no difference, even though global virtual team suggests a broader virtual environment, where team members are working from different international locations, including different management chains and possibly from different organizations. According to this notion, diverse types of formations close to virtual teams have been identified and can be grouped up to organizational virtuality (Hertel et al., 2005; Dubé and Paré, 2001) but remain slightly different from virtual team in regards to the retained definition in our work:

● *Telework or telecommuting teams:* members complete their own tasks partially outside the main organization location and work from home most of the time. The terms were introduced in 1975 by Nilles, where telecommunications replace transportation to the office.
● *Virtual work groups:* different tasks and teleworkers that report to the same manager are combined.
● *Virtual teams:* members are gathered and interact thanks to technology and ICTs. They share common interests, accountability and goals.
● *Virtual communities:* larger entities of distributed work where members interact via the Internet, share also common interests and goals, but they are not committed to an organizational structure, and are usually implemented by one of their members.

1.4.2   Specific Dimensions to Define Virtual Teams

Some researchers such as Shin (2004) argue that organizations present different levels of virtuality based on four dimensions: temporal, spatial, cultural, and organizational dispersion. O'Leary and Cummings (2007) considered the same dimensions but also introduced, however, the notion of 'degree dispersion' in regards to those four dimensions. The more dispersed the team is, the more complex and virtual it is. They distinguished spatial distance and purely geographical distance with cultural or linguistic distance, known as social distance.

For Kirkman and Mathieu (2005) virtuality indicates the sharing of virtual tools or the dependence on such tools which are needed for the virtual team processes, 'the amount of informational value provided by such tools, and the synchronicity of team member virtual interaction'. Gibson and Gibbs (2006) call it 'electronic dependence' but also add the notion of 'structural dynamism' in reference to frequent changes. Chudoba et al. (2005) widen the mentioned dimension and include work practices as a part of virtual team diversity. As a matter of fact, the work practices may greatly vary within a virtual team, depending on its input characteristics. Chudoba et al. (2005) propose a series of indexes to measure the level of virtuality of a team, based on the concept of discontinuities or changes in expected conditions negatively affecting team cohesion. The discontinuities refer to the dimensions, quoted previously, grouped into team distribution (*distance*), workplace mobility (*dispersion*) and the variety of work practices (*complexity*), partially or totally interrelated. For example, they suggest the following ratios to assess the geographical distance: share of work at home during standard working days, share of work while travelling, share of collaboration with people located in various sites, share of collaboration with people who have been met face-to-face. It is relevant to be able to assess or measure the virtuality of the concerned teams because the level of virtuality directly affects the typology of these teams, as well as their processes and consequently, their performance. Chudoba et al. (2005) point out some examples of index used to estimate virtuality. For example, virtuality at a corporate level may be measured according to the proposed training programmes and best practice recommendations in regards to virtual teaming. At the organizational level, the degree of virtuality may be assessed by the investments assumed by an organization in collaboration with the tools to support virtual teaming (computers and various equipment), communication tools (video conferencing, the Internet, and intranet), additional software (group support systems) and training for specific skills. Recent findings take into account three dimensions to assess the virtuality of a team or its virtual distance results, as mentioned by Schweitzer and Duxbury (2010). The first one is the share of time spent by team members working virtually, named 'teamwork virtuality'. Virtual teams whose members work full-time in a virtual mode do not demonstrate the same level of virtuality of those virtual teams whose members work only from time-to-time in such a mode. The second dimension is the share of members within a team who work virtually, in contrast to those who are working co-located. The virtual team management differs if all the virtual team members work in virtual mode as compared to only a few of them working in virtual mode. This dimension is called 'member virtuality' by Schweitzer and Duxbury. The third dimension is the degree of virtual distance between the team members, also known as 'distance virtuality', which includes social distance and possible subdimension such as psychological distance (Wilson et al., 2013).

One additional subdimension could be taken into consideration. The fact that virtual team members frequently belong to several different virtual teams today intensifies the complexity of virtuality, because these virtual team members have to participate in various virtual contexts in a reduced timeframe (Chudoba et al., 2005). The impact of distance on the virtual team boundaries is very different if the virtual team members belong to the same country and culture as compared to being disseminated across continents. The virtual distance comprises the physical, the operational or the daily issues that disturb the virtual team members. It also includes the affinity distance between virtual team members. Affinity distance is the degree to which virtual team members share cultural values, communication style, work practices and social capital (Lojeski and Reilly, 2008). At this level, it is critical to consider that distance and virtuality

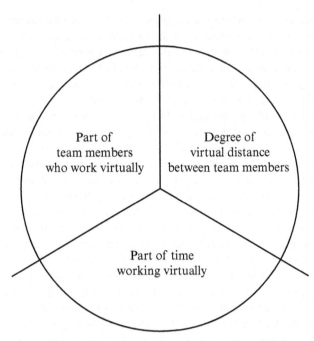

Adapted from Schweitzer and Duxbury (2010)

Figure 1.1   Dimensions that define the virtuality of a work team

alter perception of virtual team members, including oneself (Wilson et al., 2013). Therefore, the dimensions of virtuality no longer focus on the degree of technological means like it did at the emergence of virtual teams. Technology is (or should be) adapted to the virtual team complexity like the degree of virtual team members' cultural dispersion, the duration of the virtual team and the type of interaction, whether synchronous or asynchronous (Jawadi and Boukef Charki, 2011). The levels of complexity introduce the idea of a graduation from a pure traditional face-to-face team to a global virtual team. The further the gradation from a face-to-face team, the more virtual the team is, taking into account that virtual teams are evolving, based on a continuum and that some areas of coexistence of both face-to-face and virtual teams exist (Dixon and Panteli, 2010). It means that research evolves and considers virtual teams on a larger spectrum, which affects the way virtual teamwork might be addressed by organizations. The cursor position shows the possible degree of virtuality for a work team (see Figure 1.2).

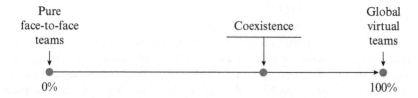

Figure 1.2   Degree of virtuality in virtual teams

1.5   KEEP IN MIND: THE MAIN ELEMENTS TO DEFINE A VIRTUAL TEAM

The definition of the terms 'virtual' and 'team' contributes to the understanding of what a virtual team is. Virtual teams gather members separated by one or more forms of distance thus influencing behaviours and characteristics that alter the group processes (Wilson et al., 2013).

- The key points to be addressed in the virtual team definition are virtual distance which includes time, space and organizational boundaries, global dispersion, degree of virtuality and webs of technology to collaborate and communicate. These critical elements shape the complexity of a virtual team and affect its functioning and performance.
- A virtual team is determinate by its degree of virtuality. Virtuality level depends on the share of time spent for virtual work, the share of team members working virtually, and the degree of virtual distance between the team members.
- The degree of virtuality affects the complexity of the virtual team and, therefore, its effectiveness. The effectiveness of a virtual team directly depends on the capacity of the individuals within the virtual team to work together toward common goals, to develop and reach performance outcomes, and to remain mutually accountable. Collaboration and coordination appear to be essential in the definition of virtual team, especially because the degree of dispersion is high and so is reliance on technologies.

The above points illustrate the reason why the definition of a virtual team evolves with time, according to the global context. Therefore, a virtual team can no longer be definitively defined in contrast to a face-to-face team.

1.6   CONCLUSION

The dichotomy between a face-to-face and a virtual team is no longer mentioned as often as it used to be in the early phase of research on virtual teams. To date, the definition of 'virtual team' as based on semantics is more explicit. We could not find any widely accepted definition of virtual teams within the academic research due to the evolution of virtual teaming. The researchers' conclusions admit that the definition goes beyond semantics and involves more elements and dimensions, such as virtuality. The assessment of virtuality in relation to virtual team or virtual teaming seems vague and difficult to evaluate and measure. However, virtuality is one of the most efficient ways to indicate the specific characteristics of virtual teams. Virtuality creates the complexity of virtual teams and has a great implication on their operating processes and outcomes. The topic is gaining prominence in academic literature.

Based on current research results, the notion and concept evoked in the global definition of virtual teams contribute determining the typology that characterizes a virtual team. Inputs, processes and outputs of virtual teams are detailed in this book to assist in understanding how virtual teams operate. We link them to the involved dimensions that affect the typology of a virtual team, the work practices, the organization and the technology. The next chapter focuses on inputs that are essential to identity and differentiate virtual teams, especially for individuals directly involved in virtual teams either as a leader or as a member.

1.7   GUIDELINES FOR MANAGERIAL PRACTICE: ASSESS THE VIRTUALITY OF YOUR VIRTUAL TEAM

One critical factor for a virtual team manager is to estimate the level of complexity and virtuality of the team to be managed. In virtual team management, complexity is defined by all elements that connect the team with dispersion along with the team composition and its processes within an organization. The share of virtual processes in the team indicates the level of virtuality, which partly increases or decreases the level of complexity of the team. Therefore, the way the team can be managed is directly impacted. The virtual team management also depends on the type of technological support dedicated to the concerned team, which is important to list in order to figure out the situation. A clear situation enables the manager to complete the necessary technical equipment when the support does not

Table 1.1   Assess the virtuality of your virtual team

Key actions	Key results
Dispersion List all factors creating distance in your team:	For example, list the:
– geographical – temporal – cultural – linguistic – social – psychological – organizational	– countries involved – different time zones – various cultures – team language – internal stakeholders – external stakeholders – hierarchical links – possible organizational change
Virtuality List all factors creating distance in your team and assess:	Percentage (%) and numbers:
– the share of time that team members spend in virtual working – the number of team members working virtually – the degree of the virtual distance between team members (e.g. affinity or psychological distance among members) *as per* the dispersion degree listed above	High Medium Low
Technology List your resources:	Available Unavailable (but necessary)
– communication tools (postal, video conference, Internet, etc.) – equipment (computer, mobile, etc.) – specific software (ERP, workflow, etc.)	
Mention separately the missing additional resources	

match the virtual characteristics of the team. The guidelines invite the virtual team manager to identify the level of complexity and virtuality of the team.

2   Emergence of virtual teams

2.1   INTRODUCTION

First, it is important to clarify how and why virtual teams appeared in the global environment because they were framed within a historical and contextual evolution. Second, it is important to define what 'globalization' means in the business context and look at the consequences of globalization in regards to virtual teamwork. Globalization implies a new approach and appropriate strategies for companies whose objectives focus on finding new solutions to compete with an increasingly demanding global market. In reaction to this evolution, a virtual environment has emerged and it has moved traditional teamwork to a more or less high virtual teamwork, supported by the development of new technologies in an ever faster context. Simultaneously with the virtual environment development, new tools and solutions have emerged and so new boundaries have emerged too. Companies' infrastructure and processes are directly affected by the evolution of the global context and they have to take into account new economic models. Within organizations, there is an implied need for new proficiencies and capabilities to integrate the advances in technologies supporting a constant rise in flow of information and new means of communication. Integration assumes processes, technology and human management adaptation. Human resources appear to be an area of high concern because individual contribution may lead to more or less successful performance. Individuals that hold the position of virtual team member or virtual team manager are pushed to integrate the virtual environment which includes adaptation, flexibility and understanding of virtuality. The change led by globalization has to meet the evolution of individual satisfaction too. The purpose is to answer the requests of organizations that are involved in virtuality at low and high levels while supporting them to reach the required agility to move efficiently across diversity while managing people accordingly.

2.2 GLOBALIZATION THROUGH HISTORY

Through 'globalization' we understand interactions, interconnectivity, interdependence and synergies between countries across the world. Those interactions were first closer to the notion of a world-system, a concept developed by Wallerstein (1974), referring to the international division of labour. This division split the world into core countries, semiperiphery countries and the periphery countries. Wallerstein tried to demonstrate the complexity of the economic networks and relationships within 'one modern world-system', whose origin took place already in the sixteenth century. The term 'globalization' can only be used after the seventeenth century which is the watershed between the phase of connected economies and the phase of globalization. This period saw a remarkable growth in Europe, even though the early stages of global economy did not start in Western countries according to Norel (2009). Progress in knowledge, skills, technologies and innovations has expanded long-distance trade to reach other parts of the globe. Land, work and capital were key factors in the growth of globalization and the evolution of these factors included flows of ideas, cultures, people and services. 'Globalization' is a term more widely used during the 1960s. The 1970s marked the end of the after-world-war economic expansion period for industrial countries. Companies were mainly concerned about how to capture the benefits of economies of scale. The 1990s launched a new approach to customers who desired customized and innovative products. This period experienced a transition from mass production to mass customization, leading to the development of service/information-oriented companies (Johnson et al., 2001). Innovation and quick execution became key factors. The hypercompetitiveness of companies caused them to be faced with severe challenges, which pushed them to engage a new orientation through total quality policy and analysis of processes. 'Globalization' achieved an utmost spike in the twenty-first century through technological advances, deregulation and disintegration of traditional industry boundaries (Harvey and Griffith, 2007). In the 2000s, companies had been focusing on their high added-value core business. They spread their production units throughout the world. The purpose was to be closer to the needed resources and to strengthen the relationships with local customers, thus accessing the global market. The production fragmentation breaks the traditional vertical-organization model of those firms. It is gradually being replaced by the model of a 'hub-firm' (Weinstein, 2011). The 'hub-firm' is based on a model where a leading firm operates as the core organization. Some specialized units are coordinated accordingly and they can be independent or dependent on the leading firm, much like subcontractors. Based on the aforementioned, we propose to understand 'globalization' as the process or the system of interactions by which regional economies, societies and cultures become bridged all over the world. This interrelation occurs through a global network of political ideas, technological, economic and cultural connectivity supported by the advances in technologies, communications, transportation and infrastructure, thus opening a wide scope for diversity.

2.3 EMERGENCE OF VIRTUAL TEAMS: ONE OF THE CONSEQUENCES OF GLOBALIZATION

2.3.1 New Approach and Corporate Strategy

The globalization of the industrial and economical work environment has led to a global framework. Along with the economic expansion, the business environment witnesses more fusions and take-overs along with more redundancies or 'human re-localization'. Companies are encouraged by a growing global competition, a need for downsizing, reduced costs and shortened product development lifecycle due to an increased velocity in time-to-market. The need for specialized expertise to complete a product or service has to be found where it is located and no longer where the company is founded. Therefore, corporations and organizations that operate through multinational connections are expanding and using more and more virtual connections. This contributed to virtual team growth. Corporate strategies are implemented and supported by different forms of international assignments such as traditional expatriation, international commuting, or more recent forms like frequent flyers, or virtual assignments. Some companies deploy outsourcing to a certain degree, especially in services and more specifically in IT services, e.g. data processing, computer programming and technical support (Brooks, 2006) than in accounting, human resources, internal mail distribution. Outsourcing, or offshoring, was not identified as a business strategy until 1989 (Mullin, 1996) but became a major driver in the 2000s for internationalization. Supported by technological advances, ICTs, cloud computing, software applications, the approach has changed over the past five years, leading to a more extended virtual way of working (Rosenberg and Kumar, 2011). This is one of the reasons why, pushed by cost reduction and a shortage of people ready for longer-term international assignments, firms reduce international assignments. As a matter of fact, international assignments appeared to be more limited in a geographical and national context. They declined in favour of more flexible alternatives for global staffing, e.g. virtual teams (Scullion and Collings, 2006). Virtual teams have the flexibility to act locally while sticking to the continuity of a global strategy without being stuck in static corporate structures. However, some global firms use other forms such as strategic alliances, joint ventures, formalized co-marketing relationships (Harvey and Griffith, 2007). Strategic positioning and responsible values shared by the corporation can also be reasons for virtual team development. 'Green thinking', derived from sustainable development policies and striving for pollution reduction, pushes companies to go in the direction of higher virtuality, as their selected operational functioning manner. The new economic approach appears to support competitive advantage. Locations are no longer a barrier to competitiveness, except for specific cases concerning some agricultural products or high-technology products. For example, Silicon Valley has developed in clusters as mentioned by Porter (2008), where innovation and research, education and high technology production are concentrated in one place. In the new economic approach, globalization introduces physical discontinuities, interrupted information flows (Lu et al., 2006), transfer of technology among countries and a rapid growth of knowledge-intensive economies (Harvey and Griffith, 2007). Companies' organizational structures need to adapt to leverage knowledge, products, and activities according to dispersion (Mohrman, 1999), which influences the companies' way of working. Adaptation requires new work proficiencies and the ability to understand globalization and deal with it, such as the capacity to create 'virtual continuities' (Dixon and Panteli, 2010) even though paradoxes emerge like virtuality versus physical presence, flexibility versus norming structures, interdependent tasks versus independent teammates and mistrust versus trust (Dubé and Robey, 2009).

2.3.2 Emergence of Virtual Teamwork

One of the consequences of strategic expansions is the development of teamwork. Work is significantly performed by teams because organizations, both public and private, saw an opportunity to produce more ideas, improve process understanding, increase motivation, and performance from an individual to a group level, and support more innovative and risk-taking decision-making (Stough et al., 2000). Teamwork became a crucial factor to productivity and a possible way to increase employee satisfaction. Initially, teamwork was based on traditional face-to-face interactions but it has moved to virtual teamwork. Virtual teams appeared to be one of the answers to the demand of the global market but were not methodically planned (Boutellier et al., 1998; Bergiel et al., 2006). They changed the nature of teamwork and provided the companies with more 'flexibility, responsiveness, lower costs and improved resource utilization' (Jarvenpaa and Leidner, 1999). Based on Trzcielinski and Wypych-Zoltowska's (2008) mathematical model, virtual teams seem financially more profitable than face-to-face teams when we consider the share of team members involved in virtual teaming and the concerned geographical dispersion. The costs of transport, travelling, accommodation and business expenses are the elements mainly taken into consideration in that model. However, organizational adaptation and coordination might be more expensive than expected, which requests deeper analysis, not yet found in the literature, but which is partly explained by the complexity of precise calculation possibilities. Virtual teams also facilitate the organization to adapt to their way of functioning towards global networks and from vertical to horizontal structures. Instead of being grouped into functional activities that usually complete sequential tasks, repeated in many different locations (vertical organization), organizations frequently joined diverse 'lateral' expertise from different departments, organizations or locations to perform the team activities (horizontal organization). Horizontal structure thus offers higher flexibility in the process. It groups the necessary expertise to perform the tasks and the virtual team members of such structure do not depend on hierarchical authority but on dispersed responsibility across various silos (Mohrman, 1999). Therefore, the managerial process and team leadership evolved too, as explained later in the book. Consequently, companies have the possibility of achieving competitive advantages, and attaining access to world-class capabilities (which implied work structure reconfiguration regarding the localization of teams). Tasks are shared by global virtual team members from their home country and are not relocated in a host base as expatriates could be. The implementations of virtual teams, although they are not the solution for every organization, enables organizations to keep the dispersed groups connected. Basically, four main reasons are often mentioned for the implementation of virtual teams as revealed by studies (Barczak and McDonough, 2003). This enumeration is not a result of specific or intentional order but for informative purposes. One of the reasons is the need for product development, or 'time-based competition' for product launches in each market (Harvey and Griffith, 2007) with the objective to develop global products to be sold in more than one country with reduced customization. Global virtual teams ensure that new product introduction in various countries and continents, prices, services and technical supports are coordinated according to the marketing and sales strategy. They contribute to the capability of following the rapid pace of globalization, thus reducing physical, cultural, and psychological distance. The second reason to implement virtual teams is to be closer to local customers, and to be able to give responses to the unique needs or specific requirements of local markets. Members of virtual teams can identify and convey different needs, whether these are global or local. Their contribution may be one way to develop complementary strategies. The third reason is that virtual teams give access to a wider range of expertise dispersed across the world. Virtual teams are one factor that reduces expatriations and international assignments in favour of an increased balance between work and private life for individuals. The extended pool of experts improves the human resources utilization to meet market demands. These experts are not necessarily employed by the companies but they are used as external resources and are, therefore, not added on to the payroll (Henry and Hartzler, 1997). This point explains the relevance given to human resources in such a context. Finally, the fourth reason concerns companies that strive for cost reduction (e.g. labour costs, logistical costs, raw material costs etc.) wherever new locations enable them to gain benefits from local favourable regulation, practices, and geographical advantages. Sometimes, this can even be a lack of regulation. The 'green thinking' and sustainable development could be an additional incentive behind the virtual team momentum, even though they are not yet clearly identified as such by researchers. Most companies consider more than one reason to develop virtual teams, as mentioned by Pandey and Sharma (2011) who designed these companies as 'prospectors', oriented to market-product innovation to reach competitive differentiation.

2.3.3 New Technologies: a Fundamental Driving Force

Since the 1980s, the growth and development of technologies has led to a wide range of technical innovations such as telephone, fax, Internet, electronic and web-based techniques. Technologies development officially started at the end of the twentieth century. It aims at making the systems more collaborative and distributed (Li and Qiu, 2006). It also creates opportunities for restructuring the traditional way of working to benefit from international competitive advantages, regardless of location, culture and language. Technologies offer high-quality, low-cost and rapid solutions to meet the complex global demand. 'Teaming electronically', or working in cyberspace supported by technologies, has created a new aspect of the team concept, moving traditional, or face-to-face teams to virtual teams (Hagen, 1999; Sarker and Sahay, 2003). Technological advances enable the virtual team members to share their work with distant colleagues and work closely with suppliers, manufacturing partners and customers. This dynamic is reinforced by the development of the Internet, giving worldwide access to the e-world (evolving from Web 1.0 to Web 2.0 technology). Information and communication technologies (ICTs) also improve and impact the economic and social sides by supporting companies' globalization and technical progress (Montel-Dumont, 2009). In less than 20 years of progression, ICTs can be considered as universal and ubiquitous in an industrial world that is moving towards a digital world. They contributed to the change of the work environment, its organization, pace and way to communicate, which is accentuated by the strong push of virtual technologies' developers. However, a digital gap exists in terms of accessibility between the most developed countries and the least developed. The implemented technology is not always compatible among some countries and the speed of information transfer can greatly vary. Thus, technological differences create disparities in access to information (Morris and McManus, 2002). Today, ICTs are part of the enterprise culture and bring a differential value to the organizations that can embed the use of ICTs in their structure. Globalization and integration are 'shrinking the world from a size medium to a size small' (Friedman, 2005), a phenomenon that has intensified since the recent economic crisis. The ICTs are shaping the relationships inside and outside of companies. More global virtual teams emerge in order to sufficiently reach performance and meet targets in a fast changing environment. Geographically distant and time desynchronized, virtual team members are more unlikely to meet face-to-face. Therefore, they need to organize themselves; and use new tools and processes, as well as an approach suitable for distant co-workers. The members have to remain a team with a common language, very often English. Technology pushes the systems to improve performance in order to support virtuality and collaborative teamwork, such as groupware. Groupware appears to create a common base between the virtual team members and the virtual environment, and is especially relevant for the more complex tasks requesting a higher level of information-sharing and collaboration supported by technologies. Groupware's contribution makes 'virtual co-location' possible (Olson and Olson, 2000).

2.4   IMPLICATION ON HUMAN RESOURCES

2.4.1   Considering Individuals as Virtual Team Members

The success of globalization went beyond technological advances. It created new opportunities to integrate human, organizational, cultural and social aspects through virtual teams. Virtual teams are part of the evolution of the organizational structure in companies aiming for quicker decision-making and higher capitalization on human resources skills, information and knowledge sharing (Brewer, 2008a). Building social relations, referred to as 'social capital' by Lipnack (1997) appears to be an essential factor. The work reconfiguration means implications for people and organizational structure, such as moving from co-located teams to dispersed ones, with few opportunities, if any, to meet face-to-face. Establishing relationships seems more difficult and less spontaneous than in traditional teams, but productivity strategy includes employees' satisfaction through innovative ways, for example, team networking, team-based strategic planning, and flexible job scheduling. In addition, the assessment and response to work, as well as affective satisfaction, look rather complex to set up in a virtual context. Employees or virtual team members do not need to travel or be relocated to participate in a global project (Arnison and Miller, 2002) which introduces a response to some pressures in a better balance between work and family life (Coat and Favier, 2000; Levina and Vaast, 2008). Team dispersion also brings some social advantages, such as job creation in areas with high unemployment rates or integration of persons with low mobility due to health or family reasons (Scullion and Collings, 2006; Amant and Zemliansky, 2008). The switch to virtual teams assumes that virtual team members are aware of the clear objectives for the team with precise roles and tasks for each member, adapted to the structure tackling the e-world. Some organizations attempt to create new individual and collective reflexes in order to develop the adequate competencies towards virtuality. However, all individuals and virtual team members may not have the capacity to work within a virtual context. The development of competencies allows the organization to embrace a virtual culture within its structure (Lipnack, 1997) to implement changes successfully. It particularly affects some types of activities where interactions between persons are important, such as design activities (Pawar and Sharifi, 1997).

2.4.2 Considering Individuals as Virtual Team Leaders

Individuals in the position of virtual team members are affected but individuals in the position of virtual team leaders are affected as both an individual and a leader. Virtual team leaders have the task of keeping a dispersed team functioning, addressing concepts not yet preponderant in team management and more critical for virtual teams. Globalization requires that virtual team leaders understand and incorporate the economic environment, especially time linked to competition that enables organizations to differentiate from one another. It is composed of a worldwide system of constraints, events and options occurring simultaneously (Arnison and Miller, 2002; Harvey and Griffith, 2007). Virtual team managers lead a global workforce that is dispersed through worldwide operations across national boundaries and have to drive the ad hoc processes to keep the team motivated (Stough et al., 2000). As pointed out by Montel-Dumont (2009) there is 'no leadership without membership'. Virtual team managers need to lead virtual teams to the expected performance, while facing unusual managerial situations such as coordinating experts that are not always directly employed by their own organization. Virtual team leaders need to align their competencies, knowledge and processes accordingly. When existent, theories about virtual team leadership most frequently study components such as trust building, social interaction etc. (Schiller and Mandviwalla, 2007). It has been determined that distance and team dispersion does in fact affect team performance and team leadership. Reasoning behind this determination is the need for the implementation of an effective communication (Smith and Blanck, 2002) for coordination, trust building, and collaboration to cope with the possible feeling of isolation, or even frustration, between virtual team members that may generate conflicts. It implies that virtual team managers are able to 'establish mutual knowledge and manage [a] geographically dispersed social network' (Ramasubbu et al., 2005). Virtual team leadership presumes proactive behaviour, along with teamworkers' collective ease with technologies and virtuality. For these reasons, global staffing policies and strategies are incorporating virtualness as a critical factor for human resources.

2.4.3 Considering the Management of Human Resources

Competitive advantages of companies emanate out of competencies specific to these companies, giving them the possibility to develop, retain, and implement values and strategies. These companies establish complex social relationships, embedded in a firm's history and culture (Harvey and Griffith, 2007). Competencies emerge from individuals and groups of individuals, along with the company's culture. The human resource management (HRM) of a company is one of the central means to explore, harness, value, manage and develop the competencies of individuals and groups of individuals. Human resource management emerged in the 1980s, resulting from an evolution of the human resources function. It evolved from personnel management to HRM and finally to international HRM (IHRM) in order to support a global staffing demand, in addition to the team distribution evolution. Virtual teams offer 'new' human resources to companies that can expand rapidly without taxing present global managerial skills while using broader human, social, political and cross-cultural capitals (Barczak and McDonough, 2003; Harvey et al., 2005). International human resource management incorporates further concepts focused on competencies, which leads to a rethinking of the function (Germain, 2011). Today, IHRM deals with 'Talent Management' or 'People Development Management' and is considered as a 'Business Partner'. This real strategic partner serves organizations' strategic control of global resources, dealing with change management, in addition to the administrative and daily human resource management. Human resources policies and processes have to harmonize their own practices in order to satisfy organizational strategy and performance-based planning in a virtual context. Virtually-based organizations bring together human resources quicker than a single-based location and face all boundaries linked to diversity. In regards to virtuality, IHRM may contribute to the development of virtual-team-specific competencies with the objective to sustain the competitive advantage, which is often underestimated. Due to the emergence of new activities, IHRM has to work on the unification of inshore and offshore sites. It results in a change in the unit of analysis, moving from national boundaries and individual sites to emergent practices oriented to a globally distributed and collaborative work, talent sourcing and knowledge development (Newell et al., 2007). Global tools are used as a support, e.g. enterprise resource management (ERM) software, because virtual teams have to reach the targeted team performance.

2.5 KEEP IN MIND: GLOBALIZATION, A RACE TO INNOVATION WHERE VIRTUAL TEAMS MAKE THE DIFFERENCE

- The concept of globalization is derived from a long historical evolution and the concept of a world-system for the contemporary synergies existing among countries across continents. It is supported by innovation in various areas but more specifically in technologies and communication.
- Globalization leads organizations into a world with new realities that encompass mergers and acquisitions, emerging markets, outsourcing and offshoring with interorganizational alliances and towards a real competitive advantage.
- Virtual teams are the result of new orientations undertaken by organizations to cope with the virtuality imposed by globalization. The momentum of virtuality has pushed people, structures and systems to deploy new proficiencies, and adequate behaviours by taking into account the broader human, social, economical, political and cross-cultural resources.
- Human resource management has evolved towards emergent practices oriented to a widely distributed and collaborative work, talent sourcing and knowledge development supported by global tools. This approach supports innovative practices and ideas from collaborative work without physical or personal restrictions. It opens the door to a wider range of inclusions such as diverse profiles and talents.

2.6   CONCLUSION

From this chapter, we understand that some factors are essential for the functioning of virtual teams. First, the context in which the virtual team developed is worthy of consideration, and it is important for the organizations to be aware of the advantages and disadvantages they may gain from virtual teams within a certain economic and cultural network context. The major acquisitions gained from virtuality are the access to global markets within shortened timescales, the identification of unique local needs, and the capitalization on dispersed resources and distributed talents. Virtual teams are one of the means by which the organizations integrate in their infrastructure to sustain competitive advantages. It requires constant adaptation from both the companies and the individuals, which leads to a second factor to be taken into account: the combination of technology, new behaviours and adapted managerial leadership. Therefore, the typology of virtual teams, their specific processes and their impacts on organizations and individuals are worthy of investigation due to a more complex set of constraints and processes. The complexity linked to the virtual network implies that the virtual team managers and virtual team members have to understand virtuality constraints in order to be able to adopt the appropriate attitudes, acquire new proficiencies, and reach team performance outcomes. International human resource management is particularly involved in the process because some specific skills prevail. Human resource management needs to develop competencies in the area of social relationships and communication, trust building, coordination in a multicultural environment, as well as technology acceptance. It is necessary for any person or structure involved in virtual teaming to have a clear picture of the attributes relating to virtual teams. The related knowledge enables to one to: select, develop and/or set up the appropriate type of behaviour or management and process, which will be clarified later in the book. The main reason is that they challenge the traditional attachment that people have to their work organization and mindset.

2.7   GUIDELINES FOR MANAGERIAL PRACTICE: ELABORATE THE STRATEGY FOR YOUR TEAM AND ITS OBJECTIVES

Once the degree of complexity and virtuality of the concerned virtual team is defined, it is useful to capture the reasons why virtual teaming is requested in the organization. When clarifying what strategy, organization and policy exists, it gives direction to the management of that team.

Thus, it enables the virtual team manager to implement the necessary managerial processes adapted to that team and the global organization objectives more clearly. Basically, the guidelines below provide the virtual team manager with the tools to identify the team strategy and objectives in cohesive reference to the corporate direction.

Table 2.1 Team strategy and objectives

Key actions	Key results
Corporate strategy	
Map the corporate changes leading to virtual teamwork	Merger, acquisition, outsourcing etc.
List the main points of the corporate strategy:	
– vision	
– mission	
– values	
Instill that strategy in to your sector with:	
– mission	
– objective	
– target	
Corporate organization	
Map:	
– the corporate organization	
– your own organization/sector within that corporate organization	
Highlight the impact of changes:	
– in your own organization	
– for the former team members	
– for the new comers in your team	
– in the team activities	
– in your way of working	
Identify the major stakeholders and their functional links to your team (other virtual teams, suppliers etc.)	
Human Resources	
List the key factors that contribute to your organizational competitive advantages:	
– new talent and competencies	
– acquisition of new knowledge	
– the innovative practices	
– impact on your cost policy	
List specific needs:	
– training	

Table 2.1 (continued)

Key actions	Key results
Human Resources – specific competencies – adapted behaviours – type of leadership Identify your HR partner(s) in the global company	

3 Mapping the virtual team research field

3.1 INTRODUCTION

A classic literature review, allows analysing only a limited number of articles which gives a partial view of the field of research. Many questions arise then: how to deal then with thousands of papers? What are the main themes of the research field? What are the paths and the dynamics of its development? This chapter presents the intellectual mapping of the virtual team research field using a scientometric technique able to treat data retrieved from scientific databases. We first explain how we collect data from various reliable sources, academic research and prior books on virtual teams, written by academics and practitioners, then we detail the successive steps based on the method of co-word analysis (COA) which consists of building clusters issued from diverse statistical classification methods that scan a selection of keywords.

Co-word analysis has been successfully used by a number of authors to explore the evolution of several scientific fields, including ecology (Neff and Corley, 2009); robotics (Lee and Jeong, 2008); information security (Lee, 2008); economics (Cahlik, 2000; Cahlik and Jirina, 2006); polymer chemistry (Callon et al., 1991); software engineering (Coulter et al., 1998); information retrieval (Ding et al., 2001); biotechnology (Rodriguez et al., 2007); and fuel cells (Hassan, 2005). When the clusters are set up, the system goes through their contents and establishes relationships with the field of virtual teams. A strategic diagram can then be created. Interactions between clusters are measured on the base of centrality and density of their content, which gives clues to read the strategic map. The map indicates the relevance of the topic in relation to the field of virtual teams and the level of discussion or analysis lead by the research community. The cluster analysis and the strategic map enable us to identify and classify the major topics that are linked to the field of virtual teams. We organize these key elements in the book, based on the model developed by Martins et al. (2004): input, processes, output. We enrich this structure by the relevant findings or models issued from research and discuss them. Our approach proposes updates and thoughts covering the field of virtual teams on a wide spectrum and underlines the topics that still need to be deeply studied by research.

3.2 METHODOLOGY

To map the intellectual structure of a scientific domain, various bibliometric analyses must be employed. Co-citation analysis and COA are often considered as the most representative methods among those techniques (Neff and Corley, 2009). Co-citation analysis leads to interesting results but it can introduce some well-known bias: 'citations must be highly skewed since only a few papers receive many citations, and many papers receive few citations. The amount of citations a paper received depends on the future, whereas a reference list of backward citations is fixed. There is also a bias for younger documents that have accumulated fewer citations than older documents' (Larsen and Levine, 2005). In contrast, co-word analysis has the potential of addressing precisely this issue. The method 'reduces and projects the data into a specific visual representation with the maintenance of essential information contained in the data' (Ding et al., 2001). Co-word analysis provides an immediate picture of the actual content of the research topics dealing with the literature based in the nature of words, 'which are the important carrier of scientific concepts, idea and knowledge' (Ding et al., 2001). The COA technique is for visualizing the structure of a research area through 'conceptual' or 'semantic' maps called 'clusters', which are generated using a classification method to analyse a set of selected words from different documents (typically research papers) (Callon et al., 1991). The method enables the structuring of data at different levels (Coulter et al., 1998): (1) as clusters composed by 'nodes' (words representing scientific concepts) and 'links' (connections between nodes); (2) as distributions of interacting clusters; and (3) as the transformation of clusters over time periods. To obtain and interpret these clusters, COA uses four main steps: collection and preparation of data; construction of maps or clusters; construction of strategic diagrams; and analysis of the interaction between clusters. The first step in our analysis was the selection of scientific literature that best represents the research area in focus. We identified the terminology used in the field of virtual teams, which is drawn from both our experience and the most relevant papers on virtual teams published in the recent year (Jarvenpaa and Leidner, 1999; Polzer et al., 2006; Montoya-Weiss et al., 2001; Griffith and Neale, 2001; O'Leary and Cummings, 2007; Hambley et al., 2007; Martins et al., 2004). We built a query with the most relevant keywords dealing with virtual teams to search databases: virtual teams,

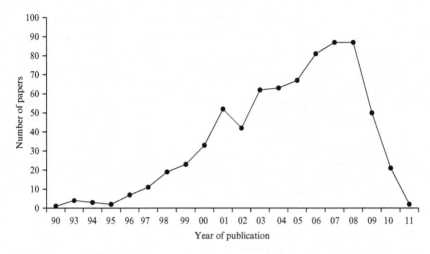

*Figure 3.1   Evolution of number of papers published over the years
                1990–2011*

distributed collaborative work, global team, virtual group, virtual teaming, virtual teamwork, distributed teams, dispersed teams, virtual work teams and virtual teamwork. We used the main sources available for the search of academic papers: EBSCOhost (Academic Search Complete, Business Source Complete, EconLit, Information Science & Technology Abstracts (ISTA), PsycARTICLES, PsycINFO, Science & Technology Collection, and Sociological Collection) and ProQuest Search.

We only extracted articles from scholarly journals whose title or abstract contained at least one of the keywords mentioned above. Those articles are reviewed using a double-blind review process and, are therefore recognized by the research community as reliable. Next, we proceeded in reading all of the abstracts of papers that pertained to virtual teams. Of those papers, 717 were finally retained and grouped in a database. Figure 3.1 shows the evolution of the number of papers published over the years (1990–2011).

As Figure 3.1 demonstrates, since 1990 the number of academic articles published on virtual teams has steadily continued to increase, except for 2002. Contrary to the left part of the curve, the decrease of publications by 2008 is artificial. It is due to the fact that the database includes items that are sometimes considered years after their publication. These articles were then retrieved from the database and placed into a central file containing the following pieces of information: title, abstract, author(s), journal, year of publication, and author keywords. Papers have been published by more than 300 different journals. Table 3.1 shows the top 20 journals

Table 3.1   Top 20 journals having published the most on virtual teams

	Journal name	Nb.	Per cent	Cum.
1	*IEEE Transactions on Professional Communication*	22	3.07%	3.07
2	*Communications of the ACM*	18	2.51%	5.58
3	*Team Performance Management*	18	2.51%	8.09
4	*Small Group Research*	16	2.23%	10.32
5	*Information Systems Journal*	13	1.82%	12.14
6	*Organization Science*	12	1.68%	13.82
7	*Information Technology and People*	10	1.40%	15.22
8	*Journal of Management Information Systems*	10	1.40%	16.62
9	*MIS Quarterly*	10	1.40%	18.02
10	*Organizational Dynamics*	10	1.40%	19.42
11	*Information and Management*	9	1.26%	20.68
12	*Information Resources Management Journal*	9	1.26%	21.94
13	*Journal of Product Innovation Management*	9	1.26%	23.20
14	*Group Decision and Negotiation*	8	1.12%	24.32
15	*Information Systems Management*	8	1.12%	25.44
16	*Research Technology Management*	8	1.12%	26.56
17	*Academy of Management Executive*	7	0.98%	27.54
18	*Business Communication Quarterly*	7	0.98%	28.52
19	*International Journal of e-Collaboration*	7	0.98%	29.50
20	*Software Process: Improvement and Practice*	7	0.98%	30.48
	Total	218	30.48%	

that published the most in this field. Bibliographic data was subsequently transferred into a web application driven by the Microsoft SQL database.

The most important components of COA are the words themselves, which we will refer to as 'nodes' from here on. In our study, we used words extracted from the titles and abstracts of articles. These words were selected in two stages. First, a list of unique words was extracted from the titles and abstracts in the database. This list is established by the totality of the words contained in both the titles and abstracts of articles. Second, a process referred to as semantic cleaning, based on the nature of the words and on their utility for our analysis, is used. For instance, articles, prepositions, conjunctions and common-sense words called a stop word list were removed because their significance to the field is very general. These constituents bring nothing useful in terms of content analysis in the field. This yielded a list of 6326 different unique words. However, a list in this raw form is unusable. Some words are synonyms, while other concepts have ambiguous meanings that depend on the context of use. Thus, a standardization process based on our expertise and aided by a thesaurus was manually performed. The synonyms were grouped together and their occurrence[1] was cumulatively tallied. After being manually validated by only selecting from the list concepts we considered having significance for research analysis: a final list was created containing the unique words used for further processing. Table 3.2 shows the occurrences of the most frequent unique words in the whole set of papers.

The next important step of COA is the construction of 'maps' or 'clusters' (Callon et al., 1986, 1991). These clusters construct relations between the nodes by identifying subgroups of words that are strongly associated with each other. The strength of the link between the co-occurring words that constitute a cluster is measured by an association index. Many types of association indexes have been used by researchers, including the 'cosine index' (Salton and McGill, 1983); the 'equivalence index' (Callon et al., 1986); the 'inclusion index' (Callon et al., 1986); the Jaccard coefficient (Coulter et al., 1995; Sternitzke and Bergmann, 2009); and the Pearson correlation (Ding et al., 2001). In our study, we used the 'equivalence index', which measures the strength of the association between two words nominated as 'i' and 'j' and that of every pair of words nominated as 'ij', storing it in a two-dimensional (2D) matrix of co-occurrences. This matrix is built by cross-referencing every word retained for analysis with the other words. The formula for calculating this index is:

$$E_{ij} = \frac{C_{ij}^2}{C_i C_j}$$

Where C_{ij} is the number of times (papers) that the words 'i' and 'j' co-occur. C_i and C_j represent the number of respective occurrences of the words 'i' and the words 'j' (Callon et al., 1991; Coulter et al., 1998; Sternitzke and Bergmann, 2009; Neff and Corley, 2009). Researchers who used an equivalence index (Callon et al., 1991; Coulter et al., 1998; Neff and Corley, 2009) have often mentioned the 'inclusion index' as another option; this index is the conditional probability that a document containing the word 'i' will also contain the word 'j' (Callon et al., 1991; Coulter et al., 1998; Neff and Corley, 2009) and it is calculated by the equation:

$$I_{ij} = \frac{C_{ij}}{\min(C_i C_j)}$$

Due to its non-symmetrical nature, the inclusion index tends to highlight central concepts rather than areas that are surrounded by concepts that occur

Table 3.2 Most frequently used singular words

Concept	Occ.	Concept	Occ.	Concept	Occ.	Concept	Occ.	Concept	Occ.	Concept	Occ.	Concept	Occ.
team	665	interaction	114	frame	72	coordination	43	community	25	workforce	16	configuration	8
work	448	implication	112	literature	71	mail	43	diversity	25	telecommunication	16	cohesiveness	8
study	295	manager	110	difference	71	discussion	42	degree	24	membership	16	instant	8
member	290	ability	110	setting	71	training	41	commitment	24	assessment	16	intelligence	8
communication	267	relationship	110	goal	70	site	39	sense	24	adoption	16	establishment	8
effect	261	product	107	decision	69	force	38	norm	23	definition	15	gender	8
organization	257	context	105	influence	67	market	37	presence	23	interface	15	personality	8
technology	255	data	102	leadership	65	measure	37	asynchronous	23	laboratory	15	output	8
research	250	level	99	framework	64	advantage	37	cooperation	23	feedback	14	workflow	8
process	219	leader	98	behaviour	62	satisfaction	37	emergence	23	economy	14	player	7
global	214	company	95	value	61	web	37	difficulty	23	adaptation	14	separation	7
group	209	concept	94	potential	61	nature	36	distribution	23	usage	14	heterogeneity	7
formation	208	factor	94	people	60	plan	35	innovation	23	selection	14	memory	7
development	207	method	93	distance	60	program	35	groupware	21	pressure	13	efficacy	7
age	205	practice	93	culture	58	effort	35	corporation	21	composition	13	disadvantages	7
project	203	trust	93	internet	58	country	35	productivity	21	construction	13	lifecycle	6

Word	n	Word	n	Word	n	Word	n	Word	n	Word	n	Word	n
information	189	problem	92	outcome	57	education	34	workplace	21	generation	13	hierarchy	6
action	181	structure	90	network	57	life	33	reality	20	partnership	12	richness	6
support	175	media	90	meeting	56	dimension	32	motivation	20	mind	11	monitoring	5
performance	166	analysis	90	strategy	56	mechanism	31	cycle	20	commerce	11	structuration	5
face	161	experience	88	experiment	53	pattern	31	conference	20	alliance	10	venture	5
time	159	theory	85	firm	52	worker	31	enterprise	19	health	10	wisdom	5
system	158	learning	83	boundary	51	barrier	30	limitation	19	facilitator	10	loafing	5
form	149	team work	81	space	51	complexity	29	medium	19	workspace	10	consensus	5
environment	148	effectiveness	80	participant	51	language	28	style	19	paradigm	9	dissemination	4
management	145	computer	79	resource	51	integration	28	cognition	18	school	9	trustworthiness	4
relation	142	tool	78	quality	50	idea	28	cohesion	17	teamworking	9	continuum	3
design	136	software	78	field	49	partner	28	dispersion	17	interdependence	9	adjournment	3
task	133	location	77	skill	47	multinational	27	creation	17	acceptance	9	miscommunication	3
success	130	activity	74	user	46	size	25	identification	17	collocation	9	abstraction	2
knowledge	120	student	74	implementation	45	evaluation	25	virtuality	17	conceptualization	9	synchronicity	2
collaboration	116	world	72	conflict	44	exchange	25	zone	17	contract	9		

less frequently (Callon et al., 1986; Coulter et al., 1998). This index is best suited for research areas organized in a hierarchical fashion i.e. where several concepts are placed on a higher level, encompassing all or almost all other concepts found on lower levels (Callon et al., 1986; Neff and Corley, 2009). For the most part, concepts in the technology and innovation field are not organized in a hierarchical fashion; instead, the field is composed of areas and sub-areas that are part of a larger group. This is why we selected the equivalence index. This index allows an equal chance of emergence to clusters with frequent concepts and to those with less frequent concepts (Callon et al., 1991) by normalizing the frequency of occurrence for each word within the cluster. Consequently, we are able to identify both the central areas and the newly emerging areas, along with their subcategories in the field (Neff and Corley, 2009). The equivalence index must overemphasize words that are used less frequently, but we can counterbalance these negative effects by 'exploring the prevalence and dynamics of both common and uncommon words in greater detail' (Neff and Corley, 2009, p.9).

After the association index has been chosen, the next phase in the analysis of word co-occurrence is cluster generation. To generate the clusters, we used a classification algorithm developed largely by a French team from the Center for the Sociology of Innovation (Ecole des Mines de Paris) whose pioneering work was published in the study *Mapping of the dynamics of science and technology* (Callon et al., 1986). This method was also used by a team of American researchers from the Software Engineering Institute (Carnegie Mellon University) and their work gave rise to other founding papers (Coulter et al., 1995, 1996, 1998). We initially generated a single cluster using the most linked unique words.

Figure 3.2 shows this cluster. The diameter of the circles shows the occurrence whereas the thickness of the line joining the words indicates the strength of their link (E_{ij}). It is evident that most occurring words (in descending order) are: 'team', 'organization', 'communication', 'member', 'technology', 'relationship', 'process', 'development', and so on. Regarding the strength of the links between words, the most linked words seem to be: 'team–member', 'team–communication', 'team–technology', 'team–organization', 'team–relationship', 'technology–communication', 'team–performance', etc. The vast number of words strongly linked to the word 'Team' is a good indicator of the main preoccupations when dealing with virtual teams.

Although unique words give a rough idea of what is important, in most cases they are part of compound concepts. In regards to our dataset, the unique word 'leadership' in reality is combined with many other words to give compound concepts such 'virtual team leadership', 'leadership style', 'leadership theory', 'leadership behaviour', 'leadership emergence',

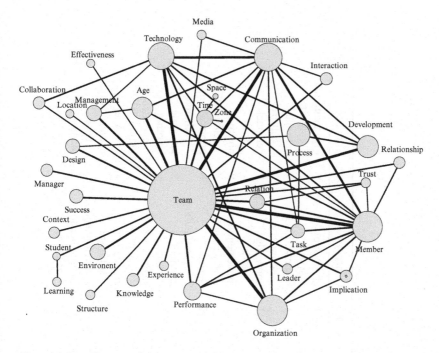

Figure 3.2   Cluster of unique words

'leadership role', 'leadership challenges', 'effective leadership', 'forms of leadership', 'leadership development', 'leadership skills', 'leadership functions', 'remote leadership', 'effects of leadership' and 'styles of leadership'. Similarly, the word 'performance' gives the following expressions: 'virtual team performance', 'task performance', 'levels of performance', 'organizational performance', 'creative performance', 'performance measure', 'performance outcome', 'product performance', 'project performance', 'individual performance', 'member performance', 'perceived team performance' and 'conventional team performance'. Compound concepts could be seen as a topic of our research field and are much more specific and comprehensive than unique words. For these reasons, we used an algorithm developed by one of the authors to extract all of the possible combinations of unique words to obtain compounds of two to five words (viz. bigrams, trigrams, quadrigrams and pentagrams) and then we computed their occurrences. The meanings of ambiguous compound concepts were checked by going directly to the text of the titles and abstracts. A final list of 850 compound concepts, of which 811 occur at least two times, is obtained. Table 3.3 shows the most frequently used compound concepts in the corpus of documents.

Table 3.3 Frequently used compound concepts

Concept	Occ.	Concept	Occ.	Concept	Occ.	Concept	Occ.	Concept	Occ.
virtual team	474	work team	18	software engineering	11	group support system	9	organizational context	7
dispersed team member	209	collaborative technology	17	social interaction	11	organizational boundary	9	national culture	7
distributed team	170	distributed work	17	time space	11	knowledge work	9	personal trust	7
global virtual team	98	collocated team	16	virtual team project	11	implementation of virtual team	9	positive relationship	7
virtual team performance	69	decision making	16	virtual setting	11	shared understanding	8	information exchange	7
communication technology	65	team building	16	virtual team structure	11	group of people	8	key issue	7
information technology	52	time zone	16	work environment	11	engineering design	8	learning	7
venture team	51	virtual collaboration	15	development of trust	11	distributed software development	8	experience	6
virtual teamwork	47	virtual team meeting	15	dispersed collaboration	11	communication medium	8	knowledge worker	6
team work	43	virtual team development	15	group decision	11			manage virtual team	6
software development	39	distributed software	15					managerial implication	6
		face interaction	15						
		project manager	15						

Term	Frequency
virtual teamworking	38
product development	36
project team	36
virtual team leader	35
team working	31
virtual team effectiveness	29
information system	28
team interaction	27
virtual team process	26
software development process	26
virtual work process	26
collaborative work	23
support system	21
virtual communication	21
project management	14
product development	14
team	14
dispersed location	14
communication media	14
virtual project team	14
work process	14
team environment	14
software development project	11
team project	10
virtual team success	10
virtual team management	10
human resource	11
information sharing	10
knowledge transfer	10
organizational structure	10
global market	10
global software	10
effective communication	10
decision support system	10
work group	10
virtual meeting	10
team problem solving	10
student virtual team	10
team face	9
business environment	8
virtual team experience	8
virtual context	8
type of team	8
traditional team	8
technology support	8
software development team	8
software team formation	7
team design	7
training program	7
team manager	7
team outcome	7
virtual team interaction	7
interdisciplinary team	6
internet technology	6
organizational team	6
organizational change	6
online learning	6
project task	6
product design	6
project leader	6
social influence	6
global economy	6
global environment	6
group decision support system	6
distributed collaborative work	6
distributed development	6

Table 3.3 (continued)

Concept	Occ.	Concept	Occ.	Concept	Occ.	Concept	Occ.	Concept	Occ.
design method	21	competitive advantage	13	team cohesion	9	virtual team composition	7	cognitive process	6
knowledge management	21	effective virtual team	13	team trust	9	virtual team context	7	asynchronous computer communication	6
knowledge sharing	21	group support system	13	virtual team leadership	9	work publication	7	process	6
team collaboration	20	management system	13	virtual team work	9	building trust	7	collaborative tool	6
virtual environment	19	concurrent engineering	12	cultural diversity	9	electronic media	7	communication system	6
virtual organization	19	cultural difference	12	development process	9	effective leader	7	conflict management	6
virtual project	19	team leadership	12	design team	9	global organization	7	concept of virtual team	6
multinational organization	19	team communication	12	communication tool	9	geographic distance	7	coordination	6
				grounded theory	9	project team member	7	problem	6

The next step is the construction of clusters from compound concepts, which is accomplished using two stages, Pass-1 and Pass-2. We invite the reader to read Coulter et al. (1996) for details on the construction of clusters. In total, 56 clusters were obtained for the entire period. Table 3.4 explains the list of generated clusters and their characteristics.

After generating the clusters using compound concepts, we analysed the content of the clusters to determine their nature and their contribution to the construction and development of the field. Figure 3.3 shows the composition of the cluster named 'Virtual teams'. It is evident that the topics the most related to 'Virtual teams' are 'Team membership', 'Boundaries space–time', 'Team performance', and 'Information and communication technologies'.

Similarly, Figure 3.4 shows the composition of the cluster named 'Team trust'.

In this case, clusters are then generally characterized based on both indexes: 'centrality' and 'density' (Callon et al., 1991; Coulter et al., 1998; Neff and Corley, 2009). Centrality measures the strength of the external links between the nodes in the given clusters and those in other clusters. The stronger and more numerous the external links, the more central is the research area represented by the cluster to the development of the field. Density represents the strength with which the nodes in a cluster are linked to each other via internal links. Density, thus measures the level of coherence and the development of a research area within itself (Cahlik, 2000). To measure density, we used the index of Callon (Callon et al., 1991) which measures the density of a cluster by the average value of the equivalence index of the internal links (strengths of the internal links, i.e. links between cluster members).

To measure centrality, we used the method employed in Coulter et al. (1998) i.e. the square root of the sum of the squared indexes of equivalence of all external links in a cluster (links from cluster members to nodes contained in other clusters). The values calculated for the density and centrality of each cluster were then used to construct a graph, known as a 'strategic diagram' (Callon et al., 1991) which positions the clusters in a two-dimensional Cartesian plane.

Figure 3.5 shows the strategic diagram of clusters. The cluster 'Virtual team' is not represented in this figure because both its density and centrality are significantly higher than that of other clusters.

The strategic diagram indicates the morphology of the field and classifies the clusters into four categories according to their position in one of the four following quadrants of the graph (Callon et al., 1991, pp.166–167). Type 1 clusters: 'central and well-developed' (high centrality, high density). As Figure 3.5 shows, topics such 'trust', 'leadership',

Table 3.4 List of generated clusters

#	Cluster name	No. of concepts	No. of links	Complexity	Percentage conn.
1	Team Performance—Style	11	20	1.818	0.364%
2	Cultural diversity	17	18	1.059	0.132%
3	Commitment	13	19	1.462	0.244%
4	Conflict management	14	18	1.286	0.198%
5	Venture team	14	16	1.143	0.176%
6	Personal relationship	14	20	1.429	0.220%
7	Team project	11	17	1.546	0.309%
8	Project management	12	20	1.667	0.303%
9	Conflict management—Satisfaction	8	20	2.500	0.714%
10	Software development	14	18	1.286	0.198%
11	Team leadership	10	19	1.900	0.422%
12	Trust	13	20	1.539	0.256%
13	Team support system	12	20	1.667	0.303%
14	Team communication	16	19	1.188	0.158%
15	Information system development	11	18	1.636	0.327%
16	Communication systems	14	20	1.429	0.220%
17	Communication media	14	17	1.214	0.187%
18	Team cohesiveness—Organizational structure	15	19	1.267	0.181%
19	Software development—Time/Zone difference	15	18	1.200	0.171%
20	Team media	5	7	1.400	0.700%
21	Virtual work	15	18	1.200	0.171%
22	Team implementation	10	18	1.800	0.400%
23	Distributed work team	14	17	1.214	0.187%
24	Distributed software development	11	19	1.727	0.346%
25	Decision making—Social loafing	13	20	1.539	0.256%
26	Team boundary—Team heterogeneity	17	18	1.059	0.132%

27	Product design team	11	20	1.818	0.364%
28	Product development team	12	20	1.667	0.303%
29	Mutual knowledge	5	6	1.200	0.600%
30	Team leadership	14	17	1.214	0.187%
31	Team design	8	11	1.375	0.393%
32	Team interaction	15	18	1.200	0.171%
33	Social identity	7	9	1.286	0.429%
34	Collaborative work	16	17	1.063	0.142%
35	Team building—ICT	15	17	1.133	0.162%
36	Online learning	9	17	1.889	0.472%
37	Knowledge sharing	17	18	1.059	0.132%
38	Team alliance	8	9	1.125	0.321%
39	Team experience	7	8	1.143	0.381%
40	Discussion board	5	6	1.200	0.600%
41	Team cohesion—Leadership style	18	17	0.944	0.111%
42	Team knowledge	6	7	1.167	0.467%
43	Cultural difference—Organizational boundary	15	17	1.133	0.162%
44	ICT—Virtual organization	15	17	1.133	0.162%
45	Team collaboration	15	17	1.133	0.162%
46	Social presence—Team size	7	9	1.286	0.429%
47	Problem solving	5	6	1.200	0.600%
48	Team formation	6	8	1.333	0.533%
49	Team environment	12	13	1.083	0.197%
50	Collocated team	13	14	1.077	0.180%
51	Virtual team context	10	12	1.200	0.267%
52	Management system	11	12	1.091	0.218%
53	Team trust	10	11	1.100	0.244%
54	Competitive advantage	15	16	1.067	0.152%
55	Building trust	7	9	1.286	0.429%
56	Virtual team meeting	10	11	1.100	0.244%

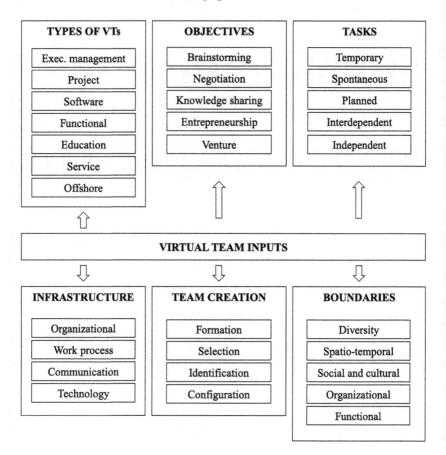

Figure 3.3   Cluster: 'Virtual teams'

'communication systems', 'knowledge sharing', 'team collaboration', 'design process', and 'implementation' are research areas that are well developed, and are also very important to the intellectual structure of the field. These topics form the core of basic ideas, definitions and concepts of the field and their positioning is strategic and foundational. They have been addressed over a long period of time by a considerable number of researchers. Type 2 clusters are 'central and poorly developed' (high centrality, low density). Topics such as 'multinational organizations', 'team effectiveness', 'conflict management' and 'virtual organizations' represent areas that have an important contribution to the field but have not yet been well-developed. These areas may include research questions that are becoming more central but have not yet been investigated by many

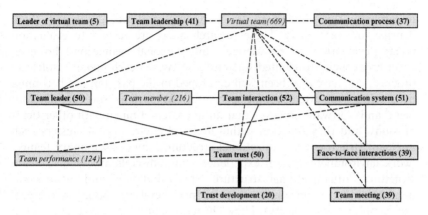

Figure 3.4   Cluster: 'Team trust'

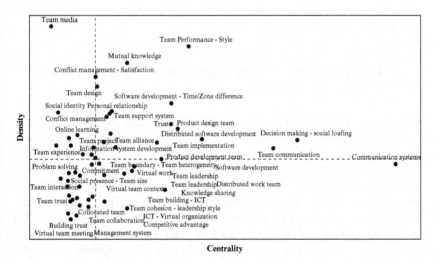

Figure 3.5   Strategic diagram

researchers. Type 3 clusters are 'peripheral and well-developed' (high density, low centrality). These research areas are related to evaluation issues ('evaluation of knowledge', 'interpersonal evaluation') however, other areas such 'distributed software', 'software development', 'software process', etc. have also been well developed in the past but are becoming peripheral. They often become specializations (such as 'software development' and 'software process') that do not interact much with other fields of study, and they function within a closed circle. Type 4 clusters such as 'team structure', 'organizational structure', 'multidisciplinary teams', 'work environment', 'team experience', 'multidisciplinary teams', 'team structure', 'organizational structure', 'team building' and 'team communication' represent studies that are 'peripheral and poorly developed' (low centrality, low density). These clusters encompass areas that are both peripheral to the central paradigm of the field and less well-developed. Based on the above information, we extract the major items related to virtual teams and classify them in typology groups based on the input/process/output model created by Martins et al. (2004). After this point, we update and develop the 'Virtual teams' typology and processes' model according to the below classification. Further key factors are to be added according to the recent research findings.

3.3   REVIEW OF THE PRIOR BOOKS WRITTEN ON VIRTUAL TEAMS

We also looked at books dealing with virtual teams. Many books have been listed on Internet bookseller lists. They have been organized into two categories: books written in a methodological academic style and books whose style has to be 'accessible' by a larger audience. The authors who target a larger audience are very often consultants or professional practitioners. They use their own managerial experiences to explain virtual team processes and propose practical advice, tips or guidance. We retain the authors of academic analysis who are mainly researchers of university faculties. The reason is that they focus on specific questions or hypotheses about virtual teams and establish some theories or new models based on studies whose results are demonstrated and approved by the research community. Their findings can then be applied by practitioners. The main topics addressed by the academic research within those existing books are the following: trust building and collaboration, process performance, learning and knowledge sharing, leadership in virtual teams, creativity in virtual teams, virtual team building and functioning, and ICTs.

Trust building and collaboration:
Beyerlein, M., Beyerlein, S., Bradley, L. and Nemiro, J. E. 2008. *The handbook of high performance virtual teams: A toolkit for collaborating across boundaries.* San Francisco: Jossey-Bass Publishing, Inc.
Kock, N. 2009. *Virtual team leadership and collaborative engineering advancements: Contemporary issues and implications (advances in e-collaboration).* Hershey: Information Science Reference.
Fong, M. W. L. 2005. *E-collaborations and virtual organizations.* Hershey: IRM Press.
Lipnack, J. and Stamps, J. 2000. *Virtual teams: People working across boundaries with technology.* New York: John Wiley & Sons.
Guilherme, M., Glaser, E., and Méndez-Garcia, M. del C. 2010. *The intercultural dynamics of multicultural working.* UK: MPG Books Group Ltd.

Process performance:
Levin, G. and Rad, P. 2003. *Achieving project management success using virtual teams.* Florida: Jossey-Bass Publishing, Inc.

Learning and knowledge sharing:
Stahl, G. 2010. *Studying virtual math teams.* New York: Springer.
Breitenöder, A. F. 2009. *Knowledge sharing in cross-cultural virtual teams: A study based on the grounded theory method.* Hamburg: Diplomica Verlag GmbH.
Godar, S. and Pixy Ferris, S. 2005. *Teaching and learning with virtual teams.* Hershey: Information Science Publishing.
Kock, N. 2005. *Business process improvement through e-collaboration: knowledge sharing through the use of virtual groups.* Hershey: Idea Group Publishing.

Leadership:
Tuffey, D. 2010. *A process reference model for leading complex virtual teams: Helping project managers improve their leadership capability.* Saarbrucken: VDM Verlag Dr. Müller A. and Co Kg.
Sobel Lojeski, K. 2009. *Leading the virtual workforce: How great leaders transform organizations in the 21st century.* Hoboken: John Wiley & Sons.
Reilly, R. R. and Sobel Lojeski, K. 2008. *Uniting the virtual workforce: transforming leadership and innovation in the globally integrated enterprise.* Hoboken: John Wiley & Sons.

Creativity in VTs:
Nemiro, J. E. 2011. *Creativity in virtual teams: Key components for success.* San Francisco: Pfeiffer.
MacGregor, S. P. and Torres-Coronas, T. 2007. *Higher creativity for virtual teams: Developing platforms for co-creation.* Hershey: Information Science Reference.

VT building and functioning:
Pauleen, D. J. 2006. *Virtual teams: Projects, protocols and processes.* Hershey: Idea Group Publishing.
Gibson, C. B. and Cohen, S. G. 2003. *Virtual teams that work: Creating conditions for virtual team effectiveness.* San Francisco: Jossey-Bass.

Communication and ICTs:
Saint-Amant, K. and Zemliansky, P. 2008. *Handbook of research on virtual workplaces and the new nature of business practices.* Hershey: Information Science Reference.
Duysters, G. Sadowski, B. and Sadowski-Rasters, G. 2007. *Communication and cooperation in the virtual workplace: Teamwork in computer-mediated-communication.* Cheltenham: Edward Elgar Publishing Limited.
Kurtzberg, T. R. (2014). *Virtual teams: Mastering communication and collaboration in the digital age.* Santa Barbara: ABC-CLIO.

3.4   CONCLUSION

We built a database from a selective and reliable dataset collection. Science mapping and co-word analysis decode the content of clusters illustrated by a 'strategic diagram' and a cluster map. Our solid and structured approach allows us to update the 'virtual teams' typology and processes' model, adding essential thoughts and permit us to update the 'Input/process/ output' model as shown by Figure 3.6. The consolidation of these results and/or further development and analysis contribute to a deeper understanding on how virtual teams function. It highlights the critical aspects of virtual teaming and helps in suggesting answers or recommendation to virtual team leaders, members, and any persons concerned by the field of virtual teams. It also gives the possibility of suggesting further orientation of research.

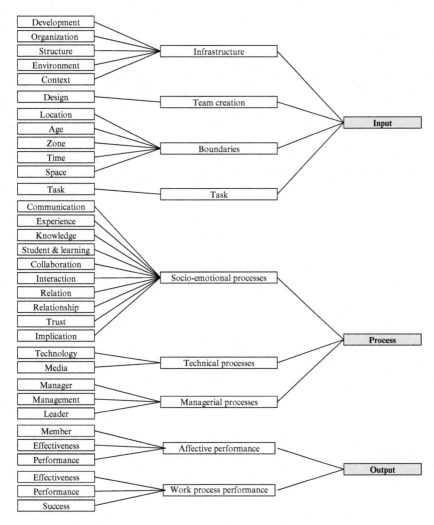

Figure 3.6   Input/process/output model update

ENDNOTE

1.   An occurrence represents the number of articles in which each word is present.

PART II

Virtual team inputs

Working in a virtual environment with virtual teams appears to be more difficult and more complex than in a face-to-face situation. Different challenges linked to virtuality emerge such as coping with distances and different time zones, along with various cultures, regulations, norms and languages. In addition to the organizational structure and virtual context, we underline in this part the importance of the attributes of virtual teams and explain why they are significant for companies, virtual team leaders, or any individuals or organizations involved in virtual teaming. These attributes bridge the already given definition of virtual teams to the organization they belong to.

This part contains two chapters. The first chapter describes and analyses the main elements supporting virtuality within an organization, whereas the second provides a comprehensive overview of inputs and characteristics of virtual teams. Figure II.1 shows virtual team inputs.

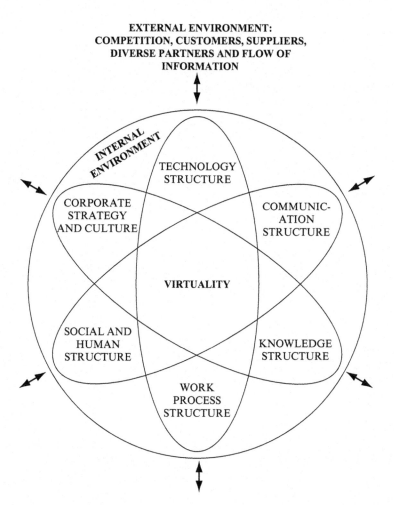

Figure II.1   Six components influencing the implementation of virtuality in an organization

4 Elements supporting virtuality within an organization

4.1 INTRODUCTION

Technological infrastructure and collaborative tools are not an easy challenge. One of the crucial obstacles to overcome is to be able to develop recognized work practices and gain members for the virtual teams, while giving to virtual team members a sense of what used to be clear and well-defined earlier. Virtual teaming requests an adapted-on-purpose framework which highlights the importance of the organizational infrastructure and its role. The organizational infrastructure prepares the architecture, which is the type of supports and resources to be implemented by the company to settle and develop virtual teaming. Basically, the organizational infrastructure provides frameworks, resources, regulation and norms. We identify and detail six main elements necessary for developing such frameworks embedding virtuality. These elements have to be considered as a connection between the organizational infrastructure and the level of virtuality within the organization. They need to integrate both internal and external relationships. They will be the support of the related processes, analysed in Chapter 6. 'If virtual teams are not planned and supported properly, their failure would be far more devastating and drastic than would have been the failure of a traditional team' (Rad and Levin, 2003).

4.2 ORGANIZATIONAL INFRASTRUCTURE

We first have to agree on the meaning of organizational infrastructure and structure in relation to virtuality and explain the connection existing between them. Infrastructure is the foundation of basic physical and organizational structures that determine how an entire organization operates (Wikipedia, 2012c; Wilson, 2003). They facilitate the activities of the organization and those activities can be physical, technical, cultural, social and functional etc. The organizational structures specify the architecture of structural components that provide a supportive framework to the organization's activities along with ensuring appropriate resources and the commitment of the organizational decision-makers (Mazze, 2008).

The structural architecture within which the company is operating comprises external and internal connections, depending on the strategy retained by the company to reach its vision. Consequently, it ensures the communication with external stakeholders and the internal side of the organization, employees or departments; you have to take into account the strategy of the organization, its structure, size, core technology, communication systems, facilities and structural connections. It is a key element that embeds virtual teams into the company organization and it is linked to internal authority, policies and procedures (Klimkeit, 2013). However, external connections assume that organizations confront an external context too and may face economical, political and competitive difficulties or opportunities.

Therefore, a new workplace strategy has to prepare stakeholders to share a variety of information, technology and knowledge to enable good performing interactions in inter-organizational teams (Larsen and McInerney, 2002). The success of organizational functioning depends on how virtuality is introduced and matches the requested processes for efficient virtual teaming, as demonstrated by the case study 'Restructuring introduces a new way of working: The case of Eks', at the end of the book. Depending on its degree of awareness, the organization may avoid internal competition or frustration when facing difficulties or opportunities outside of the usual business centre. In addition, it cannot be dissociated from the organizational values, policies and resources of the company (Mazze, 2008) which might depend on historical and contemporary influences pushing for more or less centralized companies (Boddy et al., 2005).

Virtual teams give organizations the possibility of reaching a flat or flatter and decentralized structure (Townsend et al., 1998). Units that are more decentralized seem to fit the strategy of the complex organization that is surrounded by high-flow information (Qureshi and Vogel, 2001) as long as an appropriate process is applied, as recommended by Wilson (2003). Wilson suggests that a virtual team's infrastructure should include the team information value chain, a process for communication deployment and a method controlling any change. The aim is to reduce misunderstandings, set the most adequate communication pattern and an efficient problem-solving process. The effectiveness of this infrastructure depends on its level of flexibility and the time needed to fulfil the processes.

Sarker and Sahay (2003) distinguished two relevant aspects of structure that are important to identify in order to set up the appropriate processes: production (involving work processes) and social structure (involving socio-emotional processes). They are necessary to perform team tasks and to develop social interactions where ICTs and knowledge transfer play an important role. The organizational structure should be considered from a macro level point of view, based on organization. Micro level focuses on human skills and behaviours in regard to relationships with human resource management and social structure. As confirmed by Duffy and Salvendy (1997) the performance of organizational structures goes beyond technologies and involves human, organizational and social aspects. The macro level of structure influences the functions performed by the teams, the definition of goals and responsibilities shared within the teams and the roles of the virtual team itself within the organization.

An organizational infrastructure clarifies the hierarchical organization and the information flow system too. It determines to whom and how a group of people report according to a hierarchical framework, based on a defined information flow between levels of management (Friedman, 2000). Hierarchical relationships are more diffused within virtual teams that group together team members from various organizations, departments or divisions. Within more complex organizations, which are often based on matrix models, virtual team members may report to multiple parts of the organization (Kimball, 1997; Malhotra and Majchrzak, 2004). Similarly, hierarchical links might not be direct between the virtual team leader and virtual team members. This aspect influences the managerial processes and the possible types of leadership.

Thus, the organization needs to provide the proper environment for virtual teamwork (Rad and Levin, 2003) and might adopt an entirely new way of working (Conner and Finnemore, 2003). If virtuality is largely spread within an organization, virtual teams are likely to be composed of members from various corporate functions and/or locations, dispersed across different parts of the organization. Therefore, diverse work cultures may orientate the organization to new work processes, including a high level of collaborative teamwork. Adapted practices may be requested (Qureshi and Vogel, 2001; Pauleen and Yoong, 2001) including more network forms of exchanges and new evaluation systems may also be needed (Furst et al., 1999).

The environment for virtual teaming cannot be sufficient. The role of the organization consists of building a strategy that has adapted to its environment, which includes virtual collaboration. For an effective organizational infrastructure adapted to the company's vision, this strategy requires a certain amount of awareness of the challenges that virtual teaming is faced with. According to Cottrell (2011), five main elements should be taken into consideration in terms of impact: (1) virtuality, (2) finance, (3) information tracing, (4) information access, and (5) shared goals in a project. Virtuality means Internet access, which may become distractions for team members and may be difficult to manage for team members and leaders. The time and effort involved to work virtually have to financially be worth it. Tracking and recording key information is absolutely requested for later retrieval and they offer the possibility of gathering disseminated knowledge. Easy access and equality in disclosure of information is essential for all team members who need the information. Finally, a shared sense of ownership to the project has to be set up for all team members working on the same project to ensure motivation and results. Therefore, both external and internal aspects have to be considered when evaluating how far virtuality is embedded in the infrastructure.

4.3   INFRASTRUCTURE SUPPORTS VIRTUALITY

4.3.1   External Connections for Virtuality

Virtuality may occur at different levels. At the external level of organizations, some networks are developed and keep a relationship with the organization and external stakeholders. For example, they concern smaller companies that develop a network as a virtual entity to collect competencies for collaborative projects. They may also take the form of outsourcing, where the organization outsources a large part of its value creation to a supplier network that may operate with virtual processes too (Riemer and Vehring, 2012). Consequently, organizational infrastructure has to be prepared for external virtual connections with major stakeholders such as customers, suppliers, competitors or any partners playing a key role with the company. The possibility of creating external and/or internal alliances brings additional resources to organizations which are not specifically based on long-term tasks but on merging high-quality and diverse expertise and/or interests (Rad and Levin, 2003).

Developing partnerships over interorganizational structure assumes there is high involvement from key players. It also implies companies have compatible structures in order to enable easy and reliable connections. The flow of information in the current economic environment increases and the time to process this flow is tight. Therefore, the infrastructure has to provide sufficient computational and storage resources, high-speed networking, accessible software, collaborative tools (Avery, 2004) and technical assistance (Chinowsky and Rojas, 2003) in order to create a workable, reliable and flexible base of systems for virtual teams and virtual organizations (Stough et al., 2000).

It implies that these partners are located in a region favourable to virtual infrastructure deployment (Morris and McManus, 2002). If not, these regions may not support such structures; or, they may not look attractive for organizations deploying virtuality because these regions or countries, with lower developed technical solutions, require an extensive investment in infrastructure development with prohibitive costs. Additionally, the organizations that develop very high-level technological infrastructures widen the gap of virtual accessibility within these regions and create 'technical' barriers. Even when implementing external connections with technologically developed countries, the organizations need to respect applied standards and follow the continuous technological development. To obtain membership from the concerned stakeholders, the organization may help them to see the benefits of virtual teamwork (Duarte and Snyder, 2006).

Consequently, external connection architecture contributes to the deployment of virtual teams. Becoming a part of the structural processes, virtual teams are considered as a new tool for the company's organization (Dubinskas and Hargreaves, 1993). Then, that new tool can be standardized or sometimes just added to the existing organizational structure when temporary issues cannot be handled by the present teams (Eom and Lee, 1999).

However, virtual work requires necessary rules and resources that should be clearly specified and integrated in the structure while taking into account the structural constraints for external relationships, ICTs, and work processes (Sarker and Sahay, 2004). The combination of technology, new behaviours and business pressure fosters fast decisions in addition to collaboration. This combination reduces the risk of misunderstanding and errors when document-sharing technologies are used (Grundy and Ginger, 1998). As a consequence, two or more organizations can collaborate when they succeed in establishing and maintaining a mutual commitment. They can develop collaboration and coordination between roles along with interaction and coordination between their activities. To reach a performance target, organizations need a level of connection capability that is high enough to achieve the desired target. To evaluate its possibility of connecting internal structure to external stakeholders, an organization has to assess the requested level of virtuality and be prepared to develop effective interconnections.

4.3.2 Internal Connections Embedding Virtuality

Internal virtual organizations refer to internal working processes based on collaboration through virtual teams. The degree of virtuality envisaged by the company determines the virtualness of a structure, which means the necessary infrastructure to support virtuality. The degree of virtuality also has a direct link to the complexity of the teams involved. When compared to conventional team management, higher virtuality means higher complexity in effective global virtual team management. It can be illustrated by Figure 1.2 showing the degree of virtuality when defining a virtual team, in the chapter 'Evolutionary definition of virtual teams'. A circle whose centre symbolizes the traditional teamwork could also help to visualize the concept. The team reaches higher virtuality the further it moves from the centre of the circle (Zigurs, 2003). Virtual teaming suggests some concepts and methods of management, coordination, communication, and technology adapted to virtuality, to be integrated into the company structure. Thus, company structures should not be a barrier to the development of virtual teams. Instead, they should make the virtual team visible to the entire organization (Roebuck and Britt, 2002). Visibility shows the link between virtual teams and organizations through various variables in different contexts. Therefore, it is necessary to understand what kind of organizational structure the virtual teams are operating in (Favier and Coat, 2002; Fiol and O'Connor, 2005). It appears to be challenging because managing organizational change in that dynamic context of being continuously reshaped, assumes that the characteristics relating to virtuality are understood. It also constrains virtual teams to constant adaptation (Qureshi and Vogel, 2001). The challenge mainly consists of successfully articulating the six components involved in virtuality development.

4.4   SIX MAIN COMPONENTS INVOLVED IN VIRTUALITY

The six main components are identified as illustrated in Figure II.1: strategy and culture, technology, communication, knowledge, work processes and human and social structures. (These elements are identified and highlighted by the map of clusters illustrated in Figure 3.2, which is mentioned in the description of our methodology in Chapter 3.) The roles of the key components cannot be isolated from one another when addressing the structural development of an organization towards virtuality. They are the base for the related processes developed and discussed in Chapter 6. The structure is most supportive when the integration of those elements in the organization is at its highest level. Integration in that context implies interconnections between the six components which are all interrelated. The analysis of each one improves the understanding of the virtuality environment within an organization.

4.4.1 Relevance of the Corporate Strategy and Culture Structure

When addressing virtual context, organizations have to develop a corporate culture that reshapes and supports transformational and structural change, and includes virtuality. Pauleen and Yoong (2001) report that differences within the virtual work environment often emerge from issues linked to organizational culture or organizational policies. The organizational culture is more likely to succeed with virtual teams when it is based on an 'adaptive technologically advanced non-hierarchical organization' than a highly-structured, control-oriented organization (Apgar et al., 1997).

Corporate culture in favour of virtuality is relevant because it gives direction and creates a dynamic for the organization (Monalisa et al., 2008). It also reflects an organizational identity that is essential to create a psychological tie that bridges virtual team members together within an organization, which contributes to relationship building (Pauleen and Yoong, 2001). This culture should leave space for flexibility to allow the virtual teams to adapt new structures if it is necessary for their successful functioning, while taking into consideration the following findings. Majchrzak et al. (2000) found that if a work group is allowed to modify its structures then it is possible that all structures may be changed.

This structural change is not constrained by pre-existing structures, even if the organizational context may not be flexible in the long term. Majchrzak et al. (2000) also mentioned that changes might be fostered by discordant events rather than by the flexibility of the organizational structures. This is the reason why, the organizational culture should not be neglected because it has a positive and significant relation with virtual team effectiveness and with team members' satisfaction (Doolen et al., 2003).

According to the chosen strategy, the organization has to structure its activities to integrate the cultural and stereotypical differences and ensure a balanced role distribution among the employees (Rutkowski et al., 2002). The company culture has to standardize the virtual way of working and get it accepted as a standard way of working. For example, in some organizations or countries, being present and seen at work is equivalent to individual performance and commitment. If the person is not present, it might easily be interpreted as 'no personal implication' (Furst et al., 1999).

Such a corporate culture cannot support virtuality or virtual teamwork deployment, and acceptance or it will make the integration of virtual teaming much slower and less effective. It might also be very complicated for organizational culture that includes values and beliefs from the corporate level such as languages, rituals and stories of that corporation (Zakaria et al., 2004).

All the elements related to the organizational and cultural environment are decisive in the approach, choice, implementation, adaptation and adoption of technical, and work processes. Among the first researchers' concerns was technology because it seemed critical that some solutions had to be found to fill the gap between the traditional team interactions and the virtual ones.

4.4.2   Relevance of the Technology Structure

Information systems (IS) are the field concerned with all aspects of information technology (IT) how IT architecture can support operations and how it can deploy information systems and computation within that framework. Information systems help people and organizations to collect, filter, process, create and distribute data (Wikipedia, 2012a; Short et al., 2005). They are often a vector of competitive advantage that differentiates companies from one another and allows certain decisions that affect companies' profitability. They are also the business of companies whose service is based on information delivery (Boddy et al., 2005). They evolved over the three eras of growth in the computer industry: data processing, micro-computer and network (Shim et al., 2002).

A strong link exists between organizational infrastructure and technology. Technological innovation enables the evolution of decision support systems and their numerous applications. A decision support system is a computer-based IS that supports a business or organization in problem-solving and in making complex decisions. For example, the management of a sophisticated database such as inventories of information assets, comparative sales figures from one period to another one, estimated budgets etc.

Technology structure encompasses data centres, computers, communication networks, database management devices and systems of regulation (Wikipedia, 2012b). However, it is particularly critical to note that technology structure cannot ensure successful virtual teaming, meaning without other factors challenging the different stakeholders who have to change their own structures, processes and human behaviour in order to adapt and adopt the large technological potential. The system can be totally or partially computerized. When it is partially computerized, it also includes human operations. This technological evolution pushes the decision-making from an individual level to a group level. Therefore, the organizations create virtual teams in order to be able to involve dispersed experts in their decision-making processes (Shim et al., 2002). The need for efficient collaborative tools and systems becomes critical to reach successful work team results. The relevance of the technology structure contributes to that success.

The flow of information between individuals and organizations is managed through IT infrastructure. The development of that infrastructure implies high expenditures in the new generation of technology, which are composed of computer hardware and software, data management systems, networking or advanced-computer communication technology and technology services. One of the key goals of companies, whether they are multinational or not, is to get easy and quick access to information and communication. The quick access of information affects the virtual context of their organization positively and more specifically due to a virtual team member's satisfaction and trust, as suggested by Larsen and McInerney (2002). To date, 'financially and technologically viable' (Chinowsky and Rojas, 2003) technologies become the bases of the virtual team structure linking the virtual team members with an optimum membership within a flatter structure.

The convergence of advanced technology supports the organization through a full 'tool box'. Digital texts, images, sounds, voice, videos data technology and systems e.g. electronic data interchange, radio frequency identification (RFID) together with collaborative tools, and all kinds of audio and visual processes and transmissions enable the needed collaborative connections. Those tools compensate the constraints linked to spatial and geographical dispersion (Jawadi and Boukef Charki, 2011) by enabling immediate and frequent interactions over geographical dispersion (Ahuja et al., 2003). Therefore, the technology structure determines the ability of an organization to grow globally through virtuality by adopting the appropriate information infrastructure and this is all because of the new technologies (Morris and McManus, 2002).

An ICT structure and collaborative technologies are sometimes referred to as 'groupware applications' to cover team collaboration design (Davison and De Vreede, 2001). Also, ICTs offer various channels and groupware to facilitate communication, support digital information storage and retrieval, and to help in decision-making (Stough et al., 2000; Eom and Lee, 1999; Shim et al., 2002). 'Product development, multi-user architectures, information-sharing and virtual teaming, negotiation and transaction management and networking' (Roy, 1998) contribute to the integration of virtuality within the organization.

The ICTs structure causes the virtual team members to replace 'real proximity' by information resources, and 'virtual proximity' with knowledgeable team members (Pliskin, 1997). Due to higher connectivity, virtual distance brings dispersed team members closer to each other and group collaboration, which is considered as being more effective than 'telecommuters'. This is what Pliskin (1997) called 'the telecommuting paradox'. This paradox is also mentioned by Dubé and Robey (2009) who underline that virtual teaming should be considered as 'normal rather than unusual'.

Those resources make it possible to approach the quasi-real-time exploration of collaboration structures (Uflacker and Zeier, 2011), which gives 'a sense of presence' (Fontaine, 2002) so it positively affects the virtual team performance. Virtual team participants share and access available resources regardless of their location and develop e-collaboration over the Internet and adapted tools (De Lucia et al., 2007), which is vital for virtual teams (Fong, 2005). All virtual team members should have equal and immediate access to the same ICTs hardware and technical support (Duarte and Snyder, 2006; Glückler and Schrott, 2007). Anderson et al. (2007) demonstrate that virtual team members speak more openly when each participant has her/his own communication equipment, even though it is less advanced than operational sharing of this technological equipment.

The dependence on ICTs by virtual teams means that IT planners build systems within IS infrastructures that serve the organizational performance including virtual teams' own performance. One factor of success for those IT planners is to listen, understand and propose innovative solutions to virtual team constraints. This is even more critical when IT services are outsourced by the organization whose success depends on the 'mission clarity, group cohesion and personal satisfaction' (Xue et al., 2004). Indeed, IT outsourcing might add higher complexity in the service to be provided. The IT planners' relevant role has to be taken into account when building the communication structure because ICTs contribute to a real added-value to organizations and to the evolution of virtual team forms, moving organizations from an industrial culture to a knowledge culture (Gignac, 2005).

Difficulties may occur in the relationships between technology and those who have to use it (Hagen, 1999). The large spectrum of processes to be integrated, and the extent of complexity may lead to unexpected issues. These issues may include periods of software adjustment, or failure, protocol violations, software bugs, and email limitations (Borenstein, 1996). Technology deployment may develop some dissatisfaction or frustration among the internal users and negatively influence the relations with external and internal stakeholders. Additionally, technology structure disseminates the knowledge and information which may destabilize the relationship between virtual team members and virtual organizations (Griffith et al., 2003). It may generate psychological and cultural barriers, fostered by the increase of abstraction for virtual teams due to the total or partial absence of face-to-face contacts (Fiore et al., 2009). Communication is a key factor to smooth out the negative impacts.

4.4.3   Relevance of the Communication Structure

Communication infrastructure has been widely identified as an essential key factor in virtual organization. Communication infrastructure is deployed by companies to support corporate strategy and a virtual work environment. Communication in a virtual environment copes with electronic mediated interactions where technology holds a large position for both external and internal connections.

Due to the lower richness in communication and less social presence in comparison to face-to-face interactions, computer-mediated communication might be a source of misunderstanding and can therefore negatively affect the team performance and relationships with external and internal partners. This may lead to conflicts inside the team that negatively affect the communication, productivity and, therefore, the performance of the virtual team (Schlenkrich and Upfold, 2009). For this reason, technology has a strong connection with communication structure in order to support it as efficiently as possible. As pointed by Ahuja and Carley (1998), information technologies facilitate lateral communication and have little regard for traditional hierarchy (Ahuja and Carley, 1998) referring thus to the notion of network and complex structures.

The communication structure for virtual teams, which is less centralized than face-to-face teams, seems more flexible so it is more adaptable to the organizational and cultural diversity. The structure adjusts the information needed for the team activity through fewer messages and more task-oriented and less spontaneous communication (Hammond et al., 2001). According to Ahuja and Carley's (1998) findings, the flexibility of the communication structure is associated with perceived performance by the individual virtual team members (not with team performance). The communication structure integrates two major types of media: sequential (redundant, serial or complementary) and concurrent (independent or complementary). For example, sequential information is information passed from one person to another one. Concurrent information belongs to shared resources that are available in a database, but not repeated to all points of the information transmission. These types of media are used by individuals depending on their communication objective: information transmission, acknowledgment request or incite for mutual interactions (Bélanger and Watson-Manheim, 2006).

In addition to information adjustment, communication structure has to consider the corporate communication policy's values, norms and beliefs. For example, a corporate strategy and culture may require specific missions like employee communication prohibition, whose non-disclosure rules might not be accepted easily by the employees (Sussman, 2008). If those restrictions are highlighted by the corporate communication policy, and their significance and necessity were explained, then they are likely to be accepted. In this case, the technology structure has to support the communication policy covering a certain level of security.

Communication structure has to provide a higher level of performance within a virtual context in order to satisfy a greater demand in information and communication applications to substitute the face-to-face interactions (Townsend et al., 1998). It implies the importance of technology but also involves virtual team leaders and their role in filling the distance between structure and processes, situational perceptions and psychological drivers, which is what Lee-Kelley et al. (2004) name 'the invisibles'.

They may be 'invisibles' but remain essential in virtual team processes, as detailed later in the book. Thus, virtual team leaders should propose a conceptual model for virtual team members to achieve goals and provide them with a link and the support to interact according to the available structure. They may use communication technology to create relationships between the team members (Flammia et al., 2010), initiate favourable conditions for virtual work and supply the appropriate dimensions to foster and support creativity within virtual teams (Nemiro, 2004). The leaders' support has to be integrated into the organizations' strategy structure, context-building, management and human resources (Mohrman, 1999) as described in managerial processes about the role of virtual team leaders.

The profile of the organization members should also be considered when introducing or developing communication structure within a virtual environment. The main reason is to anticipate the members' preparation for well-performing virtual teams, as either a virtual team leader or virtual team member. Some individual characteristics are likely to be more valuable than others when working in within a virtual context and fostering a 'virtual behaviour'.

A training programme (including online software-based programs) prepares people to work in a virtual environment, or encourages certain personality traits that seem to increase proficiency, assuming that training and preparation are beneficial to virtual teaming. They might not be implemented in each company involved in virtual teaming, unless they are aware of the challenges involved for that way of working. As a matter of fact, training and 'team learning' (Moran, 2005) are recognized to develop the virtual team members' multicultural and virtual perceptions, viz. improving the effectiveness of communication within a virtual context (Warkentin and Beranek, 1999). The 'soft skills' appear more challenging to learn than technical skills.

Some training sessions offer a set of best practices with the objective of developing awareness on virtuality, communication and its boundaries

(Rosen et al., 2006; Larsen and McInerney, 2002; King, 2007; Lurey and Raisinghani, 2001). The organization should offer training in addition to possible universities or educational organizations. Training that is embedded in the technology and communication structure can benefit from the computer-mediated technology, e-learning (Olson-Buchanan et al., 2007) and Web 2.0 advances, such as those issued from gaming environment and using avatars. The purpose of training is to effectively communicate inside and outside of the organization, while transferring knowledge is seen as another significant factor within the organization structure.

4.4.4 Relevance of Knowledge Structure

An organization that is able to create and disseminate knowledge in a short timeframe can provide a competitive advantage, particularly in rapidly changing environments that request timely innovation and response (Grant, 1996).

Knowledge structure can be organized under three basic topics: (1) relevance to virtual teaming; (2) consisting of declarative knowledge; and (3) procedural knowledge and structural knowledge. Declarative knowledge is the expressed knowledge on the function of an organization, how and why the different elements are working, their names and location as well as the mechanism relating them. Procedural or operational knowledge details the various steps or activities requested to perform a task or a job, thus reaching a standardization of processes. Structural knowledge or problem state knowledge focuses on problem-solving, with plans and strategies for necessary procedures and instructions when possible failures occur (Dictionary, 2012a).

Knowledge structure is extended through the knowledge management system defined as an IT-based system; it was created to support and enhance organizational knowledge management processes (Alavi and Tiwana, 2002). In regards to knowledge management, knowledge transfer is seen as a significant factor of risk in virtual team management compared to technology failure or communication barriers. The reason is given by the researchers Reed and Knight (2010) as they consider that implicit or informal knowledge transfer appears to be at a lower level in the virtual context. Knowledge needs to be transformed into explicit information to be used in an efficient way by virtual teams. Additionally, it should be embedded into the organizational structure. It is more complex to obtain than within co-located teams. Therefore, it is important to understand how knowledge structure is designed.

Thus, the organizational knowledge structure goes through three interrelated processes: knowledge creation, knowledge codification and knowledge application and acquisition (Alavi and Tiwana, 2002; Bourhis et al., 2005). Some researchers, for example, Sole and Edmondson (2002) note that virtual teams facilitate the acquisition and application of knowledge to critical tasks especially because they give wider access to diverse expertise and perspectives. Virtual teams widen the understanding of global customers, operations and suppliers. However, some knowledge is not always formalized, such as tacit knowledge taking the form of know-how, expertise, individual intuition; this is called 'cognitive knowledge' by Davidson (2013) and it might be difficult to embed it into organizational routines (Bourhis et al., 2005).

The lack of formalization may also concern 'situated' or 'situational' knowledge, which is knowledge issued from site-specific work practices. Proximity is a major reason for local collaborators to skip formalization because they compensate with face-to-face relationships to exchange local knowledge. When confronted with virtual teaming, situated knowledge plays a relevant role in learning because it requires virtual team members to consider team tasks and issues with solutions which were not obvious for some of the virtual team members (Sole and Edmondson, 2002). Interorganization or inter-site communication contributes to make those practices available to the rest of the virtual team.

Learning to create or to increase knowledge in virtual teams and in 'virtual learning spaces' is recognized to enhance an awareness of virtuality (Jones et al., 1999). Bringing both internal and external knowledge to virtual teams enables them to transform this knowledge into improved performance more successfully. Consequently, knowledge management, in addition to collaborative work, appears to be a considerable lever to innovate and create new capabilities within a virtual team and, therefore, within an organization (Sole and Edmondson, 2002).

The knowledge management shows that a virtual environment enables an organization to reach wider, diverse and specialized knowledge. However, there are constraints to the integration and application of that expertise, which highlights the need for an adequate structure (Bourhis et al., 2005). When the structure is well-adapted, virtual teams can share a concern, problems or an expertise about a topic and may even develop a 'community of practices' contributing to effective performance (Bourhis et al., 2005). Communities of practice are 'groups of people who share a concern or a passion for something they do and (intentionally or not) learn how to do it better as they interact regularly' (Etienne et al., 2002).

The knowledge-based view of an organization asserts that although the lifespan of a virtual team may be limited to a particular project's duration, the 'learning' that takes place through the team process may create organizational benefits in two ways: First, virtual teams enable employees to expand their social networks within or even outside organizations. Second, the work processes of a virtual team can become an important part of the organization's knowledge repository or 'organizational memory' (Walsh and Ungson, 1991).

4.4.5 Relevance of Work Processes Structure

The work processes structure addresses the elements that concern the organization of the work within an organization. It refers to the different steps in which a job or an activity is subdivided into manageable work elements or tasks. The work structure displays the relationships between tasks from the beginning to the end of the concerned assignment objective. It designates the task owner and responsibility, the required resources and the necessary time that is required. Work processes structure also refers to the work environment, e.g. physical location and conditions applied to process the tasks or activities; example of activities are work practices, working from home, policies and contracts related to work (Dictionary, 2012a).

In the virtual context, the work processes structure is highly dependent on the technology structure because work processes usually rely on systems developed to model, control and manage the activity, which is known as workflow systems. The purpose is to support and enforce the collaboration between virtual team members according to a logical process between tasks or activities through the execution software (Zhuge, 2003). There are three dimensions identified in regards to workflow: workflow as software tools, workflow systems defining the technical architecture, and workflows organizing business processes.

In a virtual environment, workflows have to be able to deal with a higher complexity of workflow management and an increased need of flexibility and coordination due to boundaries of space, time, geography, discipline, and diverse cultural values and norms (Limburg and Jackson, 2007; Workman, 2005). A work culture will then develop to regulate behaviours and set up the approach of the managerial control. Similar, to the case of technology deployment, the implemented work culture may generate both resistance and adaptation to the work processes (Rasmussen and Wangel, 2007). Processes are relevant and require an appropriate managerial approach to gain membership of diverse stakeholders, which also relies on human and social structure.

4.4.6   Relevance of Human and Social Structure

Social structure in this kind of work refers to the structure of social relationships and social networks that bridges individuals or organizations; it
is mainly focused on computer-mediated communication and interactions
between virtual team members or virtual teams. Social structure can also
make reference to the way norms and procedures influence the behaviours
of stakeholders or human and personal interactions within a social system
structured through time, space, and specific locations (Britannica, 2013).
However, a moderating factor is applied for organizations embedded in
virtuality because they are not connected, or are less connected, to specific
locations or times than non-virtual teams. As a matter of fact, work can
be performed within a virtual framework despite location and time (Jessup
and Robey, 2002).

Interactions between members of virtual teams are essential for an
optimum performance to socialization within an organization. Socialization
is defined as 'the process of learning behaviours and attitudes necessary for
assuming a role in an organization', and it is seen as a continuous process
carried on by various sources (Ahuja and Galvin, 2003). According to
Duffy and Salvendy (1997) organizational and human factors account for
a high percentage in the possible variation within the processes of socialization of a virtual organization.

In addition to the components previously mentioned in this chapter,
the proximity of virtual team members appears to be an essential variable in building, renewing or maintaining social ties and social presence.
Social presence is 'the degree to which a medium facilitates awareness of
the other person and interpersonal relationships during the interaction'
(Roberts et al., 2006). Creating such a presence or ties in an environment where geographical distance and group size matter is relevant and
challenging. Distance and group size influence individual physical and
interactive expression and, therefore, affect the virtual team interaction
processes (Roberts et al., 2006) which may lead to difficult team communication and possible conflicts. Therefore, it demands a more effective
virtual team management (Schlenkrich and Upfold, 2009) increased by
the virtual characteristics of dispersed teams as detailed later in the book
(Roberts et al., 2006). To avoid a critical social situation, some researchers e.g. Shin (2004) propose a 'person–environment fit framework' where
individual skills that are required to work within a virtual environment
are identified.

They should be supported by the social structure. We note that
an effective social structure is based on an architecture deployed for
social exchanges fostering communities of practices and organizational

mechanisms that enable the renewal of social aspects within a virtual team (Kotlarsky et al., 2007). Such structure that is based on social and information exchanges positively influences knowledge-sharing and integration within virtual organizations (Tiwana and Bush, 2001) as well as improvement of collaboration (Oshri et al., 2007). It is pertinent though to understand what information is exchanged because it is the foundation of socialization processes.

Virtual team members can be trained, as Beranek and Martz (2005) demonstrate that training on virtual team communication increases virtual team members' ability to exchange information. Connected to communication and organizational culture, the social structure may integrate the building of social ties through face-to-face activities, a project lifecycle or shared stories within the virtual team in order to create and strengthen these social ties (Oshri et al., 2008).

4.5 TO KEEP IN MIND: THE RELEVANCE OF THE ORGANIZATIONAL INFRASTRUCTURE

The organizational infrastructure is the frame that supports virtuality and carries out internal and external exchanges across various places, time zones, stakeholders and organizations.

The settled architecture is particularly relevant in regards to virtuality because it directly affects the functioning of the whole organization in a virtual context. The driver to success depends on the capacity of the global structure to build, deploy and adapt efficient interrelationships between key elements, such as corporate strategy and culture, technology, communication, knowledge, work processes and human and social structure.

A smooth articulation among those elements positively influences the deployment of virtuality and virtual teams in the concerned organization. It also contributes to virtual team members' involvement and satisfaction, virtual teamwork, and the global performance of the organization through the effectiveness of virtual teams.

4.6 CONCLUSION

We outline the importance of the organizational infrastructure to embed virtuality through the main identified components. If we refer to the strategic diagram (see Figure 3.5 in Chapter 3) we can see that this topic is a central one, which confirms the relevance of organizational infrastructure. There is no model and no unique organizational structure. Structures with distinct strengths, limitations and specific applications build organizations that are more or less adapted to virtual teaming, depending on the virtual awareness developed by the organizations in question. Working in a virtual context requires particular attention when implementing the appropriate environment, tools, communication and adequate processes regarding virtual teaming. As virtual teaming might not be spontaneous, training all the stakeholders solves the possible difficulties or even barriers, which particularly exist in social or communication areas. No proven results from research show when the organizations prepare their employees for virtual approach by offering specific and adequate training. Would they offer training before their collaborators are involved in virtual teaming or implement more training when they detect a crisis or a critical situation negatively affecting team performance? Employee profiles and the typology of persons who follow a specific training session could be analysed too.

In any case, the investigation and understanding of the context is relevant to determining what kind of virtual team, processes and outcomes are expected. Embedding virtual teaming within an infrastructure with values, vision, and cultures requires strategic projection in order to reach successful performance and outcomes. Based on their knowledge of virtual team typology and specific characteristics, organizations and e-leaders can set up the pertinent and performing processes to virtual teaming.

4.7 GUIDELINES FOR MANAGERIAL PRACTICES: KEY LEVERS SUPPORTING VIRTUALITY WITHIN AN ORGANIZATION

Mapping the organization in which your virtual team is embedded allows the possibility of highlighting the existing levers that contribute to efficient virtual teaming. Thus, the organizational infrastructure provides resources, the decision-making path, the usable internal and external connections, policies and processes that may more or less directly affect the virtual team management. These guidelines, see Table 4.1 below, help the virtual team manager to identify the efficient levers that may support or enhance the virtual team management.

Table 4.1   Assess the virtuality of your virtual team

Key actions	Key results
Organizational infrastructure	
Map the hierarchical organization	– listed resources; and – decision-makers.
Describe the information flow system and your environment for virtual teaming	– internal connection technology; – external connection technology; – information access; – information tracking; – Internet/intranet policies; and – technological resources (inclusive platform open to all, including for example, the hard-of-hearing).

Levers supporting virtuality within the corporate organization
Analyse the six following elements in order to figure out if virtual teaming is a standard way of working in your organization

– Corporate strategy and culture: is virtual teaming integrated and standardized?	– Can you telework? – Are best practices regarding virtual teaming transmitted?
– Technology	– Describe the quality and reactivity of technological assistance, the size and composition of your 'tool box', the proposed e-solutions, level of security.
– Communication	– Can you share databases and documents? Are you aware of the global communication policy about virtual teaming?
– Knowledge	– Is information stored and easily retrieved? Are processes and procedures clearly communicated?
– Work processes	– How work is organized: do you access global systems, such as ERP, workflow?
– Social and human structure	– How developed is the socialization process of the corporate organization? – Do these processes reduce social distance? – Do communities exist and are they recognized within the organization?

5 Inputs and characteristics of virtual teams

5.1 INTRODUCTION

Virtual teams have been widely defined by the research community in terms of concept but the understanding of the formation and configuration of these teams is also essential to address the key factors of their processes and the adequate managerial behaviour. Therefore, virtual team attributes cannot be isolated in the virtual team management analysis because they constitute a part of virtual team agility, structure and degree of virtuality (Sharp and Ryan, 2011).

In this chapter, we analyse the main characteristics by objectives and missions conferred to virtual teams, their impact on virtual team composition, the type of teams and tasks. We clarify the virtual team attributes and then we define the different phases of virtual team creation, the factors to be analysed when forming, staffing, configuring a virtual team. Then we address essential factors to consider when building or developing a virtual team, constituted by the various boundaries affecting the functioning of that team.

5.2 ATTRIBUTES OF VIRTUAL TEAMS

Figure II.1 presented at the beginning of Part II, illustrates the six main pillars that group the characteristics of virtual team inputs. It introduces the relevant inputs that constitute the particularities of those teams and gives an explicit idea of the complexity of virtual teams. We can locate therefore the main differences with co-located teams too. Each pillar is detailed later in the chapter.

5.2.1 The Relevance of Virtual Team Characteristics

A leader of a virtual team has to be able to identify the key characteristics of his/her team and situate the team in its virtual and structural environment. The connection between inputs and processes emphasizes the importance of virtual team leaders when assessing precisely the type of virtual team they lead. The purpose is to run and lead that team effectively without non-understood, misunderstood, or non-expected managerial barriers; this can be done by implementing an adequate strategy and processes, and identifying the appropriate levers they may need.

The reason is that the differences and diversities within the group increase the complexity of the virtual team characteristics and, therefore, its management. E-leaders play a high role in the configuration of the operating structure, more specifically at the creation phase (Gibson and Cohen, 2003).

The six pillars that represent the attributes or input variables are really viewed as essential and critical during the phase of building the group. They represent the capability of the team to produce, assemble the necessary elements such as material or human resources along with the individual and social characteristics of the team (Driskell et al., 1987; Gluesing et al., 2003; Martins et al., 2004).

Initial inputs outline the link between virtual teams, communication technologies and team outcomes and, thus, bridging virtual team characteristics and processes at different levels: individual level, team level and organizational level (Martins and Schilpzand, 2011). Indeed, those basic elements are to be considered for the 'starting conditions of a group' for an efficient and performing setup as clarified by Martins et al. (2004); Piccoli et al. (2004); Gluesing et al. (2003).

Some researchers split virtual team characteristics in two major categories: communicative and structural (Timmerman and Scott, 2006). In this book, we use a categorization that includes all key characteristics determining a virtual team and, thus, influencing the processes and outcomes of the team. Defining the characteristics of a particular virtual team is rather complex because various factors have to be analysed and might inter-react with each other.

We discuss each of the six pillars, the first of which is related to infrastructure and the object of Chapter 4 about elements supporting virtuality. Then, we address the different types of objectives and missions assigned to a virtual team, and identify the possible forms of virtual teams along with the types of tasks required to meet the mission and objectives. Next, we go into the phase of creating the virtual teams and the phase of staffing those teams, as well as the questions linked to the virtual team identity and configuration. Finally, we investigate the boundaries that have emerged from virtual team characteristics and their consequences on virtual teaming.

Objectives and missions determine the types of virtual teams. Virtual teams have modified teamwork in various aspects, which brings larger flexibility in global relationships but also a wider range of constraints.

Virtual team members tend to shift from one team to another, instead of being committed to one group as face-to-face teams used to be. Thanks to their geographical and organizational distribution, virtual team members share their work and tasks with different teams at the same time, either in the inter-organizational context or inside of their own organization as co-located teams. Since it may become complex, the decision-maker should be able to answer the question of why the organization needs virtual teams and for what objectives and mission, before building up a virtual team.

Different objectives might be fulfilled by virtual teams as recognized by researchers:

- *Idea generation or brainstorming:* where virtual team members seem more productive and more satisfied than in face-to-face teams (Aiken and Vanjani, 1997; DeRosa et al., 2007) most probably because participants feel liberated from any possible pressure, either psychological or hierarchical.
- *Intellective (knowledge transfer) or negotiation:* gives lower results but the team performance may improve over time. Tasks in these virtual teams usually request a higher coordination level than face-to-face teams in order to minimize operational flow failures due to computer-mediated communication that slows down interactions (Caldwell et al., 2008).
- *Entrepreneurship, venture or business:* few findings specifically mention those objectives running in virtual teams. We assume that virtual teams within a global organization enclose a part of this objective but more research on entrepreneurship or venture could be done in order to measure the benefit and challenges of virtuality in this case. An illustration of such a situation is presented at the end of the book (in the case study 'Fashioning virtuality: The case of Eco Fashion World').

Typology and objectives of virtual teams are intrinsically linked. The type of virtual team is based on the mission assigned to the virtual team and the mission might also be adapted to the type of virtual team. Depending on their objectives, virtual teams may be formed on a continuous basis rather than being limited to a starting and ending period. Additionally, the virtual team typology is also based on the virtual team members' roles, the complexity and nature of the tasks, the boundaries, the temporal distribution, and the lifecycle of the virtual team (Kimball, 1997; Bell and Kozlowski, 2002; Cohen and Bailey, 1997; Duarte and Snyder, 2006). The main typologies of different virtual teams are listed below, issued from the analysis of academic research results:

- *Networked teams:* team members rotate on and off the team depending on when and where their expertise is needed. Team members may not even be aware of all the individuals involved, work teams or organizations in the group.
- *Parallel teams:* a parallel team is different from a networked team because the virtual team members are clearly identified from the rest of the organization. This type of virtual teams is often used for business recommendation group works or domestically used when expertise cannot be found in one location or in one organization.
- *'Executive teams'* or *'management teams':* bring together leaders and/or managers that hold positions with functional responsibilities within an organization, and often across national boundaries. Team members are more oriented to strategy commitment and decision so, they usually 'meet' frequently and collaborate on a daily basis. They are based in regards to their functions and not to their location.
- *Project teams:* group together team members for a common task within various contexts but oriented to innovation and development of new products or projects and information systems, or processes for users or customers. They are also identified as 'networked teams' and, for a defined and extended period of time, their objective is to 'facilitate transnational innovation process' (Gassmann and Zedtwitz, 2003). Virtual team members have the authority to make decisions, not just recommendations as would be the case in a parallel virtual team. Virtual project teams offer the most effective decision-making support in comparison to individual contribution and traditional teams (Schmidt et al., 2001). However, the effectiveness of project teams depends on the degree of project coordination; this is the case from decentralized self-organization to a centralized coordination team whose members work together for the duration of the project. Coordination is linked to the degree of innovation and the nature of the project, along with the mode of knowledge and the available resources (Gassmann and Zedtwitz, 2003; see also Malhotra et al., 2001). These teams can be created rapidly and may not last longer than the project itself, as they are project-based so they have a limited duration in time (Cohen and Bailey, 1997). Membership is often broad and fluid, which requires an adapted leadership for creative work that involves non-routine-problem-solving tasks.
- *Software teams:* offer innovation, production and services in the area of software development, by gathering talented developers

from around the world. Virtual software teams are often referenced to and used as example in the research work on virtual teams, and the reason is likely because these kinds of virtual teams emerged among the first ones in the history of virtual teaming. Virtual software teams are an important asset for software development (Zhang et al., 2009). Some researchers, e.g. Chan and Chung (2002), proposed a few tools to support dispersed software teams in their process management; an example is 'Integrating Process and Project Management', which can also be applied to non-software-development teams because their process is very similar to any other virtual project teams. They highlight the fact that adequate process management, appropriate applications of the processes and effective control of the project execution are necessary for these teams. Communicative practices though are stressful for virtual software teams because they are responsible for tasks such as bug and error notifications, detection and correction, and to update notifications where effective communication is vital.

- *Functional, process or work teams:* team members' tasks are more oriented to action, problem-solving, negotiation and dispensing quick answers, especially in emergency situations. They usually perform regular tasks in one function with a clearly defined area e.g. production, venture, finance, research, purchase or marketing. Their membership is rather stable, usually working full-time with well defined tasks (Cohen and Bailey, 1997). They may be a part of a virtual team chain including research and development (R&D), project or product development teams, thus collaborating in parallel teams with different other functional teams. Managing such teams, with various functional perspectives and backgrounds, raises the complexity for virtual team leaders (Barczak et al., 2006). Intense problem-solving teams are usually composed of members with specific expertise to achieve a sustainable solution. Since the work process is rather complex, those teams require knowledge transfer and enriched communication (Rentsch et al., 2010).

- *Educational teams:* virtual learning is a crucial element in regards to the knowledge-based society and performance development. The challenge is to get individuals to learn how to work and operate in virtual teams that are focused on learning, which does not always require interactions between the learners. The instructor is expected to encourage collaborative process and develop teamwork. Because the participants are challenged by the quality and stability of technology, they need the necessary basic knowledge in computer literacy and have to adopt behaviour in proactive learning. Thus, they can use what is known as 'extracting knowledge' (McFadzean and McKenzie, 2001; Lau, 2007) for their own purposes. Rolstadas' experience (Rolstadas, 2013) shows that training based on technological support and virtual content appears to be significantly more effective than in traditional concept. Ferris and Godar (2006) demonstrate the importance of moving 'from e-learning to learning in virtual teams', which means that collaborative learning is efficient when 'students' are responsible for another student's learning. This approach fosters the transfer of learning and knowledge because the 'students' are sharing a common academic goal and one student's success contributes to the success of others. Based on that reasoning, the researchers note this approach as one way to develop or increase members' social relationships. Interactions are thus encouraged and give a positive impulsion to the finality of e-learning. The virtual and business contexts also need to be taken into consideration to attain efficient e-learning in such an environment. Some 'rules' are to be implemented, such as the assessment of the educational goal, the educational hardware and software, and the financial conditions. Pedagogy has to meet the virtual environment and reach an understanding of the desired training and professional development within a business context offering structure and course support (Olaniran and Edgell, 2008).

- *Service teams:* these teams are mainly dispensing advice and services that usually take place at call centres, such as customer support, data maintenance and network upgrades. They provide assistance 24 hours a day thanks to the distribution of team tasks, which are organized in a way so that one team is always operational. Their expertise and experience are usually offered to several organizations or locations, and joint efforts contribute to the completion of a project on a continuous basis. They might also be 'action team' that offer immediate responses, often to emergency situations. Time difference becomes an asset in this case by enabling companies to meet the market demand for the concerned service without disruption. The business model of those teams relies on the team members' capability to transfer the tasks to teammates. Consequently, transfer procedure should be clear, transparent and allow optimal hand-off (Gupta et al., 2011). Little research has been found on that topic in comparison to virtual project teams but, again, high-levels of collaborative work are deemed as critical in order to keep the customers satisfied.

5.3   TYPE OF TASKS IN A VIRTUAL TEAM

A team activity is composed of individual tasks that must be completed in order to accomplish the activity. The type of task affects the typology of virtual teams because it may increase or reduce the effect of virtuality (Martins et al., 2004). Therefore, some tasks seem more suitable for the virtual environment than others in comparison to face-to-face teams, such as an idea generation or a brainstorming type of task (Aiken and Vanjani, 1997; DeRosa et al., 2007; Glückler and Schrott, 2007). In those cases, virtuality requires less demanding coordination but really efficient communication tools. The tasks can be classified according to the level of dependence to each other and determined by the work itself or by virtue of team members' behaviours to the execution of their work. Some tasks might be highly independent, such as, for instance, in a sales team. Each sales person performs in one specific area independently from the other virtual team members and is rewarded for his/her own result. Once consolidated, those tasks globally contribute to the team performance. Other tasks can be more or less interdependent, more or less complex and organized, more or less unstable, ambiguous or innovative, more or less long, more or less spontaneously created (Wageman, 1995; Bell and Kozlowski, 2002; Gibson and Cohen, 2003; Vlaar et al., 2008). Here is a proposed classification of tasks in virtual teams based on their level of dependence to each other:

- *Pooled task interdependence:* concerns virtual team tasks when each member's individual contributions serve the common team objectives before the consolidation of the outcomes. The success of the virtual team's outcomes depends on the contribution of each individual or entity.
- *Sequential task interdependence:* is recognized when the virtual team members operate their tasks in a predetermined order. Each task output is necessary to perform the next one.
- *Reciprocal task interdependence:* occurs when each member's work depends on the others' contribution and from the information shared in close cyclical collaboration. For example, this is the case for a virtual team creating an advertising campaign, which requires writers, graphic artists and project managers to work closely together. Virtual teams operating with these type of tasks require specific management, including the highest intensity of interactions and skills adapted to the internal network complexity.
- *Task integration integrates different competencies to achieve the team objective:* an example can be, tasks that request the combination of 'knowledge to develop a new product', which 'requires extensive

internal social capital' and, therefore, a wide internal relational network (Gibson and Cohen, 2003). Integrated tasks often lead to the constitution of common best practices within virtual teams.

- *Task differentiation concerns customization to meet the demand of different markets:* which 'requires extensive links outside of the virtual team' (Gibson and Cohen, 2003).
- *Task duration:* can be permanent or temporary.
- *Task creation:* can be spontaneous or planned.
- *The higher the level of task interdependence:* then the higher the need for collaboration, coordination and communication is. Task interdependence might translate the level of interactions related to work between team members (Bosch-Sijtsema et al., 2011).

Indeed, collaborative communication is a crucial factor to consider seeing that the fit between the type of task and the implemented communication affects virtual team performance (Rico and Cohen, 2005). Therefore, the choice of communication technology is critical and should be optimized in order to facilitate the teamworking space and team capabilities to meet the changing demands of task interdependence (Rico and Cohen, 2005). With the appropriate technology, task interdependence presents an advantage in regards to virtual team management strategy. It is one way to foster cooperation among the team, especially at the start-up level of a virtual team (Hakonen and Lipponen, 2007) in addition to clear communication on what tasks will be the responsibility of the team. Role and context clarification is essential. It is very important to clearly explain to virtual team members so that they understand their tasks and environment, and create understanding especially 'when acts of sense-giving and sense-demanding are complemented with instances of sense-breaking' (Vlaar et al., 2008). It highlights the fact that organizational transparency contributes to performing teamwork and team membership but is not a smooth path, especially within a virtual context. Discontinuities may occur frequently, which increases the difficulty of sense-making and clarification at various levels.

5.4   CREATION OF VIRTUAL TEAMS

5.4.1   The Formation of Virtual Teams

The way that the team is formed at the inception level seems critical as it contributes to the effectiveness of virtual teams as 'a result of more openness, flexibility, diversity and access to information than in conventional teams' (Nemiro, 2001). (This is illustrated later in this book by the case study: 'Fashioning virtuality: The case of Eco Fashion World'.)

Researchers' first results on virtual team formation were focused on the difficulties that virtual teams could bring to organizations. Wong and Burton (2000) note that, when implementing or designing a virtual team, organizations should consider current situational needs and the coordination complexity while tolerating some possible errors. The addressed questions concern virtual team effectiveness and capabilities, in comparison to traditional face-to-face teams, to create comparable teamwork and exchange of information for a longer duration (Warkentin et al., 1997). To avoid these concerns, fundamental factors have to be considered when considering the formation of a virtual team: understand the reasons, objectives and mission as well as the conditions of virtual team implementation, the interactions of the virtual structure and the processes linked to that virtual team, including the type of requested tasks (Chinowsky and Rojas, 2003). Lifecycle models have been suggested, like the one proposed by Hertel et al. (2005). The researchers consider five phases to create a virtual team: preparation phase, launch, performance management, team development and disbanding, if needed. The preparation phase includes the mission and task assignment, staffing, reward system set up, choice of technology and organization integration. The launch phase is designed to kick-off the team activities and get team members interconnected, for example, through face-to-face team-building activities. It is the opportunity to clarify goals and intra-team rules. Clarification on the purpose and objectives of the virtual team to be created is necessary and should focus on 'a team charter, role clarification, operating guidelines and implementing technology protocols' (Nemiro et al., 2008). Performance management enables the establishment of the adequate leadership, to manage motivation, knowledge and communication. Through team development, the leader assesses the specific needs or issues in the virtual team process, such as individual or team training, and the effect of that training. Finally, if the virtual team is built on a temporary basis, the leader recognizes the achievement of the team activities and possibly the re-integration of the team members into the organization in the disbanding phase. When this is established, it is necessary to critically look at the 'virtual team task and the virtual team operating environment, its size and performance metrics' (Martins and Schilpzand, 2011). The team size influences the individual's behaviours, their commitment, participation and knowledge about the team strategy and purpose. Consequently, social interrelationships might more or less develop. The social dimension is also a key factor to be considered early in the phase of virtual team creation (Lin et al., 2008; Joy-Matthews and Gladstone, 2000). This dimension contributes to the team well-being and influences the interactions within the virtual team, including members' roles along with power and political relationships (Ratcheva and Vyakarnam, 2001). Most of the researchers underlined the need for a face-to-face meeting before or during the start-up phase of a virtual team in order to facilitate the social relationship crucial for group of individuals (Chinowsky and Rojas, 2003). It assumes that inter-organizational virtual teams develop according to specific patterns described as 'cyclical self-energizing processes' by Ratcheva and Vyakarnam (2001) where repetitive and cyclical actions or initiatives foster confidence in the project's success, and where individual satisfaction and ability to learn from one another allows for continuous improvement.

Accurate analysis of team inputs fuels the team process. These inputs are thus generating a different dynamic than in face-to-face groups. The research took the orientation to 'collaborative shape conceptualization' (Horvath and Rusak, 2001) demanding further consideration in terms of collaboration, trust building, synchronous communication and in the selection of technological tools. It requires a level of coordination that is much higher in consequent virtual teams (Martins and Schilpzand, 2011) because they embrace a wider degree of virtuality, which impacts their functioning. Martins and Schilpzand (2011) add 'respected and competent team members who have command over resources' and multicultural skills, in addition to a 'diffusion instead of a clustering of members across locations', which may request the expertise of a facilitator trained in virtual team processes. Staffing the virtual team is another step that contributes to virtual team typology. However, virtual teams are frequently not created for specific activities but as a response to organizational strategy to fulfil activities in globalized context. In this situation, virtual teams should be built up through the integration phase, rather complex if the virtuality is high. It should take into consideration diversity at a higher or lower degree, such as culture, organizations, habits, systems, companies, products etc. The relevance of virtual team members' integration here takes a clear dimension in terms of staffing the team.

5.4.2 The Member Selection or Staffing of Virtual Teams

Two other fundamental factors to consider when building up a virtual team are staffing the team (Nemiro et al., 2008) and the investment in people in terms of planning, training and informing. At inception, individual and interpersonal skills were not prioritized because virtual teams emerged from a consequence of globalization, and were the result of adaptation to a new environment. Virtual team members were selected for their technical skills or because they 'were already doing the job', even though technology and communication were prevalent issues requesting specific competencies.

However, it seems today, learning from past experiences, more preoccupation is given on how to integrate the best resources within virtual teams and how to remove critical barriers that may lead to virtual team failure. One challenge is to overcome the dispersion of collaborators who may constitute 'hidden profiles' that can foster a 'dispositional rather than a situational attribution' of the virtual job position within a virtual team (Cramton, 2001).

The fact that some of the virtual team members might work in different locations, e.g. a home office, hotel, while travelling, commuting, partner's office and business unit office, adds complexity to the team context. Knowledge transfer, coordination of information and team activities deemed alignment and integration of the whole team's activities through adapted infrastructure and managerial processes (Bosch-Sijtsema et al., 2011). This is also the case when one member is added to the core team, an example being a member with a different native language than the one that is usually practised in the team. Adaptation is requested to avoid possible misunderstanding in communication, especially when it concerns detailed messages (Watson-Manheim et al., 2012).

Geographical configuration of virtual teams, the number of sites and the numbers at different sites, may result in unbalanced staffing and create minorities within the team. However, Bazarova, Walther and McLeod's (2012) research shows that a virtual team member who holds a distant minority opinion may positively influence the whole team opinion. The condition lies in offering consistent arguments that generate higher majority change and improvement in majority. Similarly, a co-located member, who suggests consistent arguments but on a minority level, may not influence the opinion of the whole team. Consequently, faultlines may not develop and, on the contrary, groups with geographical isolates are likely to experience a positive dynamic.

The appropriate team selection could enlarge the global outcome of the team and develop optimal performance. Working in a virtual environment is not suitable for everyone, which leads Gibson and Cohen (2003) to define essential criteria. They identify personal characteristics to be critical, such as being able to set personal goals, work autonomously and take initiative.

They point out a further dimension that involves emotional control, tolerance for ambiguity and openness to new challenges. Critical skills are highlighted by researchers based on multiple forms of intelligence identified by Howard (1983): logical-mathematical, verbal-linguistic, interpersonal, intrapersonal, visual-spatial, bodily-kinesthetic, musical and naturalistic. Martins and Schilpzand (2011) focus their analysis on the following, summarizing the specific skills for virtual teaming:

- The requested intelligence: analytical, practical, creative and/or cultural.
- The identification of the learning style and educational level to adapt the right method.
- The level of general expertise and more specifically the functional expertise.
- The ability to adapt oneself to the environment, this includes communication ability within a virtual environment, especially when confronting the lack of feedback or participation, different time perception and a cross-cultural sensitivity. Diversity will affect the group dynamism, its way of functioning and reaching performance. It will enhance team creativity, team members' stimulation and collaborative teamwork while smoothing or exacerbating critical factors (Ocker, 2005; Bosch and Zhang, 2010).
- The experience of virtual teams, the virtual environment and the related technology.
- The network capacity and interpersonal awareness: virtual work requires team members' commitment 'beyond a job description to ensure connection, purpose, meaning and right focus' (Hoefling, 2003). A better balance between technical and interpersonal skills, especially communication skills, is beneficial to virtual teaming.

The list does not fit all organizations but highlights the skills, experiences and behaviours that are favourable for teamworking. To complete the staffing process Nemiro et al. (2008) recommend that virtual team leaders are tasked with selecting the right mix of individuals in the team to target effective team collaboration. The factors to be concerned are skills, cultures, experiences and any other asset that each individual can bring to the team. Socio-demographic characteristics can be embedded in the virtual team composition and, thus, integrate high levels of female-to-male ratio, low mean age and any national diversity (Muethel et al., 2012a). Thus, integrating diversity drives its acceptance and offers access to its benefits. The aim is to reach the necessary skills and talent richness to perform team activities and exploit market opportunities while reducing as much heterogeneity in team composition as possible. Some specific tools exist, for example, personality assessment systems (e.g. Myers-Briggs Type Indicator (MBTI) preferences, one of the most widely used personality assessments) which could give some clues on how individuals of a team can interact and collaborate together as suggested by Chinowsky and Rojas (2003) and Kirkman et al. (2002). Diversity in team composition is an asset when coordination is efficient. As for recruiting individuals, two approaches co-exist: the experience-based interview and the situational interview. The experience-based interview focuses on how the candidate *used to manage* the virtual team of which he/she was in charge. In a situational interview, the candidate is asked to explain how he/she *would manage* and solve hypothetical issues in a virtual team (Gibson and Cohen, 2003). One of the newest approaches to virtual team selection is the 'panel interview' and selection assessment done directly by the virtual team members. Thus, by being involved, virtual team members will later show a higher sense of welcome and socialization with the recruited candidate (Kirkman et al., 2004). However, one question can be raised about how frequently practitioners use these methods for team formation and how well leaders, and members are trained to use them. Staffing a virtual team is not the final objective in virtual team formation, as managers need to also give an identity to that team in order to make it extant within the organization.

5.4.3   The Identification to a Virtual Team

The individual identification of a group is the perception for the individual to exist as one entity within that group, in relation to the other team members and the organization. They feel like they are 'belonging to a social category' (Ashforth and Mael, 1989). This sense of 'belonging' or the need for affiliation (Mukherjee et al., 2012a) is critical for team members that are dealing with a lack of face-to-face meetings. The reason being that sense of 'belonging' is one of the key factors necessary to build team cohesion, which is crucial for virtual teams functioning while engaging membership. Decentralized and multiplied subidentities or subgroups may generate affective conflicts. Therefore, it negatively impacts the effectiveness of the group as Rezgui (2007) demonstrated the existence of a relationship between the virtual team identity and the effectiveness of a team.

For this reason, identification to a team and an organization is a necessary factor to be taken into account for virtual team characteristics. A virtual team should find its own identity as a group that is identified and recognized within the organization, to which virtual team members belong, or within interorganizational structure, in which they are embedded. Creating group identification, might be more or less problematic depending on the richness of the communication media and the complexity of the organization, which can be a home organization, different organizations or inter-organizational groups (Rockmann et al., 2007). Creating a group identification is more difficult for virtual teams than it is for face-to-face teams. Indeed, developing team awareness and membership is more complex in virtual settings, especially due to the impact of cultural differences of interpretation and language barriers, involving both oral and written communication.

Furthermore, individual identification to a team of an organization depends on the degree to which the individual identifies himself or herself with the concerned organization. The capacity for such identification includes the frequency of contact between the team member and the organization, and the visibility of the organizational membership, as well as the visibility of the concerned virtual team within the organization (Au and Marks, 2012). The individual's main motivation to identify oneself in groups is self-enhancement, while the reduction of uncertainty appears to be more strongly needed in virtual teams (Fiol and O'Connor, 2005). Individuals tend to bond with others when they recognize similarities among each other, on physical, cultural, geographical and social levels. Salient diversity existing in virtual teams reduces the similarities and, thus, offers a fertile ground for cultural stereotypes. Diversity does not necessarily make multinationalities an assumption. Intense cultural diversity within one country exists and the awareness of such diversity also helps to avoid mistaken assessment. For instance, India cannot be considered as one homogenous unit but as a multifaceted one. There is a high level of regional, linguistic, cultural and religious diversity across the country (Gaan, 2012). Researchers (Au and Marks, 2012) find that diversities push distant collaborators to create social relationships with local and co-located colleagues, which can lead to subgroup identities. The introduction of each team member is essential through communication of their personal values, experiences, profile and expectations within that team, which serves to build trust within the virtual team. It may improve team cohesion. Identification to an organization or a team might present sensitive effects. Hakonen and Lipponen (2007) have pointed out the existence of a link between virtual team identity and the perception of fairness regarding outcomes distribution and the decision-making process. Virtual team members are more sensitive than face-to-face team members to the perception of equity and recognition within the organization, considered as a crucial clue in the identification process. Fairness and trust has a strong correlation with the affective commitment of the virtual team members to their group and their experience with the socio-emotional processes (Powell et al., 2004). Affective commitment fosters job satisfaction, respect and pride to belong to that group while building a relationship inside the team. Therefore, the organization and team leadership need to create and maintain the identification processes. The process includes the promotion of strong psychological ties between virtual team members as well as shared goals to avoid the negative effects of reduced or non-existent identification. One of these effects may create a feeling of isolation. The fact that the organization values a team member as an individual directly impacts the individual's involvement in teamwork and satisfaction. It is then that the individual identifies to that team, which contributes to a higher quality of social relationships. Actually, teams with high levels of identification reach higher degrees of loyalty and trust (Au and Marks, 2012). In any case, the identification process is fostered by the team configuration, playing a key role as facilitator.

5.4.4 The Configuration of a Virtual Team

Configuration refers to the way that virtual team members are organized across sites, independently of the spatial and temporal distances among them (O'Leary and Cummings, 2007). The configuration gathers diverse cultures, preferences, organizations and experiences toward common interests and goals. It defines the virtual team's architecture and specifies the 'properties of the persons involved in the team', roles and responsibilities assigned to each member, skills, organization, authorization level, access control and document templates (Dustdar, 2004). The configuration of a virtual team defines the need for diversity and virtuality. An effective configuration supports team cohesion and may generate a dynamic in the group if each virtual team member has the appropriate skills to achieve the team goal. It stabilizes and sustains the virtual team within the organizational structure that supports the team configuration by linking appropriate learning capabilities to process-aware collaborative systems and resources (Dustdar, 2004). If not effective, the virtual team configuration may not cope with high heterogeneity generated in the team, which will negatively affect the team performance (Bosch and Zhang, 2010). Virtual team members might feel more or less isolated. They may create subgroups to compensate and balance geographical distances.

Some researchers imagined 'faultlines', a supposed frontier, between the subgroups that results in weakening the team effectiveness, especially by reducing communication, trust, identification, transactive memory and by increasing conflict and coordination problems (Polzer et al., 2006). It is especially true for the smaller sub-groups where identification is more problematic (O'Leary and Mortensen, 2010). In such a case, team management is crucial in the team formation process and especially when introducing the team members.

Managers have to make sure that the individuals identify themselves to the whole team and not to one subgroup only. The three following elements are therefore crucial for virtual team configuration: people, team purpose and connections that are much more developed than in face-to-face teams thanks to the ICTs. Therefore, team configuration and team formation have a strong impact on the group dynamic, more specifically in group identification, group transactive memory, conflict and coordination problems.

5.4.5 The Boundaries Influencing Virtual Teams

The virtual distance and virtuality intensify the number and the complexity of boundaries at the work and social level, fostered by possible mistrust in technology. Researchers consider that virtual teams have to intensify efforts to smooth disparities emerging from multiple barriers (Ratcheva and Vyakarnam, 2001; Shachaf, 2005).

Boundaries characterizing virtual teams continuously evolve through a dynamic phenomenon of continuities and discontinuities, such as breaks in information or communication flows. Continuities and discontinuities impact virtual teams and their members, whose perception and weight might be different and, thus, not always considered as problematic (Watson-Manheim et al., 2012). However, discontinuities are recognized by virtual team members as a disruption and request minimum concentration and attention to be overcome.

When discontinuities are considered as a standard environment that is embedded in virtual work, then they do not present a barrier to virtual teamwork and become continuities. The process of transferring discontinuities to continuities is more obvious when virtual team members are aware of the existing discontinuities. The more visible the boundaries, the more proactive the virtual team members can be. They adapt their behaviour to reduce problems associated with varying conditions in order to perform team activities effectively and efficiently. Continuities are necessary key factors for the successful performance of virtual teams.

Some situations may contribute to the implementation of continuities. Watson-Manheim et al. (2012) mention the case of collaborators working temporarily in a partner company. They may provide more continuities with distant colleagues from their own company than with local colleagues from the partner company, as common practices and understanding are expected. Our study retains the most sensitive boundaries for virtual teaming, identified as spatial (geographical and temporal) boundaries, cultural and social, organizational and functional barriers. Additional boundaries could be added, such as political, administrative and economic, whose level of differences may increase distance between some countries but we are keeping focus on the process of virtual teaming. Most of the time, researchers link the barriers below or a part of them together as they are interrelated (Lee et al., 2006):

- *Geographical boundaries:* physical distance is a dimension commonly studied by researchers when dealing with virtual team topics and it is often associated with geographical and temporal boundaries. Geographical means some distance among the virtual team members with different distances of physical separation, which reduces the possibility for the virtual team members to meet regularly. Therefore, computer and communication technologies play a relevant role in linking the team members and in making virtual processes possible, which would have been very challenging some decades ago. Both distance and technology may generate conflicts inside the team because virtual team members are sharing less common context than in a face-to-face context (Hinds and Bailey, 2003). It also makes the individual and team management more sensible to the feeling of frustration due to distance. Managers need to adopt the necessary skills to lead those dispersed teams. The key issue for individuals and team leaders to overcome that challenge is to successfully build a shared meaning and a common context in order to moderate the communication breakdowns (Bjørn and Ngwenyama, 2009) and to implement an effective coordination (Cummings, 2011). Some managerial techniques can soften those distance boundaries. The lack of shared context can be reduced with the acquisition of complementary skills, the creation of a collaborative platform with shared goals, temporal coordination and social integration, taking into account the cultural differences (Persson and Mathiassen, 2010). One difficulty in those techniques is to benefit from the cultural diversity and use it as an asset rather than a barrier. Geographical distance brings valuable contribution to IHRM by offering the opportunity to hire the most suitable employees located anywhere in the world (Townsend et al., 1998).
- *Temporal boundaries:* virtual team members operate from different locations across the world and are, therefore, working within different time zones. Time difference offers an advantage for some organizations, an example being for customer service because a virtual team can meet the demand on a 24-hour time frame and reduces real-time problem-solving (O'Leary and Cummings, 2007). However, temporal dispersion is a sensitive aspect to be handled in virtual teams. The higher the degree of dispersion in different time zones, the less synchronous the communication is. It requests higher coordination within the team, which affects the virtual team members' interaction behaviour. Moreover, interactions become even more difficult to reach if the team works under shift pattern (Espinosa and Carmel, 2003). Temporal separation appears to have

a greater negative impact than spatial distance as far as team performance is concerned. Extended geographical dispersion can create coordination problems, which indirectly impact team performance in a negative way due to time differences. However, when coordination problems are smoothed out, the negative effect of time zone differences on team performance significantly reduces (Espinosa et al., 2012). If successful, temporal coordination is positively associated to the team performance, even though coordination is not the team performance driver (Massey et al., 2003). It moderates the temporal barriers and risk of conflict through mechanisms such as 'scheduling' (setting deadlines that help to design, organize and execute projects and tasks), 'synchronization' (balancing the effort within the team) and 'allocation of resources' (defining the time to allocate on specific tasks) (Montoya-Weiss et al., 2001).

Additionally, other actions contribute to the reduction of temporal boundaries such as the control of the projects' and tasks' advancement with correction of discrepancies, social integration managing the cross-cultural differences and technical integration, including technical compatibility across the organizations. Synchronization determines the group rhythm based on the cycle or frequency when the team synchronizes and co-relates. Some tools are developed in order to create the awareness of availability or non-availability, for instance, showing or not the team member's presence via computer-symbolic and coded cues or calendar sharing. The temporal dispersion is directly affected by the geographical dispersion when the virtual team members' location is extended on broad time zones. Furthermore, cultural diversity comes as an additional factor because the perception of time is not the same as it is for different cultures.

- *Cultural and social boundaries, sometimes referred to as transnational:* cultural boundaries have a direct influence on interpersonal communication (Montoya-Weiss et al., 2001) and are considered to be, with temporal boundaries, the most relevant obstacle to project success due to its diversity and complexity (Lee et al., 2006). The research community suggests various definitions of culture. For the purpose of this book, we consider culture as a term that includes all capabilities, habits, ideas and values that characterize a group or society, acquired by a person within the group or society. It demonstrates the way of life of that group or society. Additionally, the complexity of virtual teams, including members from various organizations, increases the multicultural aspect. However, virtual teaming may reduce problematic cultural differences as long as these differences are recognized and valued (Connaughton and Shuffler, 2007; Symons and Stenzel, 2007). Cultural and social boundaries are often presented through diversities such as context and social area, work practices, gender, language, tradition, uncertainty avoidance (the degree to which cultures accept uncertainty, risks and ambiguity), sets of values, and dichotomies. These dichotomies are identified by Hofstede (1980) as individualism–collectivism, high-low context, monochronic–polychronic, long term/short term-oriented and masculinity–femininity. Individualistic cultures value the individual demands, responsibility and initiative, which show the level of the group integration within an organization, while collectivism rewards the actions of the group (Jarvenpaa and Leidner, 1999). Collectivist orientation seems more favourable to virtual team processes (Mockaitis et al., 2012) but further research should confirm that statement. High-context culture communicates easily through an implicit mode based on personal relationships while low context culture prefers explicit and concrete language, and does not look for multiplying personal relationships. Low-context cultures, e.g. Anglo-Saxons, Germanics and Scandinavians, are more task focused, and prefer written, unequivocal, literal, structured communication, and make a clear distinction between social and professional communication. However, virtual means of communication do not hide the cultural differences (Mockaitis et al., 2012). Differences between a monochronic and a polychronic culture issue from the perception of time and the way that time is used to perform tasks. Time perception impacts the individual sense of emergency. Monochronic people usually do one thing at one time, are committed and concentrate on their tasks, respect privacy, and other group members' working sphere and, in most cases, are low-context communicating persons. Polychronic people deal with several tasks, consider schedules with a more fluid approach, can change tasks easily, give importance to relationships and, in most cases, belong to high-context communication. At the team level, the rhythm of task completion, in respect of planning and synchronization within the virtual team and with other virtual teams, is influenced by social diversity. As a result it affects the team performance (Martins and Schilpzand, 2011). Cultures presenting high masculinity characteristics value the male assertiveness and competitiveness in contrast to femininity, where modesty, interpersonal care and caring prevail. Team members who are a part of the feminine culture tend to be less competitive and aggressive when interacting with their teammates. Women's groups have a longer duration and seem more satisfied of the group collaboration and can resolve conflict easier than teams that are composed of men (Martins et al., 2004). These differences help to predict the individual and group behaviour in reference to their national culture (Pauleen, 2003b) but shows at the same time the complexity of diversity and possible conflicts or feeling of discomfort. Jain and Singh (2013) suggest from their studies administering a questionnaire to measure the level of comfort existing between local culture and foreign culture within multinational companies. They demonstrate that this level of comfort varies among countries, which highlights one more time the complexity of dealing with diversity and virtuality. However, culture is not static and the above-described cultural attributes should be considered as general cultural trends. Culture may operate at a conscious and unconscious level (Symons and Stenzel, 2007). Not all individuals behave as expected by the identified culture, group or society but still, stereotypes might prevail. 'Statements about cultures are not statements about the individual' (Hofstede et al., 1991). The wider and the most diverse the team profile is, the more complex the communication at the team level is (Martins and Schilpzand, 2011). A common language needs to be determined. English is the predominant business language, which requires language skills including the ability to express and understand ideas, and technical processes, in a language different to one's native language (Shachaf, 2005). The adaptation of spoken and written communication plays a key role as well. A lack of skills in those areas may easily build misunderstandings and barriers. The communication mode needs to be balanced and adapted to the group profile, as well as to the leadership of the team. The team leader needs to adjust his/her communication strategy accordingly and find a balance in the group. It strengthens the performance of virtual teams facing cultural differences (Montoya-Weiss et al., 2001) and avoids some breakdowns in group collaboration and trust building. The awareness of different value orientations within the team is essential. Such awareness means to be able to identify the dominance inside the group without neglecting the minorities, and to propose appropriate operating guidelines on the methods of working. DiStefano and Maznevski (2000) suggest three steps to create value within a virtual team: (1) identify and describe the differences among the virtual team members; (2) consider and explain the differences to each member; and (3) integrate them by monitoring collaboration and developing adapted ways of working.

However, it is often difficult or even impossible to identify the origin of the cultural discordance within multicultural virtual teams.

The challenge is 'to find the suitable managerial behavioural process' (Symons and Stenzel, 2007) and a realistic timeframe in a constantly changing virtual context. Cross-cultural education and training is relevant in the that respect it enables behaviour adjustment because it should lead to an acknowledgment of the cultural diversity, which is a starting point for behavioural adaptation. This is also one way to decrease stereotypes about each other that are often related to cultural beliefs of the status within the company about the function that the virtual team members represent (James and Ward, 2001). The more experience virtual team members are gaining in the virtual work environment, the more willing they are to know about the other members' culture and to share their own culture (Anawati and Craig, 2006). This learning develops intercultural competences, which is only possible through the existence of cultural diversity within the virtual team (Bartel-Radic, 2006). Anawati and Craig (2006) proposed some recommendations in favour of cultural adaptation among which team socialization, cultural differences awareness and acceptation are essential. Learning from differences may push virtual team members to develop and adapt the appropriate behaviour to approach the team diversity, as supposed by Martins and Schilpzand (2011) (who have not found though proven results within academic research).

- *Organizational boundaries:* the emergence of virtual teams created new models of organizations incorporating new ways of working, integrating technology, computer-mediated communication, and a wider range of potential talented employees. The aim was to respond with capabilities requested by the virtual environment and to extent the initial organization to suppliers, customers, development partners, or any stakeholders involved in the virtual team project. The role of an organization is to anticipate the evolution of its context towards virtuality. 'When team members are co-located, they are not likely to interface through virtual means' and they have not developed the adequate behaviour (Kirkman and Mathieu, 2005). The organization should prepare and develop a culture toward virtuality, even if virtuality does not mean dispersion of individuals in every case. However, some of the co-located members may interact with virtual means and should be prepared for it (Kirkman and Mathieu, 2005). As the use of ICTs is one of the major characteristics of virtual teams (Mihhailova, 2007) the appropriate choice of an efficient communication and an effective coordination can influence the virtual team members and the different stakeholders to lever the weight of those barriers. Further findings consider the organizational barriers as a challenge to human resource management because they are more or less able to capture the implicit knowledge. Organizational boundaries are part of a context where organizational structure and strategic governance are a prerequisite to the success of the virtual team's process and development, interrelated with the other critical barriers. Pauleen and Yoong (2001) demonstrate that the differences in organizational cultures and policies are building some organizational barriers.

• *Functional boundaries:* a functional organization is based on a hierarchical structure where tasks and functions are clearly identified and separated e.g. production, marketing, human resources or accounting. Cross-functional relationships are those existing between virtual team members from the same hierarchical level but with different functions and interrelated tasks. A virtual team might be organized with a clear separation of functions or tasks that it performs, including non-routine tasks such as those mentioned earlier. A highly functional categorization within a team is able to bring a higher level of collaboration within the concerned group. The reason is that team members of a highly collaborative team tend to use the same terminology and mode of communication. For example, a virtual R&D team composed of scientific experts and technical specialists share the same goal e.g. the use of a complex tool, or a common interest in results. It gives them a level of autonomy but cross-functional barriers are likely to appear when the categorization is strictly delimited between different functional groups (Kauppila et al., 2011). The collaboration between those groups becomes more difficult, especially if the power distance is high because reducing the inter-group exchanges will negatively influence the team performance. Poor communication and collaboration across groups reduces the responsiveness of the virtual teams, which is not in line with the rapid change environment that usually frames virtual teams. If barriers are overcome, they improve the composition of the virtual team by having experts, in their respective fields, generating diversity in capabilities between the functional groups (Paul et al., 2004a). One way to reduce functional boundaries is to clearly explain the role of each member. Lower ambiguity reduces functional barriers and internal conflict, especially if members hold various roles (Bell and Kozlowski, 2002). Consequently, a team mindset can develop within the team. It is, however, rather complex to implement in a virtual team, more than in traditional co-located teams (Breu and Hemingway, 2004).

Overcoming all these boundaries gives specific characteristics to virtual teams, such as flexibility, adaptation and responsiveness (Bell and Kozlowski, 2002) with one main challenge to be able to set up team cohesion and apply the appropriate managerial processes. This cohesion can be sustainable if an exclusive-culture-to-the-group is created (Bell and Kozlowski, 2002) in addition to a regular assessment on the team progress in order to keep benefiting from the advantages of the virtual team.

5.5 TO KEEP IN MIND: THE RELEVANCE OF UNDERSTANDING THE VIRTUAL TEAM CHARACTERISTICS

The identification of the virtual team attributes is relevant in understanding the context because the essential characteristics of the concerned virtual team and the possible barriers that may hamper a leader to effectively conduct that team to the expected outcomes. The members of a virtual team need to be aware of the set of member groups they belong to, how the subgroups or the whole team system are interrelated, and how the member, as an individual is linked to the team and to the other member groups. It is crucial, when building up such teams, that members conceptualize the team system and understand the effect of their actions and behaviour. The reason is that the virtual teams' attributes influence the virtual teams' processes and outcomes.

The accurate identification of the virtual team inputs allows a leader or an organization to use the adequate levers to manage the virtual team and maximize the benefit they can gain from virtuality and virtual teaming. Adler et al. (2003) highlight the importance of explicit training, which can be on-the-job or outsourced training, to improve understanding and adaptation to virtual teamwork.

5.6 CONCLUSION

The virtual team input analysis is essential because it leads to an understanding of virtual team development. Virtual team inputs determine the complexity of those teams and their uniqueness or difference to each other through diverse ways, such as gender, thinking style, function, culture. According to the virtual team setting, specific and adapted models, and methods for the most suitable approach of virtual teaming need to be considered. When the team attributes are clarified, it makes easier for the virtual team leader to clearly communicate the goals, organization, and identity of the team. Virtual team leaders may also identify the possible dysfunction and conflicts inside the team more easily. However, one question with no answer found yet in the academic research is how often practitioners use these tools, models and methods to build virtual teams, and communicate within and outside the team environment. The same question also remains for organizations as to whether they are willing to adapt the infrastructure to virtual teaming. We assume that it depends on the culture and training that the companies develop in their organization but this remains a hypothesis as no proven results have been found. It may rely on the business pressure too, the willingness and the capacity of an organization to anticipate and remain competitive. In most of the studies, the analysis of virtual team attributes is done with experimental teams e.g. students involved in educational systems or with virtual teams already existing and embedded in an organization. We suggest that future research may look deeper into the possible application of their findings to teams that evolve from conventional to virtual team. The complexity of change versus creation of virtual teams may request different managerial processes within such global teams. One last point that we suggest for further analysis is the cost for boundary issues and coordination that organizations are facing, as well as investment in technologies, communication and training. How profitable are virtual teams to organizations in regards to money or when do they start to be financially profitable? Could it depend on the efficiency of the virtual team processes?

5.7 GUIDELINES FOR MANAGERIAL PRACTICES: MAIN INPUTS AND CHARACTERISTICS OF A VIRTUAL TEAM

When the virtual team is more clearly framed within an organization and its architecture, the virtual team manager needs to focus on the characteristics of the team. The virtual team manager should detect the type of virtual team she/he manages to possibly adjust her/his managerial style in order to reach the desired objectives. Therefore, the purpose of these guidelines are to facilitate the identification of the team attributes, along with its main missions and objectives. The virtual team manager can list the possible barriers and levers, and explicitly communicate to the team members the team they belong to.

Table 5.1   Six main attributes to characterize your team

Key actions (Analyse your team as follows)	Key results (Complete the following)
– Infrastructure	– See previous guidelines (Chapter 4)
– Objectives and missions	– List the main activity of that team (e.g. education, entrepreneurship, sales, brainstorming etc.). – List the main missions.
– Type of virtual team	– Networked or parallel, executive or project development, educational etc.
– Type of tasks	– Permanent or temporary, spontaneous or planned, interdependent or independent.
– Team creation	– List the reason for the team creation. – Detail its composition and configuration. – Precise: if the team members have been prepared/trained for virtual teaming.
– Team boundaries and diversity	– Name geographical distance, time zones, and cultural and social diversity within the team. – Describe the organizational and functional architecture (e.g. vertical and horizontal).

PART III

Virtual team processes

The concept of a virtual team is to date rather well-defined as a result of extensive academic findings. The understanding of virtual team functions and key processes is more limited due to the constant evolution and adaptation of this way of working as well as the context in which those virtual teams operate. The next three chapters are dedicated to the processes of virtual teams and demonstrate how virtual teams work, what processes are critical and at which levels they are involved. Even though some researchers have argued that co-located and virtual teams require the same skills and processes (Nemiro, 2001), this cannot be totally validated today due to the complexity in which virtual teams evolve. Researchers highlight specific skills and processes for virtual teaming, which are longer and more difficult to create, more delicate to set up and maintain than in the case of co-located teams as summarized by Berry (2011). We identify three main categories of processes: socio-emotional, technological and managerial, as shown in Figure III.1 below. They are strongly interrelated and cannot be dissociated but are addressed separately in the next trio of chapters of Part III.

Chapter 6 investigates the socio-emotional processes, which include communication and collaboration processes, knowledge management and trust building. Whereas Chapter 7 addresses technological and work processes. Chapter 8 focuses on virtual team leadership and conflict management in the virtual context.

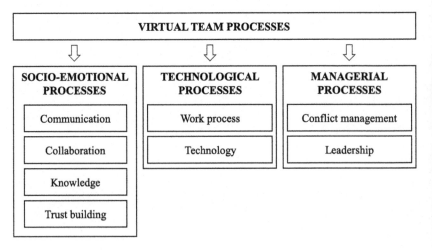

Figure III.1   Virtual team processes

6 Socio-emotional processes

6.1 INTRODUCTION

This chapter investigates the socio-emotional processes which includes both communication and collaboration processes, viz. knowledge management and trust building. The communication processes are closely linked to the choice of media and quality of communications that have a direct implication on virtual team's social and interpersonal relationships. Communication in a virtual context requires adaptation to virtual team members and managers. Virtual team leaders may use communication as a lever to facilitate an adequate level of communication that enables them to create or maintain necessary social dimensions and an adequate communication structure. As for collaboration, researchers consider that virtual team members spend a considerable degree of their time in coordinating, communicating and collaborating activities, which decreases real productivity time. We define the meaning of collaboration for virtual teaming, explore its processes and role, and highlight the critical challenges when building collaboration in a virtual context. Knowledge management is another element within the socio-emotional processes that play a key role. It is relevant to understand the role of knowledge for virtual teams and organizations, the different types of knowledge and the processes linked to knowledge. Finally, we underline the reasons why it might be difficult to develop, maintain and sustain knowledge in virtual teams. A communication adapted to a virtual team goal, collaboration and knowledge transfer cannot occur without a certain degree of trust in virtual teams. We propose to look on the different forms of trust existing in virtual teaming, the role of trust in virtual team processes and how to build trust within a virtual environment.

6.2 COMMUNICATION PROCESSES IN VIRTUAL TEAMS

6.2.1 Definition

Virtual and collaborative communication, or e-communication, can be identified as computer-mediated or electronic communication that is the advanced technological way of transmitting information between sender and receiver to enable action, or move contents to remote locations through diverse forms. It is characterized as an 'interactive, complex and limiting process' (Burlea, 2007) to be considered not only as intraorganizational but also as interorganizational, including external relationships with stakeholders. The exchange of information and knowledge as well as the speed of that exchange increases the volume of interconnections and might lead to possible leaks and complicated negotiations Sussman (2008). Therefore, the communication infrastructure of the organization influences the communication processes within that organization. The purpose is to monitor the virtual exchanges, with the appropriate choice of media and the requested level of communication quality, as well as the social and interpersonal relationships. The virtual team leader has to cope with the virtual communication challenges and measure the consequences.

6.3 CHOICE OF MEDIA AND QUALITY OF COMMUNICATION

The type of media is decisive in the communication processes because it contributes to the communication efficiency and quality. Two decades ago, at the earlier stage of virtual team building, the choice of media was pretty much linked to technological limitation. At that time, computer-mediated communication was seen as a lean electronic communication that led to numerous breakdowns and thus, to high frustration and great criticism (Reza et al., 2006; Sadowski-Rasters et al., 2006).

Today, communication media can offer both high richness and social presence, which fosters interactions between virtual team members and positively affects the social relationships within the team (Andres, 2002). Richer media (video or audio conferencing, instant messages, web conferences etc.) bring significant improvement because they convey more cues, e.g. tone, pauses, expressions (Malhotra and Majchrzak, 2005). However, breakdowns can turn a virtual team process into very poor results. The quality of the selected media appears as essential but the reasons for breakdowns are not limited to technology issues. The existing level of trust, interpersonal relations, cultural differences, membership and leadership influence the quality of communication too (Daim et al., 2012). Virtual communication is a medium used to temporarily coordinate actions, and perform tasks but might be limited to conveying visual cues and it is often asynchronous.

Media that conveys asynchronous communication is frequently used for information transmission while synchronous communication is preferred for knowledge, idea and meaning sharing. In fact, synchronicity assumes frequent interactive communication supported by ICTs, which is one way to reduce feedback delay and bring rhythm within a virtual team (Kirkman and Mathieu, 2005; Walther and Bunz, 2005; Jawadi and Boukef Charki, 2011). Synchronicity or asynchronicity might be preferred by some cultural dominance and that impacts the choice of media, according to Martins and Schilpzand (2011) based on Massey et al.'s (2003) work.

Rich media and synchronous interactions are preferred by the individualistic, low-context and low uncertainty avoidance type of cultures who use explicit communication. Reciprocally, lean media and asynchronous communication is more naturally used by the collectivistic, high context and high uncertainty avoidance type of cultures, which is more at ease with implicit communication and written messages that reduce cultural and linguistic differences. The quality of communication and the effectiveness of information exchange are not only dependent on technology and characteristics of communication, but also on the social relationship level in the virtual team.

Thus the socio-organizational context of virtual teams requires different forms of communication media (Sadowski-Rasters et al., 2006) which can offer lean or rich communication. Lean media reduce 'social context cues' and the rich media allow the transmission of 'high level of non-verbal cues' (Sadowski-Rasters et al., 2006). Technology advances offer a 'portfolio of Information and Communication Technologies (ICTS)' (Jawadi and Boukef Charki, 2011) and different tools: e.g. white boards, collaborative document editors, instant messaging, hands-up features, podcasting and team rooms to create a virtual workspace as similar as possible to a face-to-face type of relationship (Malhotra and Majchrzak, 2005).

Audio conferencing tools enable virtual team meetings via telephone, where individuals dial a telephone number, enter a meeting identification number and join the meeting. They usually offer some features e.g. individual or all participants' mute application, toll-free national and international conferencing numbers and meeting management tools, which requires a connection to a PC through an organization network or via the Internet.

Meeting tools are shared documents and slides viewing, common notepads or white boards, hands-up features, participant lists, 'chat' possibility during the meeting and a 'team room' that is a virtual space where the team members can share calendars and store common files. Chats or instant messages are usually used for informal types of communication while emails and discussion boards or forums are chosen for deeper or professional communication because they give extended access to data and information (Gareis, 2006).

The choice of communication media is not limited to a role of message transmission. It has wider goals e.g. 'message acknowledgment, enhancement of mutual understanding, and participation in multiple communication interactions'. Therefore, virtual team members use multiple types of media to reach 'specific communication goals' (Bélanger and Watson-Manheim, 2006) and flexible communication practices adapted to the virtual team activity (Paretti and McNair, 2008). Tools develop continuously, thus, offering any-time-any-place accessibility: wireless laptop, mobile phones, 3G or 4G connection and smart phones, touchpads etc. Technology gets continuously adapted to the latest contextual parameters taking into account the major obstacle that prevents certain categories of people from working virtually. Thus, the hard-of-hearing can participate in an e-meeting thanks to equipment translating sounds into transcribed text (for example, the Tadeo Platform system). This is also the case for persons who face verbal difficulties. They can be technically assisted in their communication with other team players. However, electronic media show some limitation on integration and socialization of members in a virtual team, especially for new-comers who tend to look for explicit information (Ahuja and Galvin, 2003). The leader has to evaluate the team need in terms of communication media according to the virtual team composition and also according to the type of tasks to be achieved by the team. The more complex and equivocal the tasks, the richer the medium should be (Rasters et al., 2002).

Researchers recommend that virtual team leaders look for alternative means of communication and draw their attention to the fact that the requested levels of communication and/or coordination would not be easy to set up, especially if a part of the team is co-located (Rafii, 1995; Rockett et al., 1998). Research is pursuing efforts to find out the best means to communicate, understand and share knowledge through tools e.g. argument mapping tools that allow the possibility for users to create, navigate and edit argument maps.

An argument map that is accessible on the Internet enables the visualization of reasoning and discussion. The distant users can follow who speaks and drives the discussion. An argument map provides more performing results when compared to a debate dashboard because it reduces misunderstanding and cognitive efforts. A debate dashboard is a visualization of consolidated and easy-to-read information discussed during the debate. As a result, distant users can share a higher volume of more complex knowledge (Iandoli et al., 2012). However, the whole benefit of such an argument map is not yet totally proven. Discussion and idea generation might not be as spontaneous as they could be since users have to follow a certain 'discussion format'. Research is ongoing about this topic. Thanks to technological advances, Timmerman and Scott (2006) suggest that the choice of communicative media is rather linked to virtual team structural characteristics and that communication is related to the team outcomes. To date, the retained criteria considered as determinant when selecting the appropriate media are the accessibility to the communication medium for all the virtual team members, the possibility for technology to reduce social distance and the capability of the media to facilitate idea and information-sharing (Sivunen and Valo, 2006).

6.3.1 Social and Interpersonal Relationships

Electronic communication enables the creation and the development of virtual relationships within a virtual context. The process is complex and is linked to the importance of the social capital existing in the virtual team. Social capital is the capacity for the team to develop and sustain social and personal interrelationships among the virtual team members. This capacity is considered as an essential contributor to the team performance (Warkentin et al., 1997; DeLuca and Valacich, 2006; Dubé and Robey, 2009; Lin et al., 2008; Badrinarayanan et al., 2011; Jawadi and Boukef Charki, 2011) depending on the team members' capacity to understand the expectations of those with whom they are communicating online (Brewer, 2008b). Researchers show that communication in virtual teams is mainly focused on tasks and work. When work develops, communication tends to extend to interpersonal and social aspects (Dubé and Robey, 2009; Lin et al., 2008). Those relationships are essential in the knowledge transfer process, that is further discussed later in this chapter. They are very useful for virtual creative activities, to set up a collaborative work climate (Ocker, 2005) and to reduce social distance (O'Leary and Cummings, 2007). It is necessary to remember this point when forming and composing a virtual team in order to grasp the challenges linked to virtual communication and be prepared to use the right lever.

6.3.2 Challenges and Consequences of Communication in a Virtual Context

Asynchronicity of communication within multicultural virtual teams is one of the main challenges of virtual communication. We previously mentioned that some cultures might be more at ease than others with time differences and asynchronous communication might be adequate to convey certain types of information or knowledge. The fact that individuals in a virtual team are dissociated by the timeframe might negatively impact the effectiveness of the interrelational communication and, as a result, might also affect trust building and performance of the team, because these are closely interrelated. Some researchers' findings show that if the temporal dissociation between individuals is low, synchronous communication is preferred by the team members (Rutkowski et al., 2007). Asynchronicity constraint is increased by the various boundaries and virtual characteristics of the virtual team in addition to a computer-mediated communication that offers lower richness and social presence than face-to-face communication. Additionally, this brake can lead to misunderstandings and ambiguity (Scullion and Collings, 2006). The reduced non-verbal and non-visual communication cues associated with increased usage of technology explain why some virtual teams take more time to make decisions, are less reactive in terms of feedback and are less able to interfere with members (Tyran et al., 2003). This point reveals two further communication challenges within a virtual team: the ability to send messages that are heard/seen by the team members and the ability to get a feedback from the recipient (Gibson and Cohen, 2003) without overloading the recipients' mail box. Provision and quality of feedback is a critical factor in affective conflict resolution in virtual teams, as criticism of virtual team members' ideas might be interpreted as a personal criticism if communication is misunderstood (Ayoko et al., 2012). Written communication, e.g. emails, should achieve a balance between 'task-oriented and socio-emotional communication' (Amant and Zemliansky, 2008) even though the efficiency of emails in the socio-emotional area is still discussed today. As a matter of fact, exchanges in email form may lead to 'information asymmetry' (Malhotra and Majchrzak, 2005) which means that the distribution list of message receivers might leave some members out of the discussion and information exchange, intentionally or unintentionally. On the other hand, keeping all of the team members in the distribution list may unnecessarily overload the message in-tray. The size of the group intensifies the level of this challenge, which can be moderated by computer-mediated technology in comparison with face-to-face teams (Lowry et al., 2006). Some subgroups may emerge to cope with group size, e.g. in a parent company and its subsidiaries. Boundaries between subgroups will reduce (Panteli and Davison, 2005) and that enables those smaller groups to improve communication, increase internal interactions (Andres, 2006) and keep the team performing positively. However, the fact that the group splits into smaller groups might also negatively affect the team outcomes. The efficiency of processes on accurate information exchange or workload sharing tends to decrease. Maintaining a common shared mindset within the whole team appears to be more difficult under these circumstances (Polzer et al., 2006). To cope with those challenges, virtual communication skills can be improved by specific training on interpersonal communication rather than on the use of software only (Warkentin and Beranek, 1999) especially in a multicultural context (Rosenberg, 2005). Relational training boosts the team cohesion and the individual perception of satisfaction (Beranek and Martz, 2005).

6.3.3 Managerial Accommodations to Communication in a Virtual Context

Effective team management is requested at this level to focus on not only the individual's technical skills or qualifications but also on the leader's capability to establish interpersonal relationships, on the 'social dimension' (Lin et al., 2008) where communication acts as a tool. To maintain performing outcomes for the whole group, the team manager has to focus on the whole group's shared identity, performance and communication rather than on the subgroup level. In that case, communication is intended and not naturally or spontaneously prompted. Thus, the manager can implement a technical know-how but also a communication structure within the team, which positively influences the performance of the team (Glückler and Schrott, 2007). Leaders and team players create norms and communication standards to ease their way of communicating (Dubé and Paré, 2001; Dubé and Robey, 2009; Gibson and Gibbs, 2006). Eventually, the interrelation among the leader's role, the socio-emotional communication strategy and the chosen technology are critical components for the collaboration and performance of a virtual team.

6.4 COLLABORATION BUILDS RELATIONSHIPS AND SOCIO-EMOTIONAL PROCESSES

6.4.1 Definition

Collaboration can also be named e-collaboration, collaborative teamwork, 'co-labouring' (Levina and Vaast, 2008) teaming and best-practices sharing. It is question of collaboration when groups with different practices, cultures, interests and skills are involved in common work (Levina and Vaast, 2008), common agreement and shared meaning. Virtual team members collaborate when they share their individual effort, resources and relationships to reach the team objective and performance while maintaining their functional independence and autonomy (Ko et al., 2011). Hoefling (2008) is more specific and mentions the need for an 'emotional connection' between members, which closely ties collaboration to communication (Turban et al., 2011). Virtual collaboration is only possible when the team succeeds in building mutual relationships and context while overcoming the complexity of coordination, rather challenging within virtual context (Cramton and Webber, 2005).

6.4.2 Processes to Build Collaboration in Virtual Teams

To build a collaborative process, it is recommended to use social conversation to set up relationships. It helps to establish factors that either enable or inhibit collaboration with the final purpose to facilitate and get team members' commitment. However, some researchers have come to the conclusion that the social context has more direct influence in a face-to-face team than in a virtual team where the members' inputs are more significant (Martins et al., 2004; Walther and Bunz, 2005) and more task focused. Collaboration in the virtual team environment does not only mean collaboration within the team but also with all the stakeholders 'outside' of the team and across different geographical and organizational boundaries identified as 'offshore collaboration' where each party shares the core competencies of each other (Levina and Vaast, 2008). It also means collaboration with possible subteams, which is not always a straightforward process because priorities and interests might differ from those of the core team (Klimkeit, 2013). This complexity can inhibit the effectiveness of collaboration because the shared context is even more reduced than in an environment with less complexity. Ko et al. (2011) suggest a deeper analysis for the collaboration processes with three steps: antecedents of cross-functional collaboration, implementation, and outcomes. Antecedents of cross-functional collaboration result in the interconnection of suitability of consensus (how efficient the virtual teammates are in reaching team consensus and therefore collaboration), organizational contexts (how advanced the organizational structure is in integrating virtual work) and innovation or project complexities (how technical and organizational infrastructure support complexity). The outcomes of collaboration can be measured through tangible results such as the achievements in time, budget and overall expected performance, and also through some intangible results. The intangible dimension is characterized by effective socio-emotional processes and more precisely by the affective satisfaction gained by the virtual team members through the innovation or project. The organizational structure can also provide necessary resources, such as authority, policies, procedures and systems to overcome boundaries and enable collaboration. Adapted groupware and collaborative systems contribute to efficient collaboration by offering a shared workspace, appropriate connections, and data access from different locations (Bravo et al., 2013; Dustdar, 2004). Thus, collaboration is enhanced through communication, coordination and workspace adapted to virtual teams. In any case, efficient collaboration depends on key drivers that consist of interdependency, interest, and motivation for the project's success (Klimkeit, 2013).

6.4.3 The Role of Collaboration

Collaboration is globally recognized by academic research to be a key driver of virtual team performance, which is the result of a virtual team culture that encourages shared awareness and open interaction (Nemiro et al., 2008; Daneshgar et al., 2004). Collaboration awareness means that virtual team members are informed of who is doing what, they understand the team activities and the status, and the relationships of each teammate in the team. Virtual team members who acquire such collaboration awareness feel comfortable in navigating and finding pertinent information, whether or not it is centralized or formalized (Sultanow et al., 2011). E-collaboration is a driver for organizations to meet the competitive demands but also enables common creativity. It can occur in virtual teams only when the team members are able to create the appropriate environment for collaboration, which assumes an adequate 'relational space' based on identities constructed by individuals (McNair et al., 2008). The concept of collaboration based on a 'change-oriented capability' enables companies to identify, integrate, monitor, apply, and improve their knowledge assets (Kock, 2009). Collaboration highlights the benefits of teamwork and pushes the group to go beyond each individual's skills to acquire group competencies and knowledge in order to develop further potential. Therefore, effective collaboration has a positive influence on group cohesion, communication breakdown avoidance, and members' satisfaction and motivation. Mainly three organizational roles can be distinguished in a virtual team involving collaboration: roles of coordination, learning, and innovation that are linked with efficiency and competitive influence. Kock (2009) suggests that organizations functioning in sectors that are less dynamic need virtual collaboration for operational purposes where coordination is relevant. Alternatively, high dynamic sectors require virtual collaboration to build strategies where learning and innovation are key factors.

6.4.4 Challenges Faced When Building Collaboration

Building a high level of collaboration in a virtual team is directly dependent on the interrelationships among the team communication, knowledge
transfer, trust building, work processes, technology, conflict and leadership management (Cramton, 2002). Those elements are integrated in
socio-emotional, technical and managerial processes. But readiness for
collaboration must be added to the list of essential factors (Olson and
Olson, 2000) as well as stability in the virtual team configuration with
clear role partitions, and assignments to the team members (Dustdar,
2004; Sadowski-Rasters et al., 2006). The main obstacle to collaboration remains to be the difficulty of establishing common knowledge and
shared context (Levina and Vaast, 2008) or shared identity associated to
trust among heterogeneity and virtuality. Each of these factors plays a
key role in positive collaboration within virtual teams on the condition
that effective coordination and adequate choice of management mechanisms smooth the negative influence of heterogeneity and virtuality. These
factors also determine the autonomy of the team to run a project (Ko
et al., 2011). Management mechanisms are adapted if analysed and settled
according to the typology of the virtual team, which are either people- or
information-oriented, as well as to the procedural constraints, which are
either institution- or project-oriented. In the absence of one of the mentioned factors and combined with coordination, it is difficult to establish
optimum virtual collaboration (Peters and Manz, 2007). Consequences
directly affect team performance. The decrease of virtual collaboration
negatively impacts performance not only at the team level but also at the
individual level. Some researchers like Blaskovich (2008) found that low
virtual collaboration may push some team members to social loafing,
which is accentuated by distance and lack of face-to-face interactions.
Social loafing is the result of lack or reduction in individual motivation
and involvement. In the presence of social loafing, team productivity and
outcomes decrease, and negatively affect team performance. The lack of
collaboration is not the only explanation for social loafing. Several reasons
might be the cause e.g. lack of recognition for individual contribution
within the team, how the fairness of decision-making process is perceived
within the team, and team behaviour that tends to affect the individual
(collective loafing might result in individual loafing as an individual
team member may tend to match the collective team behaviour) (Turel
and Zhang, 2011). Team leaders take a role and are supposed to use their
position and resources to facilitate efficient collaboration across constraints and boundaries (Levina and Vaast, 2008) and prevent situations
of conflict. Their roles in regards to collaboration should be oriented in

the development of individuals' behaviour in favour of interpersonal trust building, implementation of socio-emotional strategies, and technology. The aim is to enable relationships between the team members (Flammia et al., 2010) because individual behaviour is one factor that challenges virtual collaboration. For example, the multicultural aspects of a virtual team may influence and support some individual behaviours looking for recognition in a hierarchical organization. In such a case, the most ascendant ones dominate the group and may jeopardize or be an obstacle to team collaboration (Ritke-Jones, 2008). Even though, McNamara et al. (2008) demonstrate that belonging to a group majority or minority in the team does not really affect the members' virtual collaboration, because it is mainly driven through technology.

6.5 KNOWLEDGE MANAGEMENT

6.5.1 Definition

Another pillar within the socio-emotional processes is knowledge management. In the organizational context, 'knowledge' is considered as the result of the human faculty to interpret information and understand the combination of data, information, and experience. It is the sum of what is known and remains 'in the intelligence and competence of people' (Dictionary, 2012a). 'The organizations that will truly excel in the future will be the organizations that discover how to tap people's commitment and capacity to learn at ALL levels in an organization' according to Senge (1990). It is also much linked to the knowledge infrastructure deployed within the organization, as seen previously in the book. Ackoff (2010) proposes a hierarchical classification of the human mind in five categories:

1 *Data, facts or figures.*
2 *Information:* using not-yet-analysed data, facts or figures, transformed through procedures, people, hardware or software in order to give sense to the receiver, and allow answers to the questions of: 'who', 'what', 'where' and 'when'.
3 *Knowledge:* applies the information and approaches strategy, practices and methods setting patterns, and add individual learning and experience. Thus, it enables the disposition of team members toward actions and answer to the question 'how'.
4 *Understanding:* assesses and interprets information and knowledge and answers the question of 'why'.

5   *Wisdom:* evaluates the understanding and materializes the foundation
    principles. Each level requires more than just the collection of data or
    information. Knowledge is a means of sharing and explaining pieces
    of information, and relationships with patterns and even possibly pre-
    pares further models. In the virtual context, knowledge is information
    perceived as credible enough to retain attention and to be consolidated
    with other information in order to create usable knowledge, i.e. knowl-
    edge that can be transferable (Brewer, 2008a).

6.5.2   The Role of Knowledge Management

To benefit from knowledge, organizations have to set knowledge management considerations to be 'a source of considerable financial advantage'
(Hanisch et al., 2009) and a key pillar that enhances organizational performance (Karayaz, 2008). The role of knowledge management refers to
technologies that gather, organize, share and analyse the collective knowledge and expertise circulating in an organization, in terms of resources,
databases, documents, and in people's mind and skills. Its role is also to
distribute knowledge wherever it can generate benefits, throughout the
cycle of knowledge creation to retention. Virtual teamwork and knowledge management are mainly based on communication, credibility and
culture, according to Sarker et al. (2005). One of the positive effects of
using knowledge management systems within a virtual environment is to
leverage the virtual team management. It helps those teams find solutions
to challenges they encountered (Karayaz, 2008) taking into consideration
that virtual teams are also relevant conveyors of knowledge. This frame
can be extended to allied suppliers, competitors and customers looking
for common solutions. They can create and share knowledge through
their virtual network and, thus, innovate (Salazar et al., 2003). It means
that knowledge has to be transmitted in the virtual team, the organization and 'outside' of the organization. Virtual team members or leaders
must develop cognitive knowledge, which means the capacity to 'combine
facts and ideas to create knowledge that will drive the organization in the
right direction' (Maznevski and Athanassiou, 2003). In comparison to
co-located teams, knowledge can be transferred informally, which does
not require computerizing all data but appears more difficult to achieve
in a virtual context. The type of knowledge to be transferred needs to be
assessed because the way it will be transmitted and the necessary technical
support may vary.

6.5.3 Types of Knowledge

Some work environments require intensive levels of knowledge where collaborators need a lot of documents and information to execute their tasks. This is more difficult to achieve in a virtual team due to dispersion and various levels of knowledge requested (Liu et al., 2013). Knowledge can already exist within a virtual team and it can be improved, or just be collaboratively created as it is not yet in the hands of the team when formed. Increased collaboration develops knowledge and leads to knowledge accumulation that supports the virtual team tasks and lifecycle and is enriched by 'improved navigation paths' (Ahn et al., 2005). Technology use and communication protocols are recommended along with adaptation processes to the team characteristics (Malhotra and Majchrzak, 2004). As a matter of fact, virtuality makes information-sharing more difficult, especially when this information is not unique, which should be taken into consideration, because efficient information-sharing contributes to the virtual team's performance (Mesmer-Magnus et al., 2011). Knowledge may appear in an explicit or tacit way. The explicit knowledge is comprised of facts, documents, policies and procedures, which is easy to transfer, and it sustains to the global team performance independently from individuals (Michaux, 2005). The tacit knowledge is strongly linked to the individual knowledge and is difficult to formalize, and not expressed in a clear and accessible form (Maznevski and Athanassiou, 2003; Karayaz, 2008) and might be located in the individuals' minds. Therefore, it is easier to share than to transfer individual know-how, e.g. behaviours, and is a part of the human contribution within the team performance. It requires strong ties between members in order to be transferred. It is important for a virtual team leader to identity the complementarity between tacit/explicit knowledge within his/her virtual team in order to identify who is holding what knowledge in order to be able to coordinate the knowledge management. It will influence the configuration of learning within the virtual team, depending on whether that learning is mainly linked to tacit or explicit knowledge (Maznevski and Athanassiou, 2003). Tacit knowledge requests more attention in the virtual context because transmission is based on human interactions and the credibility level that exists within the members of the virtual team (Maznevski and Athanassiou, 2003). Tacit knowledge transfer can be facilitated by face-to-face interactions, team tasks and job engagement (Cao et al., 2012). If tacit or informal knowledge is not shared on a large extent, it will lead to a lack of knowledge transfer that represents a risk for virtual teams, and negatively impacts trust in the virtual team and its performance (Reed and Knight, 2010). Despite the type of knowledge, deploying knowledge within virtual teams require adapted processes to the target need.

6.5.4 Processes to Deploy Knowledge

The operational knowledge processes define the activities that the virtual team needs to perform in order to successfully execute its mission. For example, they can be the use of tools. Basically, the operational processes, mainly roles and tasks focused, require a certain level of trust among the virtual team members along with tasks cohesion. The exchange of information and messages, thus, reduces the risk of misunderstanding (Cramton, 2002), positively influences team collaboration and is interrelated with the team-shared context, identified as 'contextual information' or 'knowledge context' by some researchers (Ahn et al., 2005; Feghali and El-Den, 2008). Contextual information is a key factor to keep knowledge interrelated with other relevant knowledge results and, ultimately, become a knowledge repository. A knowledge repository is defined as a computerized system that enables the creation, capture and the organization of knowledge, and contributes to knowledge creation and utilization within the virtual team lifecycle. Unless the virtual team members face a lack of the company's support and misuse the virtual communication channels and tools (Breitenöder, 2009), they may elaborate common transactive memory. Transactive memory is a process through which teams collectively encode, store, retrieve and share knowledge issued from individual learning or expertise. In our context, transactive memory is the result of 'how organizations come to develop "group minds", memory systems that are more complex and potentially more effective than those of any of the individuals that comprise them' (Wegner et al., 1985).

Transactive memory helps the group to better use the knowledge that members have collected and can lead the team to a higher performance level than without such processes (Nevo and Wand, 2005). The virtual team members may develop a relational knowledge by remembering 'who knows what', based on relationships established between virtual team members and stakeholders (Wegner, 1987; Davidson, 2013). However, it takes some time to be effective in virtual teams due to virtuality and the difficulties of establishing personal interactions. Standardization of work, frequent exchanges and rotation of virtual team members may contribute to reach transactive memory in the team (Martins and Schilpzand, 2011) as well as processes achieving a shared meaning, learning climate, coaching (Hong and Vai, 2008) and mentoring. Giuffrida and Dittrich (2013) add the importance of understanding how the communication network operates within the team and, finally, the role of social software. To understand the whole processes of the knowledge development, Griffith and Neale (2001) proposed a conceptual model showing the 'transition from nascent knowledge to transactive memory and group outcomes'. From information, social and value diversity, nascent knowledge emerges and develops if it is not hampered by barriers e.g. psychological safety, lack of social identity or cultural differences in values, practices or institutions that influence specialization, coordination and credibility (Jarvenpaa and Keating, 2011). The progression of nascent knowledge enables the virtual team members to share and refine knowledge, which may lead to possible conflicts inside the team. When overcome, the progression continues and finally fosters transactive memory. The aim to develop common transactive memory is to reach a minimum threshold of trust and psychological safety that is necessary for knowledge transfer. Knowledge is successfully created in virtual teams when knowledge-sharing and trust develops within the team (Curseu et al., 2008). Virtual teams are not 'technological' (Maznevski and Athanassiou, 2003) but social systems, which refers to the social capital of the virtual team. Based-on-deputy-system work, social capital, spatial and temporal boundaries and affordances of collaborative technologies knowledge contribute to the emergence of coordinative knowledge practices or shared knowledge (Franssila et al., 2012). This is why some researchers point out the importance of the social processes or socio-emotional processes first, rather than on the importance of sharing and managing the content of knowledge. Those processes facilitate a 'shared construction process' that fosters 'knowledge creation' (Leinonen and Bluemink, 2008). The team members will assess each other on their respective level of knowledge and individual expertise through the use of standardized templates and methods that support knowledge transfer. Knowledge transfer or knowledge-sharing means dissemination of knowledge within the virtual team in order to bring back new knowledge (Rosen et al., 2007) that is enriched by experiences that can be reproduced, improved, and then transmitted inside or outside of the organization. The fact that virtual teams are geographically dispersed is an opportunity to scan and collect information on a wider scope, especially in case of tacit knowledge (Maznevski and Athanassiou, 2003). In that case, it needs to be supported by adequate and up-to-date technology (Gillam and Oppenheim, 2006). Virtual team members can easily access and use the local knowledge for problems that occur locally. When the problem occurs in distant sites, virtual team members need to identify, and adjust their practices with the available knowledge (Sole and Edmondson, 2002). Team members need to develop a 'mutual knowledge' (Cramton, 2001); that is knowledge shared between the individuals of the group in such a way that they are aware of this common knowledge and this is a critical factor of success within a collaborative virtual team (Leinonen and Bluemink, 2008). Sharing knowledge is a complex social, based on a global collaborative processes (Mohrman et al., 2003) and a continuum aiming to 'capture and transform knowledge into a global asset through the management of people' (Pauleen, 2003a). Knowledge transfer and trust emerge in virtual teams when the social capital of the group reaches a high level, namely in network ties and shared vision. Thus, leaders and managers of virtual teams that are aware of the effects of social capital can use it to improve the processes of knowledge sharing and, consequently, contribute to the virtual team performance (Liu and Li, 2012). A knowledge management system offering real-time applications through easy-to-use and accessible databases, through an efficient keyword list, could improve knowledge sharing (Karayaz, 2008).

6.5.5 Barriers to Deployment of Knowledge

In addition to being a complex system, knowledge transfer has to face time pressures in order to offer quick, elegant and effective solutions, which is especially challenging for virtual teams that are grouped for temporal tasks or projects. Because it is challenged in virtual teams, knowledge transfer is more or less facilitated depending on the complexity of the virtual context, such as the number of virtual teams, the degree of virtuality, the development of advanced ICTs, and the degree of organizational centralization. Additional factors that increase difficulties in capitalizing on knowledge and expertise in a virtual environment are change management and culture (Khan and Woosley, 2012). In a 24-hour knowledge team model (model of teams running their activities on a continuous base), efficient knowledge management and knowledge transfer are particularly critical, depending on suitable tools designed for efficient transfer. Those tools provide a complete knowledge database that enables intelligent usage for maximum performance of the team activities. Thus, the activities can continuously progress and collaboration between virtual team members is effectively supported, with a reduced communication and less coordination. In that case, team productivity is enhanced (Gupta et al., 2011). The main challenge faced by virtual teams is the emergence of uncertainty that might be generated by fast knowledge dissemination. Keeping control of uncertainty is crucial in order to develop or maintain a mutual knowledge (Daassi and Favier, 2007; Cramton, 2002). Daassi's work demonstrates that mutual knowledge can be initiated through the operational processes and the relationships existing in the virtual team. Other possible barriers to knowledge are failure to communicate, heterogeneity in information distribution, the difficulty of identifying relevant information and inequalities in information access. McNair et al. (2008) recommend the creation of a 'relational space' to facilitate information and knowledge exchange, which enables the setting-up of a base for social knowledge construction. This base allows the virtual members to evaluate their teammates' knowledge, such as expertise (Leinonen and Jarvela, 2006) and avoids solutions that are reinvented due to inaccessibility of existing knowledge (Tiwana and Bush, 2001). If trust exists in the team, the knowledge processes perform faster through a mutual understanding and enhance sharing. If successful, task-oriented communication volume reduces, and the processes integrate transactive memory. It requires the team members to be qualified in their communication ability and interpersonal relationships capability, especially towards mutual trust and respect, in order to carry forward that knowledge. Therefore, knowledge management requires some attention and a need to gather some essential elements at the implementation phase, which is the same as for collaboration development: common social group identification, clear role assignments in accordance to tasks characteristics, interpersonal relationships and ICT support (Michaux, 2005). Virtual team managers need to be aware of knowledge-sharing among the team members in order to use it as a key lever to performance. A successful organization is the one that can understand, get committed, and has the capacity to learn at all levels of the organization. Those organizations access the level of 'Learning Organization' (Senge, 1990) 'shifting from competition to cooperation and collaboration' (Gignac, 2005) which positively supports the knowledge management globally and not just individually. They are able to set strategies that are adapted to the organization itself, elaborated by headquarters, and executed at the global or regional level or elaborated by regional organization and locally executed (Khan and Woosley, 2012).

6.6   TRUST BUILDING

6.6.1   Definition of Trust

The definition we use is the one suggested by different researchers for virtual teaming based on interpersonal relationships, as there might be a lot of others recommended by sociologists, psychologists and scientists etc. Trust is one person or organization's confidence in another person or organization regarding ability, integrity, strength, surety or character (Dictionary, 2000). It is the willingness to open oneself to another, therefore, achieving a certain level of vulnerability without taking advantage of another even when the opportunity is available (Zolin et al., 2004; Brown et al., 2004; Muethel et al., 2012b). 'By trust, organizations really mean confidence, a confidence in someone's competence and in his or her commitment to a goal' (Handy, 1995). Academic researchers stipulate that trust is a key factor for 'understanding interpersonal and group behaviour, managerial effectiveness, economic exchange and social or political stability' (Hosmer, 1995; Brown et al., 2004).

6.6.2   Different Forms of Trust

Throughout academic research findings, various types of trust are mentioned: cognitive and affective trust, swift trust, knowledge-based trust, socially based trust and situated trust. Trust acquisition incorporates a temporal dimension within virtual teams, which is more or less reduced depending on the level of cognitive and affective trust in the teams (Wilson et al., 2006; Greenberg et al., 2007).

Cognitive trust is the assessment of ability and integrity. It is related to the level of confidence that team members have regarding competence and reliability of their teammates based on social cues. Affective trust consists of the assessment of benevolence (disposition to trust building) or personality-based trust. It is linked to emotional relationships among virtual team members, and assumes reciprocal concern and care among members. Both cognitive and affective trust can be measured through the level of collaboration within the virtual team.

Some virtual teams may reach a 'form of swift trust' (Jarvenpaa and Leidner, 1999) which is a quick acquisition of trust among virtual team members based on the member's role even if the person is unknown (Zolin et al., 2004). Swift trust is generated by early perceptions of trustworthiness by virtual team members on how their colleagues deliver and convey reliable information (Zolin et al., 2004).

This perception is based on external signals such as reputation, roles and rules, as well as intrinsic factors such as benevolence (Greenberg et al., 2007). Swift trust can occur early in the virtual team implementation but may remain fragile (Greenberg et al., 2007) and is difficult to sustain even though team activities help to maintain trust by generating confidence. If the level of task interdependence is high, then the interaction level is also high, which contributes to developing or maintaining trust (Wilson et al., 2006).

The team acquiring swift trust is more able to manage uncertainty, and risk vulnerability (Jarvenpaa and Leidner, 1999) and, if it is established at the start-up of the virtual team, it appears successful in the virtual team's functioning. According to these researchers, swift trust can be established for a specific, common and short-timeframe task that does not allow team members to raise expectations on the other members. An example can be the case of virtual teams that perform emergency actions. Their members need to establish immediate interpersonal trust through feeling formation, perception of social presence, self-assertiveness

(Altschuller and Benbunan-Fich, 2008). The team can be composed of team members that have very little experience with each other, or even none at all, but are sharing actions and enthusiasm, showing individual initiative and responsiveness rather than waiting for the other member's suggestion. Knowledge-based trust is trust that appears when swift trust declines. It happens when the virtual team members acquire enough information to assess their teammates' trustworthiness (Robert et al., 2009). In this case, the virtual team reaches a higher level of interpersonal relationships and knowledge on teammates' needs, preferences and points of view on how to handle team issues (Hernandez and Santos, 2010).

Socially based trust (Henttonen and Blomqvist, 2005) or characteristic-based trust (Nandhakumar and Baskerville, 2006) is focused on the well-being of others and is concerned with creating a common culture and procedures. Action-based trust or process-based trust is built through actions, shared goals, quality of procedures, reliable feedback, promises and commitment. This trust is essential to create a dynamic within virtual teams.

Institutional-based trust is related to infrastructures, which is another basis for trust in virtual teams. Therefore, we can notice that trust develops at individual (personal trust relation) and organizational levels (impersonal abstract trust) (Nandhakumar and Baskerville, 2006). Situated trust refers to a type of trust relationship mutually discussed and jointly built, and emerges with the situation (Panteli and Duncan, 2004). In comparison, swift trust has to exist when the activities of the virtual team start. Situated trust assumes there are constant discussions and interactions throughout the virtual team activities or project.

6.6.3 The Role of Trust

Trust is fundamental to the successful functioning of any work team. It is one of the roots of socio-emotional processes, and often associated to geographical dispersion although that is not necessary. Essential to the success of virtual teams, trust develops mutual understanding, respect, openness and cohesion among virtual team members. These conditions enable the virtual team members to develop the necessary interactions and transactions to learn dynamically, improve and adapt their activities to the context. Trust positively involves virtual team members in the team goal while reducing uncertainty, doubt and control (Brown et al., 2004; Muethel et al., 2012b), increasing collaboration and decreasing the efforts and costs of coordination (Henttonen and Blomqvist, 2005). Trust is, therefore, the foundation of virtual collaboration. However, it is not an exercise that is straightforward to achieve for those dispersed teams confronted to boundaries of virtuality (Smith, 2002; Zolin et al., 2004; Thomas and Bostrom, 2008). It affects virtual teams in diverse ways depending on the social characteristics and values along with personal traits of the virtual team members including their propensity to trust (Brown et al., 2004), and the different situations and contexts (Jarvenpaa et al., 2004). Therefore, trust building follows certain processes.

6.6.4 Trust Building Processes

As for virtual teams, direct supervision needs to be replaced by formalized team procedures or self-organization, creating the required social space for trust building (Rasmussen and Wangel, 2007). If swift trust does not develop, virtual team members and leaders need to find ways to build trust and this is especially critical at the first stage of team development. First, team members improve their knowledge about their teammates. They can predict their behaviours that might, however, be based on reputation and categorization (team members with prominent reputation are trusted). Second, trust appears when they are able to establish social interactions leading to social solidarity within the team (Sarker et al., 2003). Trust building evolves at different levels along virtual team development and adjustment, and seems more fragile in weak structural situations (Staples and Webster, 2008). Trust cannot be considered as constant and needs to be regularly re-stimulated. Therefore, virtual team managers should play an active role in building and sustaining trust by fostering a positive perception of each other within the team and by monitoring the trust building processes (McNab et al., 2012). Message- and behaviour-based stereotypes look more relevant for trust building than technical skill-based stereotypes in the early stage of team formation, and sometimes the team development. Trust may take various forms with diverse impacts. Globally, the most relevant impact is the positive association of trust with virtual team performance, perceived cohesion between team members and overall satisfaction (Walther and Bunz, 2005; McNab et al., 2012). In virtual teams, due to the lack of presence, trust is mainly based on teammates' perception of competences, ability, reliability, integrity and benevolence, which gives a certain fragility to trust building (Piccoli and Ives, 2003; Baskerville and Nandhakumar, 2007; Greenberg et al., 2007). Perception may lead to stereotypes based on behaviours and interaction styles. However, Henttonen and Blomqvist (2005) identified four components needed to develop and build trust in virtual teams: viz. behaviour, goodwill (moral responsibility and positive intentions), capability (technology and business related) and self-reference (ability to make coherent decisions).

Those components interact in a context where conditions influence trust building according to a varying degree, such as geographic dispersion, computer-mediated communication and national diversity. Consequently, identifying the contextual conditions in which virtual teams operate appears relevant to understanding trust-effectiveness relationships within these teams. Trust is, therefore, not always beneficial as such but can become a critical driver to virtual team performance, especially when geographical dispersion, ICTs and national diversity are high (Muethel et al., 2012b).

The reduced number of common social networks or the lack of common social networks challenges the potential capability for virtual team members to build trust. This is partially due to the difficulty for virtual team members to think about their communicative behaviour, recognize the coexistence of different communication habits and constraints, and learn from it, in order to adapt to an appropriate communication behaviour (Jarvenpaa and Leidner, 1999; Piccoli and Ives, 2003). Reduced 'inflammatory communication' contributes to the development of trust within virtual teams (Wilson et al., 2006).

Behaviour control contributes to increased vigilance and highlights incidents that generate unexpected reactions by teammates. Therefore, behaviour control negatively influences trust that fails or declines (Piccoli and Ives, 2003). For instance, it occurs in cases of reneging (real trust failure) and incongruence (perceived trust failure). Further analysis has come to the conclusion that behavioural control amplifies the salience of all behaviours, thus weakening the impact of reneging and fulfilling (increased trust beliefs) behaviours on trust (Dennis et al., 2012).

Certain norms should be adopted, such as setting an automatic 'out-of-office' reply message in order to avoid wrong interpretation of silence (Henttonen and Blomqvist, 2005). The researchers notice that high-trust virtual teams group together members who demonstrate a high level of confidence and optimism as well as individual initiative, thus, positively influencing interactions with their teammates. Higher interactions foster open innovation among virtual team members (Muethel et al., 2012b).

The initial perceptions of trustworthiness are particularly critical in trust development in the virtual context. Similarities, for example, belonging to the same culture, encourage trustworthiness, which highlights the difficulties that may appear within virtual teams due to diversities and heterogeneity (Zolin et al., 2004; Newell et al., 2007). In a virtual context, communication that evaluates, meaning that it takes into account and respects the diverse cultural roots, values and beliefs among team members, may lead to successful trust building (King, 2007). However, distance- and technology-mediated communication make it more difficult to set up.

Virtual team members may rely on their first negative impression of

perceived trustworthiness because reliable information on distant teammates is lacking or is difficult to interpret. In addition, virtual team
members are less familiar to each other regarding relationships and work
processes (Zolin et al., 2004). Reduced interactions make it difficult for the
dispersed teammates to identify who holds the information and knowledge
that they need. Therefore, team performance decreases due to missed deadlines, lack of cooperation (Newell et al., 2007), and so on.

Clear relationships link the communication medium with trust building.
No direct connection could be identified between individual perception of
trust and task interdependence operated within certain conditions such as
time pressure and task complexity. The common factor remains to be the
communication medium, which implies a particular attention when building trust (Olson and Olson, 2012).

Wilson et al. (2006) demonstrate that trust starts at a lower level in
virtual teams compared to face-to-face teams due to computer-mediated
communication, visual isolation and cultural diversity. Electronic communication reduces interpersonal relationships, therefore, virtual team
members feel more anonymous to each other. Then the trust level either
gradually increases to a level similar to the ones found in face-to-face teams
or exceeds that level and remains rather stable once established (Zolin
et al., 2004). However, long-term trust building is not based on impersonal
relationships but rather on personalized repeated trust interactions for
continuous teamworking (Nandhakumar and Baskerville, 2006). This personalized trust seems to be a solid base for trust sustainability in a virtual
context if connected to face-to-face meetings. Communication behaviour
providing openness and social presence fosters trust development in virtual
teams. Shared values, common culture and goals, various forms of socialization inside the team, integrity, and keeping commitments and promises
are critical factors to developing socially based trust (Henttonen and
Blomqvist, 2005). Failure of trust development is linked to communication
failure and more precisely to failure in retaining information.

A strong relationship exists between trust and knowledge-sharing, and
knowledge-sharing and team performance, especially when task interdependence is low (Newell et al., 2007; Staples and Webster, 2008). Exchange
of information is determinant on trust building and, reciprocally, trust
is necessary for knowledge-sharing because it often depends on personal
interactions. Additionally, system infrastructures support trust building.
The use of workflow systems enables such an exchange because it allows
virtual team members to see their teammates' work progress.

Therefore, virtual team members' trustworthiness can be improved
(Thomas and Bostrom, 2008). Trust has a direct positive organizational
influence on a virtual team's performance and collaboration. It may even

smooth functional diversity and increase performance relationships (Peters and Karren, 2009). Trust is more likely to be initiated through engaging communication that is established in the first steps of team creation or project start-up. Effective socio-emotional communication strengthens trust that is associated with higher job satisfaction and improved working relationships (Furumo et al., 2009). This is a key point to be addressed by virtual team managers.

6.6.5 Managerial Influence in Trust Building

Virtual team managers can positively influence trust building in their team through technology adaptation, relationship management, collaborative team environment and through style of management (Newell et al., 2007). Coppola et al. (2004) suggest four key factors for trust building by virtual team managers during a virtual meeting: set the communication quickly, develop a positive social atmosphere, strengthen predictable communication, and take action to structure activities and involve team members in tasks.

The virtual team leader needs to motivate, encourage and require participation. He/she may use templates for communication including time management, feedback, conflict and task completion as suggested by Remidez Jr et al. (2007). However, templates may appear as behaviour/ process controls, and can negatively influence successful outcomes, in addition to the fact that they might be interpreted differently due to diverse cultures. The virtual team leader's role also consists of creating opportunities for the team members to assess trustworthiness among teammates (Zolin et al., 2004) and focusing on trust building at the initial stages of team creation or collaboration between teammates. They need to maintain trust level or repair trust when is has been interrupted. Effective communication, time guidance and no time pressure, a result focus rather than a time focus, and high supervisory skills contribute to building trust in virtual teams (Cascio, 2000). Trust can become sustainable through consistent and repeated communication, positive leadership, successful transition from social to task focus and slow reaction to crisis (Jarvenpaa and Leidner, 1999). Therefore, a facilitator-type or inspirational-type style of management, rather than a command-and-control style, is preferred to develop trust (Amrit and Van Hillegersberg, 2008; Thomas and Bostrom, 2008; Joshi et al., 2009). It requires the team leader's involvement in relationship management in order to reduce the influence of possible negative internal relations within the group (Henttonen and Blomqvist, 2005; David et al., 2008), such as ineffective communication, lack of clear procedures and roles, or lack of individual commitment (Jarvenpaa and Leidner, 1999).

6.7 TO KEEP IN MIND: INTERRELATION BETWEEN THE KEY FACTORS OF SOCIO-EMOTIONAL PROCESSES

Virtual communication enables the exchange of information, knowledge and collaborative interactions within virtual teams, intra- and/or interorganizations thanks to a portfolio of ICT tools. Supported by technologies, it offers some advantages to build trust and collaboration and smooth the multiple boundaries characterizing virtual teams. Depending on the media, communication can be lean or rich, offer access to a more or less wide spectrum of activities, may reduce the social distance and facilitate the interrelationships inside the virtual team if the social capital is high enough. However due to its complexity, particularly asynchronicity, virtual communication requires a high level of coordination, and specific virtual communication skills for team members and team leaders, in order to foster team performance and avoid possible conflicts.

Collaboration in virtual teams occurs when the members reach a level of trust, communication and knowledge that is high enough to share common agreement and practices with the willingness to reach the expected team outcomes. Collaboration enables them to overcome the virtual team coordination complexity, benefit from competencies across the organization and enter the cycle of 'coordination, learning and innovation'.

Knowledge management is essential in virtual team evolution, especially because knowledge is disseminated in such an organization. To build collective knowledge, companies need to support knowledge access, retrieval and deployment in order to be able to transfer that knowledge. The main obstacle within virtual environments remains the lack of common knowledge, shared context and organizational systems, as well as appropriate managerial processes. Successful collaboration depends on the capacity to establish mutual knowledge while taking into account feedback processes and their dynamics. Additionally, virtual teams enable the awareness of a larger spectrum of situated knowledge, and improving work processes and practices, thus contributing to the team performance globally.

Trust building is the foundation of virtual team functioning. Different forms of trust influence virtual teamworking and trust building. Institutional trust contributes to sustaining virtual teamworking for shorter periods, whereas, personal trust based on social relationships is a key factor for longer periods. Frequent communication and virtual leader's skills are relevant to maintain trust because it dissipates over time, especially if face-to-face social interactions decrease or are non-existent. Understanding the impacts on virtual team processes help virtual team managers to facilitate and improve virtual teamwork and performance. Trust is a determinant factor of satisfaction, employee retention, balanced work and private life, creativity and productivity.

6.8 CONCLUSION

If we refer to the cluster map about virtual teams, we can note that the main areas of the research's interest are those which characterize the socio-emotional processes. They include team and communication, members, development, organization, technology and processes. We need to add the smaller areas that appear relevant for virtual team socio-emotional processes and where research is currently being developed as well. They concern relationships within the virtual team (e.g. interactions, relationship and relation developing a shared context and team cohesion), trust, collaboration, knowledge and implication. Socio-emotional processes demonstrate how virtual teams articulate their inputs to provide outcomes and satisfaction at team, and individual levels in direction to global performance. Socio-emotional processes are crucial in this articulation, in regard to the correlation with technological and managerial processes because they act as a facilitator in team processes. Disruption in the socio-emotional processes may lead virtual teaming into a real frustration but, if well managed, they transform coordination and planning activities into high-added-value virtual teams and efficient realization of their potential. The main challenge is to succeed in managing the virtual team members' emotion through virtuality. Rules and norms should optimize the virtual team processes. Being able to start activities immediately creates dynamic and relational opportunities between members and a most efficient use of time. Frequent communication and messages of acknowledgment reduce uncertainty, maintaining trust among members and information flow quality. Team members should explicitly communicate about what they are doing and thinking, and revise and respect deadlines (Walther and Bunz, 2005). Efficient virtual team leaders cannot skip these processes because socio-emotional processes help them to maximize the benefits of dispersion while minimizing its disadvantages. When monitored, the socio-emotional processes contribute to the stability of the dispersed teams, to the increased virtual team performance and to efficiently resolve conflicts. The academic research still needs to provide a deeper understanding for e-leaders and organizations in order to implement appropriate strategies and policies, taking into account that the external context faces a continuous change. How far will the external context influence the virtual team processes? Would virtual teaming become a standard way of working supported by technologies that are continuously developing? Research should further analyse the possible gap that may emerge between higher or lower degrees of virtuality within such environment and virtual team stakeholders' adaptation.

6.9   GUIDELINES FOR MANAGERIAL PRACTICES: SOCIO-EMOTIONAL PROCESSES

Among the major processes in virtual teaming, the socio-emotional ones are revealed to be essential in virtual team performance. Virtuality and complexity of virtual teams make these processes difficult to implement and analyse. However, its level of implication on the concerned virtual team needs to be assessed and monitored. These guidelines propose to pinpoint and qualify the four main elements in the socio-emotional process that can be used as key levers to lead the virtual team to perform through appropriate actions that positively influence virtual teaming.

Table 6.1   Socio-emotional processes

Key actions	Key results
Communication	
List and qualify:	
– The communication technology (as listed in guideline 1.1):	
○ Is it adapted to the concerned team?	Yes/No
○ Is it accessible to all team members?	Yes/No
– The type of communication mainly used.	Synchronous/asynchronous
– The email policy.	Restrictive/not restrictive
– The communication standards if extant.	Protocols etc.
– The implication of communication in the team social cohesion and team collaboration (for example, how social conversations create a sense of presence).	Low/Medium/High level
Collaboration	
Assess the level of collaboration:	*Share (%) of collaboration contribution in:* – team coordination; – learning; – innovation; – common knowledge; and – shared context and identity etc.

Table 6.1 (continued)

Key actions	Key results
– in the team; and	High/Low
– with other stakeholders.	High/Low
List the existing systems that support collaboration and knowledge-sharing.	Databases, e-room, documents, models etc.
Knowledge management	
Define the knowledge type existing in the team:	*Based on:*
– explicit;	Facts, documents, policies, procedures etc.
– implicit;	
– name the persons who hold knowledge and what knowledge in the team; and	Personal experience, know-how, behaviours etc.
– list the possible barriers to knowledge transfer (within and outside of the team).	Uncertainty, fear of knowledge dissemination, technical aspects, failure in communication, difficulty to retrieve information etc.
Trust building	
– Define the type of trust existing in the team.	(Cognitive, affective, swift trust, knowledge-based trust etc.)
– How do you qualify that trust?	Sustainable or fragile? Needs to be stimulated?
Implemented trust in the team is the result of:	Yes/No
– positive behaviour toward trust;	
– goodwill (positive intention to trust);	
– capability (technology and business-related);	
– ability to make autonomous-decisions; and	
– team members' job satisfaction.	

7 Technological and work processes

7.1 INTRODUCTION

Among virtual team processes, technological and work processes support socio-emotional and managerial processes. Virtual teams can exist only because technological processes are well advanced. Technologies offer 'a structure that facilitates result-oriented team spirit' (Symons and Stenzel, 2007) through a range of tools that allows effective connections and enable operations within the involved processes. Processes organize technology the way that activities and operations have to be conducted. We do not cover hardware, installation or programming because that is out of scope of our book, but look at the implication and roles of technologies in virtual team processes. People involved in virtual teams need adequate systems to fulfil their missions in accordance to the infrastructure in which virtual teams perform because they are confronted to a large variety of different types of tools. Virtual team leaders need to overcome challenges directly linked to technologies at the individual, team or infrastructure level. To meet that request, they need appropriate technologies to develop efficient collaborative work processes. It implies that developers clearly understand their 'customers' needs and that they provide the expected level of involvement and expertise. Work processes are interdependent with technological processes that enable the development of adequate systems. Work processes support the structural bases on which virtual team members perform their tasks. Depending on the elaboration level of the system, team activities might be more or less integrated, which influences team collaboration efficiency. We explain the role of work processes through workflow systems and a collaborative way of working pointing out their influence on virtual teaming.

7.2 TECHNOLOGIES AND PROCESSES

7.2.1 Definition

Technologies enable 'virtual team members to use media and combine the characteristics of ICTS so they can take full advantages of their objectives features' (Jawadi and Boukef Charki, 2011). They should enhance virtual team members' relationships rather than substitute human interaction (Morris, 2008) which implies specificities. Technologies in the virtual context correspond with a variety of tools and applications whose function is to replace and simulate face-to-face interactions and integrate work processes. Terms used to designate virtual technologies are e-technologies, collaborative technologies, 'computer supported collaborative work' (Ferris and Minielli, 2004) within 'distributed electronic work environments' (Qureshi et al., 2006). We indifferently use this terminology in the book, and we generally refer to the term 'technology'.

7.2.2 The Roles of Technologies

The main roles of technologies that serve virtual teams are split in two main categories: decision support systems and group support systems (Ferris and Minielli, 2004). Decision support systems are not dedicated to one group but assist an entire organization in the decision-making process. Group support systems include a range of technologies that support group activities, processes and coordination through organizational communication (Davison and De Vreede, 2001). Both cases impact virtual teaming in a company in its efficiency to achieve its missions and to perform its activities and tasks.

Virtual technologies enable virtual team members facing the characteristics linked to the boundaries of the virtual team to execute, coordinate and manage virtual team activities (Pauleen, 2004; Massey and Montoya-Weiss, 2006). Therefore, enough resources should be available to enable sufficient communication and be adapted to the frequency and regularity of interactions (Jawadi and Boukef Charki, 2011). As seen in the previous chapter, virtual technologies are a necessary contributor to information, paperless documents and knowledge-sharing, communication and collaboration within a virtual team.

If adequate, accessible and advanced, technologies give organizations, virtual teams, virtual team members and leaders a high level of performance and satisfaction through efficient socio-emotional, managerial and work processes. Multiple tools and systems exist, which implies that companies invest in technologies and duplicate hardware, where the cost of new system implementation rises, even though the cost of basic technology reduces.

7.2.3 Diversity in Technologies

The selection of the correct tools and technologies is essential to get virtual teams performing efficiently on work processes and team performance levels. Various factors affect the choice of technology, as underlined by Martins and Schilpzand (2011).

The virtual team structure influences that choice, in relation to the complexity of its activities and timeframe, its members' dispersion and cultural diversity, its members' level of knowledge and skills which may require training to be quickly operational. The corporate organization influences the choice of technology as well. As demonstrated by researchers, small- and medium-sized enterprises (SMEs) display a more limited technological infrastructure, thus reducing their access and experiences to global networks. In SMEs, however, collaboration efforts are enhanced when Web 2.0 tools are available (Michaelides et al., 2013; Nyström and Asproth, 2013).

Massey and Montoya-Weiss (2006) underline that virtual team members may select a monophasic or a polyphasic structure depending on the virtual team context. In the monophasic structure, the users work with a single medium at one time, whereas, the polyphasic structure benefits from a various range of media at a time.

The antecedents of virtual team creation also play a role in technology selection and proliferation. If a virtual team is created from the fusion or accumulation of diverse organizations, each entity may operate with their own systems, different from each other. Thus, it explains the existence of multiple collaborative information technologies within a team and, therefore, the complexity in technological process management (Bajwa et al., 2005). This is why the assessment of the virtual team profile is relevant and influences, among other factors, the decisions taken in regards to technology deployment.

The organizational infrastructure and strategy play a role in technology architecture. Infrastructure needs to support the virtual team profile for efficiency. Additionally, infrastructure needs to consider the required level of security, the allocated budget, the availability and compatibility of the different types of technology more specifically. The company's decision also depends on its strategy towards virtuality. When the organization considers virtuality as critical and important, it grants a higher investment for supportive technologies.

Supportive technologies are more oriented to collaborative and communicative tools to compensate for one of the highest challenges to be overcome in a virtual context. Collaboration and IT offer solutions to foster collaborative teamwork. Collaborative technologies empower virtual teamwork processes and enhance virtual team members' interactivity and independence in work processes (Townsend et al., 1998). Gaan (2012) highlights the bridge existing between collaborative tools, demographic diversity within a virtual team, trust, and team effectiveness. Collaborative tools belong to a groupware.

Groupware, also designed as computer supported cooperative work (CSCW), computer-mediated communication systems (CMCS), or group support systems (GSS), is a 'software with a primary aim to support group/ teamwork' (Nedelko, 2008). A groupware integrates information and messages exchange, collaboration, mainly group discussions and scheduling. The major software brand names are LotusNote, MicrosoftExchange, Netscape Communicator, Habanero and Novell Groupwise.

Groupware are classified according to time dimension, whether they are synchronous or asynchronous tools. They are also classified according to location, whether team members are co-located or dispersed. Although it is also used by co-located teams, a groupware constitutes a central part of the supportive and collaborative technologies for virtual teams. The reason is that they provide a huge structured database that can be accessed by a large number of authorized persons; virtual work processes are elaborated because of it (Nedelko, 2008).

If a groupware operates efficiently, it facilitates communication, supports information storage and retrieval as well as supporting decision-making and overcoming the virtual barriers (Stough et al., 2000; Bajwa et al., 2005). A groupware conveys communication with preferred channels depending on the type of communication to be transmitted, which is not only based on communication tools but also on database systems that store the information for quick retrieval. A groupware is one way to link virtual team members and reduce administration, such as meeting minutes, document distribution and, therefore, contributes to increased team productivity as analysed by Bravo et al. (2013).

The various tools provide a new area of technologies applied to a wide range of stakeholders and integrate computer-mediated communication technologies. Additionally, various technological tools planned to complete a task are considered to be more efficient than just one tool or just one technical solution because it reduces misunderstanding and ambiguity (Dennis et al., 2008; Lee-Kelley and Sankey, 2008; Jawadi and Boukef Charki, 2011).

Technology diversity includes equipment that supports online meetings, e.g. digital white boards, packages to facilitate online presentations, project management software and document-sharing. As listed by Ebrahim et al. (2009) in the solution panel, we find the following examples of tools: web conferencing (e.g. NetMeeting, Microsoft LiveMeeting, WebEx, Meeting Space, GoToMeeting, Genesys Meeting Center); file transfer (file transfer protocol (FTP), collaborative websites, intranets), phone (two types: Plain Old Telephone Service (POTS), or Voice Over Internet Protocol (VOIP). We can add instant messages (e.g. Yahoo Messenger, MSN Messenger, AOL Instant Messenger, Skype etc.) and remote access and control (e.g. NetMeeting, WebEx, Remote Desktop, PCAnywhere etc.).

The Internet; XML coding (extensible mark-up language) a set of programming rules used to encode documents in a textual data format, human-and-machines readable; extranets, business-to-business (B2B) systems, business intelligence and knowledge management applications and systems, such as enterprise resource management systems (ERM) or customer relationship management (CRM) systems: all contribute to technological development (Bal and Foster, 2000). An ERM system associates back-office functions and all transversal processes from the organization, viz. finance, sales, production, plant maintenance, human resources, etc. Those systems are largely used and developed by SAP, BAAN, JDEdwards, PeopleSoft, Oracle and Lawon. They present diverse characteristics and types: text-only, audio-only, text-video or audio-video. Baker (2002) points out that the apparition of the video in the set of tools contributes to a real improvement in the virtual team communication, which is enhanced by the development of the mobile tools 'any time and any place' support (Nosek and Mandviwalla, 1996), mobile e-services, and wireless Internet protocols (Shim et al., 2002).

Supported by Web 2.0 technologies such as wikis, blogs, forums, social networks, opinion polls, community chats; collaboration within virtual teams is enhanced through new possibilities (Turban et al., 2011). Web 2.0 technologies enable high-speed communication and also the emergence of generative learning processes, transforming individual contribution into team contribution, opening virtual team members to new ideas and to new ways of interaction. Collective knowledge is enhanced but collective intelligence and emotional intelligence also appear in online settings, along with virtual communities of practice and innovative outcomes (London, 2013).

This is one way for smaller companies to access mass collaborative tools. Thus, they can implement collaborative relationships with major stakeholders, partners, customers and suppliers (Turban et al., 2011). Still, one point that is not really discussed in mentioned researchers' work is security and confidentiality issues, which may hinder companies to widely use those Web 2.0 tools. It also explains why companies tend to use tools that are secured for their own activities or even develop internally their own systems.

Emergent technologies also try to make virtuality a 'physical reality' by introducing a three-dimensional collaborative environment, as outlined by Montoya et al. (2011). Based on 3D virtual world technologies developed for the gaming environment such as Second Life from Linden Lab, or ProtoSphere from ProtonMedia, the virtual world environment offers a wide range of communication and interactive tools within a shared life-simulated space for virtual meetings, information-sharing and learning where users are presented by avatars (digital representation of themselves).

Users can create their own avatars in their imagined environment that they imagine where they can socialize and connect using free voice and text chat. A new and richer level of collaboration is driven through the collaborative process modelling, where animation, visualization in 3D and presence are simulated. For instance, the position of participants' avatars in the virtual workshop indicate who is present, who is working with whom, who is working on what (Poppe et al., 2013). Virtual world systems are controlled by a virtual operating software and maintained by distant developers (Oyedele and Minor, 2011).

Companies can use this kind of platform to integrate new collaborators from distributed areas, to train their collaborators, to present and discuss product development and innovation, or any conference and idea sharing meetings. The use of such tools enables reduced travel time, pollution and costs. The virtual world environment simulates a sense of presence, a psychological involvement (mental energy used by a user on simulated actors) and a behavioural engagement (perception of the user on his/her contribution with the simulated actors) (Oyedele and Minor, 2011).

However, these recent technologies moderate team performance for the business world because the degree of provided service and technologies may vary from one provider to another. Also, some business activities might be more adapted than others for 3D collaborative environment. Product innovation, decision-making or learning sessions fit rather well into that context. Nevertheless, further research regarding the possibilities and benefit brought by challenging 3D collaborative technologies to virtual teaming is still necessary.

Evaluation on the benefits gained by the virtual team indicates the fit of the technological tools to perform the team activities notably in the decision-making process and team outcomes performance. Technology improvement continues while will bring even more diversity while widely giving access to technologies that partly already exist (e.g. cloud computing, 3D web, semantic web etc.)

7.2.4 Impact on Individuals

When introducing new technologies or technologies that users do not know, users might not be so excited to use such software so it may require a certain experience beforehand. This is especially the case with 3D collaborative technologies. For instance, users may need some experience in manipulating objects in 3D-space that entail multidirectional and cognitive efforts before they become familiar with these kinds of platforms (Saunders et al., 2011).

Thus, individual satisfaction might not increase as expected unless the virtual world setting is very close to a real world setting (Sutanto et al., 2011). This means that companies need to create conditions to maximize user immersion (Goel et al., 2012). They need to promote these technological platforms and show the benefit they may bring to the concerned work processes. They should take into account three major possible user profiles, as suggested by Oyedele and Minor (2011), in a virtual world customer typology. Profiles differ from those who are 'virtual-skeptic', those who are on the contrary 'virtual-enthusiastic', and comfortable with virtual world transactions, and finally those who have real abilities to connect real world and virtual world experiences.

An improved environment for the development of group decision support systems, which are cost-effective and easier to maintain with the introduction of XML languages, positively influence technology accessibility (Mtshali and Korrapati, 2000). Mobile technologies also increase accessibility and reduce distance. Therefore, virtual teams and their members become contactable any time and any place. The accessibility to data and connections looks easier and brings work closer to home, as noted by McCord and Boone (2008), 'teleworkers can install very capable home technology infrastructures at modest costs'. The advances in global networking have resulted in the e-workers' reliance on technology.

Team processes are largely supported by Internet-based collaborative technologies (Babar et al., 2006). Virtuality and dispersed teams assume there is a possibility of technology diversities within the group or organization, which implies the need for technology standardization. As a matter of fact, each virtual team member in a team needs to get the same basic technology, for example, a laptop computer, modem, mobile phone, Internet access and an email account, along with the same groupware systems.

Despite this need for standardization, Gaan (2012) notes some disparities in the computer-mediated context related to age differences regarding professional commitment and gender differences related to social constraints, a sense of affiliation to the team, and cognitive disparities. This disparity should be taken into account when collaborative tools are selected and when team members are trained to work with those tools.

But deeper research on the subject should be performed in order to confront results. Some further analysis points out that the diversity of technological solutions tends to push virtual team leaders and members to develop their skills at adapting ICTs. This is true as long as they find technical solutions to their team activities (the receiver) and the communication technology that matches the content of their messages (the sender)

(Beise et al., 2004). This is also one of the reasons why technology developers need to improve technical solutions on a continuous basis and provide practitioners with tools that are updated accordingly.

7.2.5 Challenges Faced by Technologies within a Virtual Environment

One of the most frequently mentioned challenges is the lack of real and visual cues. 'A groupware system does not have the same capacity to convey the multiple cues that characterize human conversation' (Montoya-Weiss et al., 2001; Jawadi and Boukef Charki, 2011). This is why systems evolve continuously to offer solutions that give 'a sense of presence'. However, possible technological incompatibility may ensue and inhibit information-sharing, which reduces virtual team performance while increasing possibilities of breakdowns and possible virus contamination. Technology can be a source of serious failure in virtual team implementation and, alone, it cannot create efficient virtual teams. They should be embedded in the socio-emotional and the managerial processes. The systems themselves are complex and have high demands on resources. Among resources, we note development such as the development of technical engines development and applications for a large range of requests that are challenged by time-to-implementation pressure.

This requests IT developers to understand the virtual team environment they are working for, along with the users' methods and best practices in order to meet their needs and offer the best suited systems and applications (Beise et al., 2004). The researchers point out an additional challenge faced by IT developers: confronted with globalization, outsourced IT development emerges with the competition of global strategies, and the relocation of IT development to lower labour cost areas. When outsourced, IT development might be confronted with an increased complexity in the understanding of expected outcomes as well as customer satisfaction process due to multicultural diversity.

Transferring the venue of IT operations to another place may affect the local IT workers and their environment. Therefore, the impact might concern the virtual team users, depending on the type of outsourcing structure and organization, as well as the location of the outsourcing supplier (Brooks, 2006). For example, the Indian software industry is a preponderant competitive market offering talents and expertise at a lower cost of human capital compared to Western countries. Although they are bridging temporal and geographical distance while offering work flexibility, those Indian companies still face, however, challenges in working with customers in a virtual context.

They face high employee turnover, difficulties in getting professionals willing to transfer from a technical position to a managerial position, and finally, lack of fundamental managerial and leadership skills in team leaders and team members. High turnover is high work pressure and an unbalanced work life, routine issued from legacy work and the challenges of running a project on time, and satisfying customers when not all resources are gathered (Agrawal et al., 2012).

Employee turnover hinders team spirit building, accentuated by all the challenges linked to virtual team processes, as mentioned in socio-emotional processes. In addition to cultural and geographical distance, virtuality challenges the project delivery and team members' satisfaction. Relationships between onsite and offshore team members is asymmetric in technical knowledge, domain experience, project management and customer management skills, which may cause possible misunderstandings, and more frequent discussions to clarify those misunderstandings.

For example, some of the Indian project team members may work onsite, close to the customer. In that case, relationships with customers and local team members may get facilitated but when they come back to their initial team in Indian, those Indian project members might be confronted to integration challenges: no promotion, salary gap between onsite experience and local ones, difficult insertion in a new team project.

The example of Indian IT services shows the complexity and challenges of IT outsourcing and virtual teamwork within a multicultural context through various organizations. The researchers Xue et al. (2004) recommend that the missions given to IT developers are clear, they get enough time to accomplish the mission and to become a cohesive group, and they are able to assess customer satisfaction in running their mission.

Additionally, multiple technologies in a team or close environment combined with traditional technical challenges, that includes the 'compatibility of systems, security, and the selection of appropriate technologies', and explains the reasons why technological processes may interfere with improved solutions and other complexities in team processes (Chinowsky and Rojas, 2003). The combination of appropriate assessment of the company or team needs, adapted technologies and already existing IT infrastructure, adequate economical structure as well as the degree of organizational preparation is essential to ensure 'fit and viability' concepts (Turban et al., 2011). Economic viability of the selected tools should not be underestimated.

7.2.6 Technology Adoption

Adapted training for the concerned stakeholders is assumed due to the complexity of the technologies supposed, as well as modifications within the organizational structure (Chinowsky and Rojas, 2003). The goal is to get the team members to feel at ease with technology and be committed by using, sharing, updating, and maintaining the information that they access, and, naturally, be operational as soon as possible. The development of online courses is one example of technology adoption leading to adaptation (as demonstrated by the case study: 'E-learning—Challenges and opportunities: Chloe's case', located in Part V Case studies).

Adapted training is also the opportunity to develop the ability to influence from a distance, create and maintain virtual relationships, work independently and manage efficient online meetings (Morris, 2008). Constant changes and version updates may create a feeling of unease and stress in the users' sphere. A lack of reliability in technologies or even fear can emerge, if the alignment is not effective. Thus, it reduces the opportunities for technology adoption (a key criterion for technology implementation success) that are presented.

This is even more crucial when various technologies are available within the group, requiring standardization. Technological standardization facilitates ICTs' appropriation and adoption by the virtual team members. Consequently, it leads to an effective use of the tools and reduces task conflict. It requires, however, a certain individual availability to assimilate new technologies during daily routines, skills and technology understanding.

Confronted to technological diversity, 'alignment with existing collaborative work practices' is necessary because it contributes to a faster technological integration (Munkvold, 2005) which influences team motivation and performance through an effective perception. Additionally, virtual team members and all stakeholders have to be aware of the available 'tool box' and the quality approach. They should use them in a quality-oriented problem-solving, and a continuous improvement mindset of products and services usage (Thomas and Bostrom, 2010).

Virtual team members need to acquire the capacity to run their activities virtually, such as problem-solving or decision-making within a multicultural environment. It underlines the relevance of assessing team inputs and, more precisely, team profiles, and team size (Ebrahim et al., 2009). Team size influences technology choice as researchers found that larger teams select technology seeking for coordination of asynchronous work, whereas, smaller teams choose technology that supports collaboration (Bradner et al., 2005; Rezgui, 2007). Team size also impacts team membership, which is directly connected with technology adoption success.

Team members have to get involved and show their collaboration willingness and ability to use the proposed technology, which might not be uniform within a virtual team due to culture, language and virtual boundary diversities. Membership across various 'social worlds' or 'working spheres' may facilitate technology implementation.

A social world is described by Ferris and Minielli (2004) as 'a collective unit or team running collective activities related to work within an organization'. Membership in an organization may create some resistance for potential users but once users from one 'social world' have adopted the technology they can introduce it to another 'social world'. As underlined by Jawadi and Boukef Charki (2011), virtual team members adopt technologies easier if their 'social virtuality' is high. The authors define social virtuality as the capacity of the virtual team members to adopt and adapt technologies to their social and communication needs.

Collaboration and integration technologies that support real-time communication, control and coordination issues in the virtual context are still under further development and, therefore, investigation (Qureshi et al., 2006; Rodrıguez et al., 2010). As a matter of fact, technical and legal adjustments are still required, especially with some tools, systems compatibility and improvements on ICT quality.

Outcomes of virtual teams and global performance are concerned with the technological processes for the aforementioned reasons. Team performance is also negatively affected by the perception transmitted by the virtual team outcomes that might be slowed down by the possible technological failures or, on the contrary, positively enhanced by improved solutions (Driskell et al., 2003). At this level, managerial processes should take action.

7.2.7 Managerial Facilitation in Technology Adoption

The virtual team leaders' role includes creating a supportive climate for the technology deployment through a socio-technical approach considering human, contextual and technical factors (Boddy et al., 2005). It contributes to the swift involvement of virtual team members' in the team activities. Thomas and Bostrom (2010) suggest that virtual team leaders should understand the 'team technology knowledge' in order to facilitate the adaptation of the technology in distributed project work.

Virtual team leaders' choice of technology is guided by four main criteria: accessibility, social distance among team members, idea sharing, and informing team members (Sivunen and Valo, 2006). The leadership style may facilitate the implementation and a team's adaptation to ICT tools. A facilitator and supportive behaviour fosters more trust and cooperation while a 'command and control' behaviour is more effective to reach team outcomes rather than technology adaptation (Amrit and Van Hillegersberg, 2008).

A prerequisite to that approach is the need for the team leaders to be aware of the level of technology knowledge within the team in order to request the adapted ICT (Thomas and Bostrom, 2010). Successful managers and teams can adapt and use rather various existing ICTs rather easily to meet their own task or process and teamwork objectives (Beise et al., 2004; Gressgard, 2011). Then the leader has to inquire as to how individuals get adapted to that technology.

In any case, technologies cannot compensate for leadership skills. Technological group support systems 'can make a well planned meeting better, and it can make a poorly planned meeting worse' (Nunamaker et al., 1996).

7.3 WORK PROCESSES

7.3.1 Definition

Work processes refer to task-related virtual team activities and the resources to enable these activities, such as the structure supporting virtual work organization, and defining work environment and its characteristics. Globalization leads to fundamental transitions in the work structure, driving an orientation to collaborative work with a reduced sense of presence. Virtual work is possible through virtual teams, remote control, simulations and digital representations. Simulations are relevant because they make virtuality more accessible and closer to physical processes (Bailey et al., 2012). Work becomes 'portable' thanks to digital representation and adequate processes.

A set of essential information is necessary for the virtual team members to proceed successfully through the virtual work processes. Task and role assignment has to be defined for the team and for each team member together with the expected team outcomes, associated to identification, prioritization and completion schedule of the major tasks. When they can visualize the expected team targets, there is higher probability for virtual team members to get involved and committed at a higher level.

Clarification of work processes and strategies are needed as they are critical in regards to the performance of virtual teams (Lurey and Raisinghani, 2001). Assessment of team performance and virtual work requires massive digital information to support remote control. Remote control may take various forms: input control, output control and behavioural control. Control can be operated through self-control, by peers or hierarchy but, within the virtual environment, control of management and work processes are often supported by information systems (Limburg and Jackson, 2011).

7.3.2 Workflow System

Technologies and digitization enable virtual work, which implies a separation between workers and objects e.g. production machines. Operators remain co-located with each other and operate through computers and control systems using symbolic and iconic representations of objects and physical work processes. Operators deal with increased analytics, data processed work and may be involved in decision-making that is traditionally reserved for managers.

The risk of virtual work is that operators may develop mistrust in digital representations and experience cognitive overload. Furthermore, managers may hesitate to transfer some of their responsibilities to operators, turning away changes in labour division (Bailey et al., 2012). This evolution implies the integration of critical elements such as new competencies to cope with changes in work design with a variety of computer-based technologies (Townsend et al., 1998; Sparrow, 2000). Supported by technology advances, work processes have been automated through workflow systems. A workflow system might be totally or partially implemented. Workflow consists of a sequence of connected tasks, steps, required information, tools and people involved in the activity or business process. It defines and organizes the logical execution sequences among virtual teams and virtual team members' activities. The system is used to collect data and information from sensors (workflow technology) located throughout a plant; for example, to synchronize the different steps of the activity process, to execute automatic administrative and production tasks, and to provide needed data and notifications to the users (workflow management).

They enable a reliable tracing of the executed or pending tasks. Such a system determines the intra-enterprise or inter-enterprise work processes through categorization (sequential work step breakdown), formalization (business rules) and automation of the business process (Bafoutsou and Mentzas, 2002; Zhuge, 2003; Radoiu, 2007; Limburg and Jackson, 2011). Thus, virtual teams can share common goals, methods and practices under the same model, associating communication and work processes as a relevant factor in the coordination of dispersed activities (Im et al., 2005). It is the basis of collaborative work.

Two types of workflow systems distinct from each other are: the operational process (or production workflow) and the situational process based on a collaborative workflow model where the virtual team members are invited to participate in the decision-making process. A collaborative workflow enables activities to be executed in parallel, thus, giving virtual team members the possibility of checking and monitoring intermediate results of the activity execution. The different steps of the activity process can be more easily coordinated by the concerned team members or the team leader through various parameters (Baïna et al., 2004).

Situational process is considered as a dynamic workflow, where the virtual team members' cooperation is classified at three levels by Zhuge (2003): work cooperation level, information-sharing level, and cognitive cooperation level. At the work cooperation level, virtual team members proceed to the tasks as planned by the work system. At the information-sharing level, teammates are able to communicate by exchanging information according to the predefined sharing model. When reaching the level of cognitive cooperation, virtual team members show the capability to distance themselves, and make abstractions, think and analyse their past experience, and use it to implement new solutions to new problems in a dynamic way. They are also able to learn from each other.

7.3.3 From Work Process Structure to Collaborative Work

Work process structure is associated with task liking, as stated by Short et al. (2005), who suggest that virtual team managers should consider the organizational context in which team members interact. Structured processes positively influence the effectiveness of virtual teams towards increased collaboration (Rice et al., 2007). When successful, we designate those processes as collaborative work processes. Collaboration implies that virtual team managers should organize and communicate with regard to work processes to get the virtual team members committed, as Powell et al. (2006) demonstrated, and create a strong relationship between work processes and trust within team members and into the process.

Collaborative work processes define how to work in collaboration in or outside of a virtual team, including rules and norms statements, while paradoxically bringing more flexibility and efficiency to the processes. Consequently, the areas of individual implication are extended and virtual team members tend to become multitask employees, thus, less closely attached to a delimited job function. Collaborative workflow can be monitored and visualized using different tools or different workflow systems at the same time, which reinforces multitasking orientation.

To enable at a collaborative work level supported by a work process structure, virtual teams need information on the status of all activities performed by the different stakeholders so that they can keep track of the work progress. They need objectives determined in accordance to the appropriate available documents and databases (artefacts) and knowledge about the framework in order to understand the relationships of all artefacts ('who, what, when, in which context'—Dustdar, 2004).

Likewise, the virtual team leader also needs access to the team progress status and artefacts to be able to measure the team progression and performance. Formalization and procedures depict rules on how collaboration operates. Because a collaborative work system gives access and distributes a lot of informative data, some authorization levels and access to control management are implemented for internal actors, administrators and external partners. This control may occur at the system level by system administrators and at the group level by group administrators. The access to this information is especially necessary for distant managers to be able to pilot the virtual team who may set adequate parameters. However, the responsiveness of a fast communicative network simulating availability should not reduce due to control needs. Furthermore, remote managers should pay attention to the fact that tracing team activity progression might be perceived as stressful by some virtual team members. Therefore, efficient and clear communication is an essential link in the functioning of the work processes, as demonstrated by Dustdar (2004) named 'Caramba'.

This collaborative model is based on the 'organizational objects' establishing the structure and responsibilities for the virtual team 'persons, roles, groups, skills, units, organization, tasks and documents' and with work and business processes led by an appropriate management. The model shows the importance of the relationships between tasks and activities, work processes and team members. It proposes a template of the best practices and rules in order to develop team members' awareness of those interrelations. Some procedures show how communication is managed within the team, and point out what main characteristics should be considered in the case of breakdowns, such as the development of social relationships. Social relationship development is considered as important to carrying forward the tacit knowledge and intensifying collaborative work (El-Tayeh et al., 2008).

The benefit is to provide a real-time visualization of the virtual team activities. It must remain agile, which is a relevant factor to keeping virtual teams operating efficiently, while sharing and processing information quickly (Denton, 2006; Tavana and Kennedy, 2006). Therefore, a deployment of modern and adapted devices emerges, such as laptops, personal digital assistants (PDAs) and even smart phones with adequate display and services capabilities (Bergenti et al., 2002). Additionally, groupware systems contribute to overcoming interorganizational and transitional decision-making obstacles through adapted framework for the agile exchange of information and, thus, the accessing databases.

One point to consider, though, is the balance of time pressure with team members' perception of satisfaction with intense virtual communication and multitasking. 'A higher level of work virtuality leads to a lower level of work satisfaction' (Mihhailova et al., 2011). However, we have not found much academic research on the relation between virtuality, technology, time pressure and individual satisfaction.

7.4 TO KEEP IN MIND: ASSOCIATION OF TECHNOLOGIES AND WORK PROCESSES

Technologies consist of a portfolio of tools and applications, namely groupware, that assist organizations in the decision-making process. Technologies enable virtual teams to execute, coordinate and manage their activities through collaborative or communicative systems to achieve team outcomes. Those systems enhance and improve communication and shared knowledge, and also contribute to virtual team performance when associated to work processes. Multicultural teams often face diversities in technologies, which may request adaptation, standardization and/or adoption, especially because technology advances increase continuously. Specific training, supportive managerial processes and adapted organizational architecture contribute to virtual team stakeholders becoming comfortable rather than resistant, to the use of technologies that facilitate successful deployment. Technologies that support virtuality must be continuously adapted to the market and companies' demand in terms of flexibility, fastness, reliability, capacity and proximity. Technologies may encounter higher failures and breakdowns because they are becoming more and more complex. To meet cost-reduction policies, technology development might be outsourced, thus, creating further constraints in 'customer–supplier' relationships that are linked to virtuality in a global context.

Work processes are necessary to organize and support virtual teamwork. They are essential to embed virtual teaming within a work environment and its characteristics, especially when automated through workflow systems, thus, reducing distance. Workflow systems are the core of work processes because they constitute the automated part of work process. The final objective of technologies, work processes and workflow systems within the virtual environment is to develop collaborative work, a key component in technological and work processes. Collaborative work tends to raise the chance of the virtual team members becoming multitask employees, therefore, visibility and control on the work progress is strengthened. Efficient and clear communication fostered by social relationships is necessary to avoid misunderstanding and stress among virtual team members, and to reach high levels of collaborative work.

7.5 CONCLUSION

Work processes supported by technologies are designed to empower virtual teams and people, and make virtuality a reality. Technology compatibility and performance still might not be at the expected level to reach successful results and might be complex, but embedded in continuous changes. They will present new opportunities and challenges. Therefore, more adaptation and training are needed for virtual team users to have higher rates of assimilation. Additionally, training should emphasize the relevance of social relationships, as demonstrated by socio-emotional processes. Connecting virtual team members is a valuable investment and a factor in good performance.

Organizations are pushed to continuous change to get adapted to their moving environment more rapidly. Work processes and advanced technologies are one of the major levers that allow global organizations the possibility of differentiating themselves. They enable a more accurate and more consistent control on work progress, and can even outsource some of their non-core business operations.

Work processes, related methods and practices can suddenly change too. The continuous changes bring some advantages to an organization confronted with fast evolution but they can be considered unstable. This instability may foster stress and anxiety among virtual team users due to time pressure becoming consistently tighter, work evolution from traditional to multitasking activities, increased productivity and competition within the virtual team. Frequently, evolution of virtual teaming is embedded in a global change in the company, which may intensify resistance from the diverse stakeholders.

The impact of intensive technologies on the virtual team members' satisfaction and performance requires more academic research. It should be associated with the impact of intensified control that is exerted by the different systems and managers. Technologies and work processes contribute to a certain simplification and flexibility in the virtual team functioning but also creates new issues. The rapid technological evolution may create a gap between the diverse profiles involved in virtual teaming and fostered by a possible generational difference. The 'Y' generation may bring an added-value in the business world, due to their transactional ability to deal with technologies, work processes and the e-world. However, monitoring technologies does not imply expertise in virtual team leadership. More research is needed to study how IHRM can deal with a new approach and integrate those differences, consequences and evolutions together with the appropriate managerial processes. Technologies that are applied to virtuality are powerful tools, when combined with adequate strategies and managerial processes.

7.6 GUIDELINES FOR MANAGERIAL PRACTICES: TECHNOLOGICAL AND WORK PROCESSES

Technological and work processes support both socio-emotional and managerial processes, which appear to be a key factor in virtual teaming. Technologies consist of a series of tools and applications that assists virtual team managers in the decision-making process and team members in team activities. The work process consolidates the collaborative virtual teamwork. The purpose of these guidelines are to evaluate how far these processes support virtual teaming within a defined environment.

Table 7.1   Technological and work processes

Key actions	Key results
Technological processes *Describe your:* ● Decision support systems. ● Team support systems.	– decision-making process; – team activities, process and coordination (including prioritization, completion schedule, targets, etc.).
● Type of technological system.	– Are one single medium or several media available? – Are some systems inherited from fusion or acquisitions? – Does standardization exist within the team and within other teams? – How quick is the response time of the system? – Do you have flexibility to develop techno-logical support (through local IT, for example)? – How well is the information protected? – Do your technological systems offer advanced technology such as 3D technology?
● Analyse the conditions for users.	– Is training possible? – Does the team manager feel comfortable with the available technology? – Do you need to convince, or encourage the use of technologies? – Do all team members use the same or very similar technology?
Work processes ● Name the type of groupware and associated services.	– ERP, CRM, etc. with services such as common database, shared team space, online meetings, communication channels etc. – Web 2.0 (e.g. wikis, forums, social networks, opinion polls, webinars).

Table 7.1   (continued)

Key actions	Key results
Work processes	
• Investigate your workflow system and the precise the levels of:	– Is the workflow implemented for the whole channel of process (production and decision-making)?
– work cooperation (task activities);	– Is work automation well-accepted by all team members?
– information-sharing level (exchange of information); and	– Do all team members trust the system?
– cognitive cooperation (analysis and improvement of the process).	
• Describe the role assignment in the virtual team.	– Tasks and roles for each member (including prioritization, completion schedule, targets etc).
• Analyse the control process.	– How is it organized (self-control, by peers, by the hierarchy, by the work process system etc.)?
	– Is the information and activities tracking flexible enough?
	– Are the procedures clearly defined?

8 Managerial processes—leadership and conflict management

8.1 INTRODUCTION

In the previous chapter, we have seen how technologies are highly relevant in the virtual team processes. New technologies do not exclude, hide or reduce the importance of managerial relationships and processes inside and outside virtual teams. Managerial processes bridge socio-emotional and technological processes with performance at the organization, team and individual levels.

We first define what management and leadership consist of, then explain virtual managerial processes through two main aspects: virtual team leadership and conflict management in a virtual context. E-leaders or remote leaders need to gain appropriate competencies and behaviours so they can move from a traditional to a virtual type of management, not only through technical competencies but also through interpersonal and relational competencies. According to their behaviour, they play different roles in the team process, leading them to common goals through appropriate and clear guidance.

We specify the relevant actions or leadership attitudes that lead a virtual team to successful performance and refer to appropriate management styles. For efficient leadership, virtual team leaders need to understand virtuality, its benefits and constraints and, more importantly, how the virtual team is situated within that virtuality. The fact that diverse leadership styles might be perceived differently, depending on situational and cultural environments, should also be taken into account.

The second point of this chapter addresses conflict management in the virtual context. We first explain how conflict in virtual teams is understood by academic research and what types of conflict may affect a virtual team. The attributes that characterize a virtual team offer a wide range of possible sources of crisis within a group. This is why we detail the impact of conflicting situations and the reasons why they are more critical and difficult to solve in a virtual context.

Then we bridge leadership and conflict management and look at their close relationship. More specifically, we identify the most adequate leadership style that can regulate certain types of conflict in virtual teams. The purpose is to understand how conflicting situations can be resolved, what kind of conflict resolutions are identified by researchers, and if conflict can in any way create assets in a team.

8.2 VIRTUAL TEAM LEADERSHIP

8.2.1 Definition

Named under diverse terms such as virtual team management, virtual team leadership, e-leadership or remote team management—virtual leadership is not a new form of management compared to conventional team management. Based on a general definition (Friedman, 2000; Dictionary, 2012a; Avolio and Kahai, 2003; Lee, 2011b), team managers or leaders are defined as persons involved in the team decision-making process, building relationships between leaders and followers. They administrate or lead a group of individuals to perform specific functions, towards common goals and outcomes.

Leadership in a virtual environment can be defined as an association of global leadership processes, a leader as a person and a specific job. Leadership processes encompass processes attached to clear communication of a vision, facilitation in the achievement of designed goals and results and encouragement of team members to operate and collaborate (Lee, 2011b). A leader should enhance virtual team members' motivation and satisfaction to achieve optimum performance at team and individual levels. For that purpose, they ensure the availability of the necessary material, cognitive, and social resources according to team priorities and performance objectives.

As a person, an efficient leader shows ability that depends on trait theory (personality traits, 'born to be a leader'), contingency theory (adequacy between leadership roles and external environment) and behavioural complexity theory (specific behaviours, different leadership styles and influence) (Zigurs, 2003; Chen et al., 2011; Pless et al., 2011). We may distinguish a team manager and a team leader. A manager might not be a leader and vice versa. Managers are more concerned with operational actions and leaders more with strategic decisions.

However, the terms 'leadership' and 'leader' cannot be dissociated as both are closely linked to leading and guiding virtual team members toward expected strategic missions, goals and results within a virtual and global business environment. In other words, efficient global leaders or e-leaders are engaged in cognitive, affective and behavioural processes, and require specific skills due to virtuality and all boundaries linked to virtuality.

8.2.2 Specific Skills Requested for Effective E-leaders

A full understanding of what virtual team management and virtual leadership are varies with diverse social and cultural context, location and time (Avery, 2004). Efficient e-leaders, who wish to respond to the international requirements, should understand that e-leadership requires specific skills and abilities that convey effectiveness in virtuality. The case study: 'Restructuring introduces a new way of working: The case of Eks' in Part V of this book, points out the consequences when the below elements are underestimated.

These abilities encompass a global business understanding with cultural sensitivity, global environment knowledge meaning capability of learning and adapting their thinking to new orientations and various team member types within a global continuum, therefore some visionary competencies.

Controversial positions consider that leadership cannot be taught because it emerges from personal traits while some argue that it may be learned or at least developed through coaching and mentoring. In fact, leadership skills refer to a wide range of leadership competencies that are linked to specific characteristics and approach, which is different than in co-located situations. Some of them can be learned, at the very least, the main characteristics implied by leadership.

Those characteristics may vary according to the degree of virtual team complexity. As suggested by Tuffley (2009) three main differentiations for virtual leadership are identified:

- **Generic leadership skills:** are applicable to any teams that are conventional, multicultural or virtual.
- **Multidisciplinary skills:** are specific factors applicable to multidisciplinary teams.
- **Specific-to-virtual-environment skills:** are applicable to complex virtually organized teams, which represent higher challenges for leaders along with required adapted skills.

In this book, we concentrate on multidisciplinary and specific-to-virtual-environment skills, which refer to a gradation towards virtuality. Virtual leadership skills in multidisciplinary teams encompass cognitive, social and behavioural capabilities. Cognitive capabilities mean the necessary skills to analyse and synthesize in multidimensional amplitude with the aim to adopt the appropriate decisions. Social capabilities refer to the ability of developing adequate interpersonal relationships within the team. Finally, behavioural capabilities concern comportments and manners that influence team members (Mukherjee et al., 2012b). Those competencies can be used more or less intensively dependent on the stage of team development, associated with other factors influencing virtual contexts. Social and behavioural skills bring high value during the maturity phases of virtual team development and highly influences the managers' role within a virtual team.

E-leaders need what Niederman and Tan (2011) call 'equafinality' (concept borrowed from von Bertalanffy who set up the principle that diverse inputs or initial states can lead to similar results). Specific competencies encompass relationship management with the ability to build partnerships that cope with function-specific knowledge as well as ambiguity (Maznevski and DiStefano, 2000; Pless et al., 2011).

In fact, e-leadership has to cope with the virtual context and discontinuities, technologies and managerial transfers such as switching from traditional leadership to e-leadership, thus, 'bridging the gap between traditional leadership theories and virtual leadership' (Zhang and Fjermestad, 2006; Al-Ani et al., 2011). Virtual leadership transfers from local offices to e-connected locations, from the same time zone to various time zones, from conventional teamwork culture to virtual teamwork culture, meanwhile, a specific-to-the-virtual-team culture has to be developed within the team.

Confronted with discontinuities, source of process issues and possible problems linked to virtual team boundaries, e-leaders may face a lack of team cohesion (Chudoba et al., 2005). Consequently, e-leaders have to be aware of virtual team dynamics and acquire the ability to manage this dynamic through technology in order to maintain or develop team cohesion. The approach of virtual team management requires a focus on results and project or productivity development rather than on time spent working at the office. Higher supervisory skills, in comparison with co-located teams, are also necessary due to higher team complexity (Cascio, 2000). However, management of interrelationships should not be neglected.

E-leadership requires efficient management and leadership similarly to face-to-face or conventional teams. However, since virtual teams present higher complexity and challenges than those encountered in co-located teams, additional specific skills are required from virtual team leaders. The main areas of competencies strive for enhancement of the responsible and global mindset, ethical knowledge, cultural intelligence, self-development and network building. More specific and absolutely necessary are building communication and cohesion in a virtual context (Pless et al., 2011).

Key competencies are highlighted by Cascio (2000) in the area of virtual collaboration, socialization and communication. More precisely, Hambley et al. (2007) point out critical elements such as being able to lead effective online meetings, to personalize virtual teamwork, learn how to effectively use the different media and give visibility inside of the team and outside of the organization.

Virtual managers' communication skills seem even more essential in an environment that has become more virtual than conventional due to the boundaries linked to virtuality (Gerke, 2006). They have to master synchronous communication: face-to-face meetings are rare and, therefore, need to be run effectively when they occur. They also have to be proficient in asynchronous communication. There are less face-to-face meetings, more scheduling, higher performance and diverse pressures while building trust in the team which cannot be covered by technologies only.

Managers of virtual teams need to deepen their knowledge and adopt appropriate behaviours and managerial processes. Necessary fundamentals keep virtual members focused on the team missions. Therefore, virtual team managers need to be capable of providing clear team objectives through a clear team charter and the means of achieving the objectives through operation principles. Virtual team managers need to understand their decision-making and problem-solving processes and analyse the consequences of their decisions within a virtual environment, the way they think and who they draw in to the processes (Lee, 2011a).

E-leaders need to keep the team agile and adjusted to constant reconfigurations. Those leaders have the ability to adjust themselves to the typology of their teams (viz. different sizes, compositions and attributes). Thus, formal structures and processes should not stop the possibility for the virtual team to reach its targets. In addition to technical skills, effective virtual team leaders demonstrate the ability to adopt the right style and leadership roles as a response to various situations within virtual teams.

It may concern time, risk-level, time orientation and cultural difference. Their ability to 'change ahead of the curve' plays a key role in virtual team leadership skills in order to lead the teams and/or other teams towards the corporate strategy (Thomas et al., 2012). It includes emotional intelligence, the capacity to create an open and supportive environment, deal with change management and a certain complexity with contradictory and paradoxical behaviours, such as simultaneously handling authority and flexibility (Kayworth and Leidner, 2002).

The remote managers' competencies and skills are recognized to be crucial because they directly affect the work and affective process performance of the team, therefore, additional skills to standard managerial skills and competencies are requested to reach efficient leadership. Leadership effectiveness can be measured through four major approaches as identified in the research literature by Chen et al. (2011).

The measures can focus on objective versus perceptual measurement, acceptance versus exclusion of the leader, individual versus group performance measurement, and productivity versus satisfaction. The measures encompass global areas as the main criteria of evaluation, including outcomes assessment, managerial interrelationships, performance and outcomes. The adapted measurement should be chosen according to the multiple missions and targets settled for the team (members and leaders) in a rapidly changing context. The managerial final objective is to achieve the necessary trust building within the team to achieve team performance and team satisfaction.

As revealed by Kahn and Ahmad (2012), some competencies for effective leadership in the virtual context seem more relevant at some levels of team management than others. At the top level of management, usually composed of executives who settled policies and objectives, team leaders need to show the ability of team building and communication because their role is to build and monitor the team along with communicating team policies and objectives. Team building skills at this level appear more important than at the middle level of management.

Team motivational skills are relevant at the low level of management because leaders must get the work done at this level and need to communicate about problems and suggestions in order to motivate the team members. At the middle level of management, communication skills are the most necessary because this level of management needs to inform both top and low levels of management. However, to show team building competencies, one must also have motivation and communication skills. It highlights the complexity of necessary skills for effective team leadership. A set of skills is required, even though one of them may be preponderant at some level. Some indicators underline the level of effective leadership.

For example, cultural intelligence is a reliable indicator for effective leadership of virtual teams and a function of the leadership context. Cultural intelligence combines integration in cross-cultural teams, international assignment effectiveness, expatriate adjustment and performance. All these elements determine the success of a virtual team leader (Zander et al., 2012).

Some ground rules should be laid down such as being able to understand, value and capitalize on the team's diversity (i.e. on cultural, social, geographical aspects etc.). It also includes the ability to expect and accept differences in personal values due to cultural diversity. Being patient with team members' efforts to communicate in another language than their native one is a key factor. Finally, showing the capacity to effectively keep the team informed about its missions, goals and results, clarify any questions or doubts belongs to e-leaders' fundamental skills. Those rules play relevant roles in virtual team processes (Levasseur, 2012).

A quick assumption could lead to the idea that born multicultural leaders can spontaneously lead multicultural virtual teams. However, this is not demonstrated by research. Moreover, social, professional experiences and specific training contribute to the acquisition of knowledge, skills, capacity, motivation and multiculturalism understanding.

Learning leadership skills is possible and becomes essential when a leader needs to acquire the capacity to develop a strong virtual team identity and create team fundamentals. More and more often, leadership training sessions are provided in a virtual mode, which saves financial and time resources, offers flexible schedules in addition to virtual experiences and reaches a wider range of potential candidates for training.

However, they are not adapted to all trainee profiles. Some trainees present higher dispositions than others to be trained in a virtual mode. Most of the time, they show high openness to experience, low anxiety or high conscientiousness, which are key characteristics of success for a leaders' improvement in virtual training. These characteristics are informative indications of how effective a leader can be in a virtual context (Eissa et al., 2012).

Openness to new experiences is linked to adaptation to change, imagination and an attraction to unconventional methods. This openness is necessary because the learning environment is rather new and requests motivation to learn in such a context. Conscientious people are highly organized, results-oriented, disciplined and most probably highly involved in job performance. Anxiety is associated with low emotional intelligence and low emotional stability.

Therefore, demonstration of anxiety is negatively related to engagement in learning experiences. Virtual training seems to be more accessible and effective to leaders showing individual psychological capital, including the mentioned psychological traits showing high openness to experience and conscientiousness but low anxiety. These personality characteristics play a key role in the effective performance of leaders in a virtual leadership.

Continuous change in the virtual environment affects managerial styles and roles that may vary from 'permanent leaders to rotating leaders' or to a 'leaderless structure' (Nemiro et al., 2008). However, the leader's role should not be confined to a rigid style or role which may lead to possible stereotypes that would affect leadership efficiency and performance.

8.2.3 Managerial Styles

Different managerial styles can be adopted depending on the team priorities, team structure, evolution and outcomes to be reached (Carte et al., 2006; Konradt and Hoch, 2007):

- **Coordinator type:** highlights stability and concentrates on control and internal focus.
- **Command-and-control or director type:** this directive style is task- and outcomes-oriented, and enhanced control and external focus. Therefore, the leader focuses on monitoring, work and performance progress (Amrit and Van Hillegersberg, 2008).
- **Transactional type:** builds relationships based on process of exchanges and rewarding or sanctioning the team members to reach goals. Transactional leaders monitor and control team members based on rational and metric means and measure to bring solutions to any possible deviations from set goals (Mukherjee et al., 2012b). Any results issued from exchanges returns, for instance, rewards announced due to higher productivity are called 'transactional' relationships. Transactional leadership, on 'demanding mode', positively affects the idea generation, but does not foster higher creativity.
- **Innovator or transformational type:** is a more 'inspirational' style that focuses on members' motivation and stimulation (Hambley et al., 2007; Davidson, 2013) so it is more concerned with people than with processes linked to ideas and values (Maznevski and Athanassiou, 2003; Nemiro et al., 2008) which is especially true for emergent e-leaders. The innovator style, an adaptive leadership, bridging virtual team members together towards common goals and vision, is more oriented towards flexibility and external focus. Transformational or innovator leaders communicate the strategic vision of the team and are task-focused. They facilitate the objectives understanding through an effective computer-mediated communication that they are able to use effectively (Tyran et al., 2003). In the case of email communication, they use a clearly and concisely written format. The inspirational style fosters more trust and collaborative behaviour in a team showing a high degree of understanding, empathy, charisma and interpersonal bonding, which are critical factors to effectively managing virtual teams. Wang et al. (2011) indicate that virtual team members' creativity is improved when managed with transformational leadership even though their performance on idea generation does not increase. This style of leadership is important in all contexts but more specifically in the

virtual context (Joshi et al., 2009) and leaders of virtual teams have to be able to inspire and motivate through computer-mediated communication (Tyran et al., 2003).

- **Transformational and transactional type:** e-leaders play the role of facilitator and supporter in the actions while building relationships and clear communication (Tyran et al., 2003). They affirm their authority simultaneously but still keep certain flexibility (Nemiro et al., 2008). They use leadership strategies and remain people-oriented to retain talent, and skills while still considering the constraints of globalization, stressed by competition and financial struggles (Zander et al., 2012). Cultural intelligence is one of the key factors in transformational and transactional leadership (Ismail et al., 2012). Those managers have the possibility of operating on a broader transactional network within the organization while taking a transformational behaviour to lead the virtual team. However, higher effectiveness due to the association of both styles is not proven if we refer to Hambley et al. (2007) who found that both styles have the same effectiveness on the virtual team interaction mode or outcomes. This leadership style leads to a greater amount of feedback positivity within virtual teams when interacted with the communication medium, more specifically with instant messaging. Positive feedback contributes to higher social presence, discussion satisfaction, group cohesion and virtual team performance. However, research finds a negative influence on decision quality (Kahai et al., 2012).

- **Facilitator or mentor type:** characterized by a facilitative, participative and supportive approach that is focused on adaptation and therefore is highly recommended for effective technology adaptation management, for instance. This type of leadership is oriented to flexibility and external focus. Nemiro et al. (2008) define the virtual team facilitator as a virtual team leader who brings tools, information and resources to guide the team to the expected outcome. They use cultural intelligence and a global mindset to leverage global team diversity (Zander et al., 2012). According to their study, the facilitator may achieve the behaviour of a mentor or coach and innovator. The mentor-or-coach-type leader endeavours to develop the virtual team members' interpersonal potential and accountability in others (Nemiro et al., 2008).

The choice of management style has to be adequate to facilitate the attainment of the virtual team targets and mission; in order to avoid any possible frustration that may happen if it is not well understood and anticipated by the manager. Adaptation to the team profile is also necessary, as some virtual team members may expect coordination and support rather than general guidance. Therefore, effective virtual team leadership can be classified according to the leader's role, more task-oriented (focusing on task completion) or more relationship-oriented (focused on interpersonal relationships between team members and their emotional needs) (Chen et al., 2011).

The e-leader has to keep in mind that, as a result of the virtuality effect on structures and organizations, the structure and the duration of the team may change. It then requests a certain level of analysis and assessment from virtual team leaders in order to adapt their managerial style to the projected team missions and the context.

8.2.4 Virtual Team Leaders' Roles

On a macro level, e-leaders of virtual teams are asked to encourage and sustain a culture of cooperation or collaboration. The finality is to lead the team to higher competitiveness through the management of international human capital and global competitiveness (Ling and Jaw, 2011). Since it is more challenging in a flatter-type organization—where the ability to coordinate decisions and actions across virtuality becomes essential—e-leaders need to also gain the membership of team members or colleagues who may be confronted with competing priorities or conflicting targets. The difficulty may emerge from matrix organizations, typical models that result from globalization, where tasks are dispatched transversely, and done by people over whom leaders may have no direct authority. To reach effective leadership within this context, e-leaders' roles convey three major actions or recommended behaviours: clear and transparent communication, agreement on cooperation process (when and how it is needed) which preserves trust and the establishment of common explicit team goals, which maintain cooperation (Forgie, 2011).

On a micro level, e-leaders' role can be defined as detecting, diagnosing, solving problems and providing the appropriate solution to the team that he/she leads (Zaccaro and Bader, 2003). At this level, e-leadership roles encompass two main functions: team performance management and team development (Hunsaker and Hunsaker, 2008), which are split in three parts: 'team liaison, team direction setter and team operational coordinator' (Zaccaro and Bader, 2003).

Leadership and team management show the roles distributed in the team 'who one is', 'how one interacts' and 'what one does' (Wakefield et al., 2008) 'who makes decisions and how they get made' (Thomas et al., 2012). More precisely and similarly for the macro level, the roles involve setting goals and priorities, communication and information-sharing, work processes and team method analysis, information and knowledge resources with the aim of reaching team outcomes.

Virtual team leaders ensure that their virtual teams acquire the necessary legitimacy to operate within the organization (Zivick, 2012) through a certain degree of influence, congruence and integrity (Lee, 2011b). E-leaders act as 'sense-makers' and 'sense-givers' in and outside the virtual team. In most of the reported research studies, e-leadership is considered a critical element in the effectiveness of a virtual team, especially when 'social presence' is concerned (Sarker and Schneider, 2009).

Effectiveness is also enhanced when the virtual team leader is able to develop communities of practice to which members are willing to belong, and where groups share their experience, knowledge and reflection about a common topic. These communities are especially effcient to foster tacit knowledge. E-leaders need to ensure that infrastructure and organization support such communities of practice, and that their team members have access to those communities. In that case, clear communication, climate favouring risk taking, trust building and open interactions operate positively to encourage innovation activities (Bertels et al., 2011).

E-leaders lead the decision-making processes in the team thanks to techniques, technologies, processes and tools for organizing and coordinating the group. Team managers and team leaders remain accountable for any situation or events engaged into by the team activities. Virtual team management plays a notable role in structuring virtual team tasks that support socio-emotional processes (Al-Ani et al., 2011). For these reasons, the start-up process for a virtual team leader is to assess the inputs of the virtual team that he/she is in charge of, and check and understand the virtuality context in order to set up the right managerial approach.

8.2.5 Approaching and Understanding Virtuality

To create the appropriate environment for virtual teams, virtual team managers should understand what they need and why. They should have the authority to get the appropriate infrastructure implemented as well as technologies that connect the dispersed members (Maznevski and Athanassiou, 2003) in order to effectively handle virtual team processes, deal with cross-cultural communication, embrace virtuality, diversity and team building with methods such as story-telling to be able to convey implicit knowledge.

Virtual team managers are confronted with either a lower or higher level of complexity, such as how to use adequate technology to enhance team performance, how to cope with the anonymous environment of some virtual teams and, finally, how to communicate social and cultural values and which protocol to base it on?

For example, in the case of participative leadership and the team's controversial position, the virtual team leader may set up an electronic poll to find out how the dispersed team members are willing to follow her/his strategy on a specific issue (Avolio and Kahai, 2003). This method is efficient if democratic polling criteria are clearly established and if the team members have equal access to the poll. The poll offers the possibility of identifying areas of agreement or disagreement, especially those possibly problematic to voice into a true multicultural group situation (Nunamaker et al., 1996).

It is recommended that virtual team managers analyse and assess the virtuality level of their distributed team which is related to the level of diversity within the team. According to Pinjani and Palvia (2013) a 'deep level of diversity' does not impact virtual teams at the same level as a 'visible functional level of diversity'. A deep level of diversity significantly influences team processes, and more specifically mutual trust and knowledge-sharing, more than visible diversity. A high level of diversity and possible issues with team processes linked to that level of diversity can be moderated by the collaborative technology developed in the team as well as the level of interdependence of tasks. We note that the level of diversity plays a key role in the team effectiveness through available level mutual trust and knowledge-sharing in the team.

Researchers, such as Pauleen (2003a) or Maznevski and DiStefano (2000) demonstrate that virtual team managers proceed or should proceed through three phases to approach virtuality:

1   **The first phase, called the 'mapping' phase:** is where leaders assess the attributes of the virtual team to understand its complexity and the way it operates. They evaluate virtual team infrastructure, objectives and missions, the type of virtual team, the composition and types of boundaries they are confronted with. The purpose is to find out the team's strengths and assets, and to set the adapted structure, ICTs, and adequate work processes. According to the virtual team complexity, team leaders assess a realistic timeframe for the completion of tasks. Virtual complexity, as well as the associated boundaries, are intensified when the leader leads cross-functional team members with different functional perspectives and backgrounds or even members from diverse organizations and companies, aiming for global common outcomes (Barczak et al., 2006).

2   **The second phase, called the 'bridging' step:** consists of evaluating the level of relationship to be developed (low, medium, high, depending

on the required personal involvement). Before starting teamwork, it is recommended that the virtual team leader engages in individual and personal relationships with the team's members in order to build a solid base for the team's processes.

3   **In the last phase, called the 'integrating' one**: the virtual team managers create strategies, choose the appropriate means of communication (e.g. Internet-based communication, face-to-face, email etc.) and generate an innovative approach to the task. They give clear and deliverable goals, roles and task assignment, create a shared meaning, along with interdependent tasks together with a global mindset. The final purpose is to engage members into the team tasks. It is often recommended to start off with 'kick-off meetings' and to invest in face-to-face meetings at the beginning of a project or when building a new project team. It prevents mistrust and possible negative stereotypes (Muethel et al., 2012b).

Once achieved, the evaluation of the team virtuality should be reported by the virtual team leader and it is no longer in a semantic form but in an evaluation grid. That grid enhances the 'involved-in-virtuality' factors based on two dimensions: technology and social virtuality, while taking into account virtual team attributes.

An e-leader can determine a 'virtuality index' based on three main clusters of virtuality: 'team distribution, workplace mobility, and variety of work practices' (Chudoba et al., 2005).

Technology and social virtuality are essential because technologies support socio-emotional processes, and, social virtuality shows the team capacity for adaptation. The level of technologies also has to be assessed because it influences procedural role behaviours. The higher technological level, the higher the focus on procedural role behaviours (Griffith et al., 2004). The evaluation grid is a solid base for the virtual team leader to identify the appropriate levers to lead the team to the expected outcomes (Jawadi and Boukef Charki, 2011).

Once the virtuality degree of the virtual team is clarified, the e-leader needs to evaluate the relationship levels inside of the team. She/he, evaluates the socio-emotional processes within the team mainly through the communication used in the team. The communication style used in a virtual team is important in determining the social distance existing within the team especially because asynchronous communication dominates. The e-leader should assess the communication level.

Then, the e-leader adapts his/her language and type of communication for adequate leadership within the team when he/she gives feedback to the virtual team members. The language can be empathetic, direction-giving, and/or mixed, which is perceived to be more effective as demonstrated by an empirical study led by Wang et al. (2009). Similarly, communication transmitted by the virtual team leader may be perceived as constructive, passive, or aggressive by the virtual team members, which might be used purposefully by the team leader in regards to the results he/she targets.

Communication or communicative performance contributes to enhancing the socio-emotional process inside the team. The virtual team leader encourages her/his team to develop an attitude favourable to virtuality by discussing the cultural differences and similarities openly, getting virtual team members more familiar with the other teammates' competencies and profiles, and by agreeing on communication norms supported by technologies (Maznevski and Athanassiou, 2003; Jawadi and Boukef Charki, 2011). As explained in the previous chapters, a leader showing an attitude that integrates the social dimension encourages collaboration, trust and sound knowledge levels.

Once the relationship level is assessed by the virtual team leader, the leader can create and establish strategies for the team. Different leadership strategies might be adopted to manage virtual teams embedded in multicultural complexities: '*laissez-faire*', 'cultural trial-and-error' or common team culture (Zander et al., 2012). The first strategy is to lead the team through '*laissez-faire*' mode, which means that the leader ignores the cross-cultural diversity of the team and relies on the team members' tolerance and self-control. We may find that this strategy conflicts with management as well. The risk with such a strategy is in creating faultlines between cultural subgroups. The second strategy is to run a process of 'cultural trial-and-error', a pragmatic way to find one-by-one solutions for cultural diversities through personal relationships amongst the team leader and team members. The weakness of that strategy is the risk of reinforcing negative cultural stereotypes rather than developing a collaborative climate within the virtual team. The third leadership strategy aims to establish a common team culture, where cultural differences are smoothed within a framework of norms and appropriate behaviours. The risk of that strategy is that the team's common 'culture' becomes the pattern and limits of the cultural exchanges.

Approaching and understanding virtuality means that virtual team leaders' skills encompass the capacity of dealing with the adequate strategy at the right time with the concerned virtual team members, whilst giving sense to the whole team. Furthermore, the appropriate way of communicating strategies is also essential because the virtual team leader may foster an affective process (this process is described in the next chapters).

Affective process is directly linked to the team members' motivation and expression of emotions. One of the challenges for e-leaders includes the management of these emotions. A functional bridge connects collaboration, trust and team cohesion with affective process and individual motivation (Zaccaro and Bader, 2003). This position is delicate because it affects the way conflict is detected and managed. For example, letting people know that workload is high and stressful should be included, and acceptable in the norm of virtual team functioning to avoid latent conflict.

Based on the fact that virtual teams evolve on a continuous basis, virtual team leaders have to be prepared for change management. Changes occur in roles, strategies, policies and procedures, technologies, work processes and plans, thus, generating uncertain and unstable situations (Nemiro et al., 2008). Change management also means that leaders are likely to deal with generational differences and diverse individual expectations, which is increased by the diversities of the team composition and attributes. Change managers should adopt dynamic systems that are responsive to changes across virtual and various contexts (Maznevski and Athanassiou, 2003) and be aware that the perception of their management may vary according to various criteria.

8.2.6   Perception of Leadership in a Virtual Team

Virtual team members perceive leadership through the leader's level of presence and effciency in team management (Zigurs, 2003). However, leadership skills might be perceived in various ways by virtual team members, depending on the team diversity and, more precisely, depending on the members' culture and perception of power distance.

Power distance, as defined by Hofstede's paradigm, is the extent to which less powerful members in the organization accept the distribution of authority. This acceptance is not equal as the cultural perception of power distance varies, which influences the way of working inside a team. It also relates to the degree to which the virtual team members challenge the leader's authority.

In high power distant countries such as Malaysia, Guatemala, Mexico, China, and India, bypassing authority is considered as insubordination. Therefore, not all virtual team members may consider the effectiveness of leadership via the same angle (Nicholson et al., 2007). To smooth out those discrepancies, e-leaders are recommended to explain the goals and outcomes expected from the team as a whole, whilst nurturing individual needs and expectations (Brunelle, 2009).

Authority might also be perceived under different considerations depending on how the virtual team leader is appointed. The virtual team leader can be assigned or emerge based on individual initiative and competencies. Virtual team leadership might be shared and some virtual teams might be self-managed. Assigned leaders have to provide real leadership competencies otherwise they are less likely to be recognized as the group leader by the virtual team members, especially in the presence of an emergent leader that shows a higher level of well-perceived communication, intelligence and collaborative behaviours (Kock, 2009).

Emergent leaders demonstrate skills in relation with' 'role performance trust' with 'high ethical integrity trust' and an 'affective bond trust' used to obtain 'reliability, consistency, quality of work, initiative and experience' (Tyran et al., 2003). One way to recognize emergent leaders in a virtual team is their communication approach and social-oriented dimensions that may seem different (Yoo and Alavi, 2004; Cogliser et al., 2012).

Studies indicate that emergent leaders send more and longer email messages than the other teammates do, mainly oriented to task activities and related to logistics coordination. The effect plays on a pleasant and conscientiousness dimension and appearance. Emergent leaders show higher initiator, scheduler and integrator competencies but no differences with their teammates in the relational and technological management messages. Surprisingly, emotional stability within a team is not related to any dimension of leadership emergence.

Virtual team members may identify more than one leader in the group, which leads to the notion of shared leadership within the group for some specific roles or tasks aiming to higher results and performance enhanced by mutual influence process among virtual team members (Ensley et al., 2003).

Shared leadership means distributed leadership, thus, contrasting with centralized leadership that indicates 'focused' or concentrated leadership. Shared leadership can be understood under two main directions. One suggests that leadership is decentralized but remains vertical and the other refers to collective leadership with the aim of achieving team outcomes due to collegiate efforts and work throughout spread organizations. In the latter case, leadership becomes more horizontal. Shared leadership is distinct from fragmented or misaligned leadership, which underlines the fact that shared leadership assumes coordination in team management (Iles and Feng, 2011).

When team members engage toward shared or distributed leadership, virtual team members tend to be self-driven and resourceful. The virtual team becomes empowered, which is one way to solve the difficulties of monitoring virtual team members' activities (Kirkman et al., 2004) and reduce the virtual distance within the team. Considered as a 'dynamic, proactive and interactive influence process', shared leadership fosters constructive suggestions from team members that are enhanced by diverse national or country-specific knowledge and expertise.

Leader's motivation might influence team leadership differently. The leader can either be team-directed proactive motivated or self-directed proactive motivated. Team-directed proactive behaviour ensures that team members contribute to the team tasks, whereas self-directed proactive behaviour makes certain that the individual contribution fits to the team interdependent tasks. Shared leadership is a positive factor for team performance because team members engaged in shared leadership set actions and means in the interest of the team performance objectives (Muethel et al., 2012a).

Some virtual teams are permanently self-managed which means that they have 'no formal leader' (Bell and Kozlowski, 2002) and have a present, rather a high performance level. Kossler and Prestridge (2003) point out the fact that high-performing teams usually demonstrate effective decision-making processes. Team members know when a decision is made in the team and they are also aware when the team leader or team members are allowed to make a decision. However, the mean age of the team appears to be relevant. A virtual team composed of young members is less experienced, and encounters less members' initiative toward leadership, feeling less capable and insecure (Muethel et al., 2012a).

Depending on the autonomy of the virtual team and its capacity to temporarily adopt a self-managed behaviour, some leaders may choose to delegate their authority to team members. Authority delegation is very often transferred to competent virtual teams, which positively impacts virtual team performance through team and individual motivation (Zhang et al., 2009).

Delegation means that one member of the team is clearly identified and authorized to take responsibilities for certain activities of the team that were initially the leader's responsibility. The delegation can occur at different degrees: (1) problem sharing with the leader and a need for leader's advice about possible solutions; (2) the need for information before making a decision; and (3) a decision being made without referring to the leader.

Delegation differs from a '*laissez-faire*' leadership because the appointed leader remains responsible for the follow-up, and is accountable for the team outcomes. Delegation is a way to efficiently manage the team resources and get the team members involved in the decision-making process, which incites them to perform their tasks at a higher level. Positive effects occur at the intrinsic motivation levels and with increased flexibility.

On the other hand, the virtual team leader needs to spend more time monitoring and coordinating the delegated tasks, although they can spend less time if team members show the adequate competencies, taking into consideration that 'walking-around management' cannot be used as a managerial process (Zhang et al., 2012). If delegation is efficiently monitored, the leader contributes to developing proficiencies within the team, and thus contributes to team performance.

The leadership role might also be perceived differently by leaders and managers themselves. Leaders may give more importance to relational and flexibility-in-work leadership functions while others may allow more concern to stability and prefer leadership functions, e.g. monitoring and coordinating roles. For example, Zander's et al. (2012) analysis shows that cultural diversity is a relevant topic held by a wide range of virtual team leaders but recognized as critical by a few virtual team members. In the same work, empowering is mentioned only by virtual team leaders, whereas mentoring, coaching and resource are increasingly used by virtual team members.

Certain situational characteristics of projects may influence the relationships between the virtual team leader and her/his perception of difficulties (Lee-Kelley, 2002) such as project objectives, team size, frequency of team changes and project duration. Some stereotypes might be reinforced, an example being those involving gender in leadership, where female-to-male ratio is low.

Even if women are as skilled as men, they might be considered as less skilled, less confident and passive as far as leadership is concerned. A high female-to-male ratio may positively foster shared leadership behaviours within a team, based on a participative leadership model as women show higher affinity to that model (Muethel et al., 2012a). Whatever the perception is, the key priority for virtual team leaders is still leading the virtual team to the expected performance level.

8.2.7 Leading a Virtual Team to Successful Performance

A virtual team leader's main priority is to drive team performance and progress to achieve the defined tasks or outcomes, assuming that the leader has a direct or virtual contact with the team members (Hunsaker and Hunsaker, 2008). The e-leader has to integrate the differences between conventional 'execution-oriented practices' and a collaborative behaviour, and knowledge transfer facilitation, in addition to providing interpersonal communication (Hunsaker and Hunsaker, 2008; Nicholson et al., 2007). They need to deal with multiculturalism. To positively influence the team performance, he/she has to provide the following items (Tyran et al., 2003; Glückler and Schrott, 2007; Davis, 2004; Lojeski and Reilly, 2008; Tuffley, 2009):

- **Personal and professional development:** to be aware of the specific competencies and skills he/she must possess to run a virtual team successfully, whilst also considering those available within the team. The e-leader then gets the appropriate training, when needed, to ensure team progression.

- **Shared vision:** created and communicated through clear and transparent strategies, vision, guidance, mission and a culture unique to the virtual team.
- **Clear goal setting:** the purpose is to develop the shared vision into a shared meaning, by creating the alignment of goals across the organizational boundaries (Maznevski and Athanassiou, 2003) and delimiting the virtual team members' autonomy. The e-leader needs to monitor the virtual team members' attention and make sure that they focus on the priorities of the team.
- **Clear role assignment:** according to the knowledge resources available to the team, he/she has to conceptualize abstractive information into problems or strategies. Clear roles are roles that are translated into deliverable task assignments, schedule and coordination. Interdependent tasks enable shared meanings and targets, necessary to encourage, foster and measure team performance. He/she produces a project plan, along with a training and competency plan.
- **Collaborative climate and global participation:** to coordinate and use fluid, engaging and interpersonal communication to choose the right process for the team and be realistic in task completion. He/she implements agreements about regular team interaction or online meetings (Mewton et al., 2005), measures and communicates the team performance and outcomes (Yates and Beech, 2006). Edwards and Wilson (2004) call that behaviour 'sharing, caring and daring' behaviour. He/she produces reports and record protocols, agrees on a system for performance measurement, sets a strategy for team evaluation and indicates a central knowledge base. Team members' engagement and global participation might be a challenge to achieve when there are no direct hierarchical relationships between virtual team members and the team leader. The virtual team members might prioritize some local tasks more.
- **Personalization of the relationships:** she/he produces personal files to make the participants feel as though they know each other, which is at least a necessary minimum to develop the team social capital. He/she develops virtual socializing skills and provides sense-making based on the Five Cs of relationships proposed by Nicholson et al. (2007): clarity, connection, candor, co-creation and commitment.
- **Interpersonal communication norming:** she/he agrees on a code of conduct, a communication protocol and a meeting protocol whilst keeping flexibility in the communication process.

- **Recognition:** she/he develops individual and team evaluation policies and systems in order to reward significant behaviours and results that positively encourage performance and sustain collaborative behaviour (Pauleen, 2003b).
- **Virtual team visibility in the organization:** to develop individual satisfaction, and avoid individual isolation that results in reduced social relationships, and get the virtual team considered as a 'real' team.

Some of the above points might be common to conventional teamwork but they challenge virtual team leaders at a higher level due to their complexities and dependence on technologies. Efficient e-leaders need to revise figures and numbers, to be able to cope with diverse cultures and to develop business, and stress results while caring for the team members. E-leaders have to continuously manage 'the head and the heart' (Davis, 2004). One of the concrete and positive achievements consists of defusing virtual team members' possible frustrations to keep them motivated (Roy, 2012). The finality is to keep a balance in the team and to avoid the possible traps that come with high complexity and virtuality, such as conflicts. Conflict management appears to be another essential challenge to virtual leadership because conflicts are difficult to detect and to solve.

8.3   CONFLICT MANAGEMENT

8.3.1   Definition

Conflict can be defined as 'disagreement among group members' (Polzer et al., 2006) or between one or more interdependent parties (Shin, 2005). Conflicting situations emerge when team participants develop the awareness of discrepancies and diversities inside the team that they cannot manage (Paul et al., 2004b) or when trust existing between teammates is violated (Muethel et al., 2012b).

Most of the time, conflict leads to deterioration, breakdowns and disruption of the virtual team's functioning. Therefore, it directly affects virtual team members' satisfaction, cognition and behaviours and, consequently, influences team productivity and performance. Different levels of conflict may appear at the organization, team, or individual level, and it may happen for various reasons.

8.3.2 Types of Conflicts within Virtual Teams

Research findings recognize different types of conflict whose differences come from the causes of the conflict. For example, cultural diversity is likely to generate both task and relationship conflict whereas functional diversity may just create task conflict (Kankanhalli et al., 2007). Four major types of conflict are identified: task conflict, affective conflict, process conflict and cognitive conflict.

- **Task conflict:** is defined as an issue-based task-related disagreement within the team. It occurs when there is a lack of understanding of the activities and tasks about work content or when mutual understanding of the activities is not shared by all members of the virtual team (Wakefield et al., 2008). Consequences are a decrease of productivity and interactions in the virtual team process and outcomes. In that case, team performance is negatively impacted. Paul et al. (2004b) and Wakefield et al. (2008) argue that virtual teams face less task conflict that conventional teams because the discussions are supported with ICTs and the virtual team members concentrate in their discussions.
- **Process conflict:** is a divergence among virtual team members on how to do the team tasks, the methods, approach and processes (Wakefield et al., 2008). Less research results have been found on this type of conflict, which requires deeper analysis.
- **Affective conflict:** also designated as collaborative conflict or emotional conflict, and refers to discordant relationships among virtual team members (Hinds and Bailey, 2003; Kankanhalli et al., 2007). It results in interpersonal disagreement on 'preferred outcomes', attitudes, values and behaviour (Paul et al., 2004b) that arises when the level of personal knowledge and understanding on the teammates' characteristics, such as cultures, personality or norms, is not high enough (Wakefield et al., 2008). This type of conflict generates frustration, anger and hostility among virtual team members (Hinds and Bailey, 2003) reduces the socio-emotional relationships and negatively affects the team performance. In comparison to conventional teams, virtual teams experience less affective conflicts due to geographical distance. But both task and affective conflicts are interrelated as they may both trigger one or the other, and both contribute to destroying trust within a group.
- **Cognitive conflict:** emerges from disagreements about ideas, content and methods or models, within the virtual team associated with the team's tasks, even though team members share common goals. This

sort of conflict positively influences team performance when discussions between team members offer greater understanding of issues and a larger panel of final solutions are adopted to solve the conflict (Ayoko et al., 2012).

8.3.3 Sources of Conflict

The origin of conflicts in virtual teams is usually triggered by factors in the work environment and intensified by the virtual context and diversity issues. These factors affect the individual's emotions and therefore their behaviours towards work and their relations with the others (Ayoko et al., 2012). For example, some of the teammates may try to dominate the rest of the group and thus, use behaviours of intimidation. Individual passions over mission, direction and vision of the team objectives may lead to a situation of conflict. Past conflicts, the dissemination of activities among team members without common acceptance, or team members who remain silent because they do not dare to express themselves, are examples of potential situations that may trigger conflicts (Cottrell, 2011).

The structural characteristics of the virtual teams and the organization they depend on play a role as a conflict trigger. In fact, the organizational and virtual environment of virtual teams might provide a source of conflict. Joshi et al. (2003) demonstrates, for example, that there is a higher probability that critical conflicts emerge between two country subsidiaries before they emerge between headquarters and country subsidiaries. The reasons might be linked to the non-acceptance of corporate strategy. But it is likely that the main reasons lie in relationships existing between workflow model, workload, and organizational hierarchy levels of collaboration among the teammates, that may lead to affective conflict.

The difficulties that motivate this type of conflict are explained by disruptions in daily workflow activities, which reduces the possibility of creating strong relationships among dispersed team members.

Organizational structure based on matrix architecture might also be another source of conflict when different hierarchical levels operate. It might be the case when a virtual team member needs to answer to his/her local manager's instruction whilst having to simultaneously fulfil the global team objectives that might be contradictory. Therefore, affective conflict is very likely to occur in multinational companies.

The attributes that characterize a virtual team seem to offer a high potential for possible team conflicts, such as the various boundaries and more precisely geographical distance, cultural differences, computer-mediated communication and the lack of shared context (Mortensen and Hinds, 2001; Hinds and Bailey, 2003; Schlenkrich and Upfold, 2009). On the other hand, technology and lack of opportunity to meet face-to-face, often reduce the possibility for virtual team members to show their emotional reactions and, thus, may hide possible conflict (Ayoko et al., 2012).

Different lines in cultural value also influence the origin of conflict and the conflict management style (Paul et al., 2005). As an example, virtual teams built on a collectivistic context show a higher level of collaborative conflict management than an individualistic-based team does. Collectivist cultures basically work on collaborative models and are therefore more frequently exposed to conflicts at this level.

Consequently, continuous cultural alignment should be considered by global companies in order to create or maintain a shared context and avoid conflicts (Latapie and Tran, 2007). One example is the implementation of a company merger-and-acquisition integration through realigned organizational cultures between the purchased and purchasing companies. If this realignment is neglected, the integration of the purchased company may lead to critical dissensions or even failure. Virtual team leaders play a critical role at this level, shaping virtual team culture and shared identity by matching global expectations whilst advancing team activities.

The level of task interdependence, complexity and degree of virtuality generate higher levels of conflicts in virtual teams (De Dreu and Weingart, 2003; Hinds and Bailey, 2003). The higher the virtual degree, the higher the impact of task conflict is on the perceived performance within the team (de Jong et al., 2008). Mutual misunderstanding or different understandings of tasks can trigger task conflicts inside a team, which might be enhanced by the heterogeneity of the group. It results in wider confusion generating 'constant surprises', which affects collaboration between teammates (Hinds and Bailey, 2003).

The degree of collaboration within the virtual team seems to present a stronger impact than heterogeneity. Communication, information transfer and coordination complexity in addition to the team diversity make the collaborative process even more complicated. Virtual teammates have less opportunity to learn about each other and create informal relationships. The opportunity to develop the necessary social capital is thus reduced. As a consequence, lower levels or indeed a lack of friendship in the interpersonal interactions foster possible affective conflicts, accentuated by the heterogeneity of the group and, when it occurs, by the disparity in resources or equipment among the virtual team members.

Computer-mediated communication that reduces socio-emotional relationships is also one other important source of conflict within virtual teams. More precisely, virtual teams request intensive focus in communication and synchronization to share the effort within the team, remove any temporal ambiguity such as scheduling and deadlines, and cope with a scarcity of temporal resources (Montoya-Weiss et al., 2001). Additionally, technology does not easily convey 'emotion' but it is more likely to get the virtual team members engaged and focused on the team activities and, thus, reduce the possibility of conflict (Wakefield et al., 2008). But as soon as technological barriers or any other type of barriers hinder effective communication: decreases in team interactions and team productivity occur (Schlenkrich and Upfold, 2009) as well as reduced information transfer and diffiulties in coordination.

It may lead to repetitive malfunctioning and disruption in the team processes which fosters dissatisfaction among the team members, and further the lack of a shared context resulting in task and affective conflict. When the level of shared context in a virtual team is not reached as detailed in the socio-emotional processes, collaboration and information transfer decrease, and communication interactions reduce, which foster a lack of synchronization. The perception of time may differ within the virtual team depending on the cultural diversity, which intensifies the lack of synchronization and lowers the rhythm of the team. Process conflict often emerges at this phase.

8.3.4 Impacts of Conflict on Virtual Teams

Virtual team conflict is not recognized by the academic research as a long-term positive and stimulative element that creates a dynamic in the group functioning. But short-term conflict may push the virtual team members and leaders to adapt the process, their behaviours and the team coordination. Thus, it can give a dynamic impulsion, resulting in procedure establishment, shared database, information retrieval, effective knowledge transfer, and higher coordination or innovation.

Pazos (2012) highlights conflict management as an essential conveyor in developing virtual team effectiveness. He establishes clear relationships between a commitment to team goals, conflict management and performance-and-behavioural team outcomes in virtual teams. Conflict management plays the role of mediator in the relationships between goal commitment and team outcomes. Therefore, commitment to team goals is a significant indicator of effective conflict management supporting team effectiveness in the virtual team context. It is especially valid for virtual team members who try to prevent and solve team conflicts, and when the concerned conflicts last on a short-term basis.

This behaviour tends to significantly increase relationships between commitment to team goals and team performance and, therefore, to virtual team performance. In this case, conflicts may generate innovative ideas, revised positions and satisfying solutions thanks to increased discussions

(Flanagan and Runde, 2008). It is however more challenging to achieve in a virtual environment as more time is needed to exchange information, instead of using this time to do the collaborative tasks (Maznevski and Athanassiou, 2003).

For similar reasons, task conflict can be beneficial for a virtual team because it often generates discussions and improved ideas associated with effective decisions according to Simons and Peterson (2000). However, too high of a level of task conflict negatively influences the team performance, and it may then lead to affective conflict, which is even more likely if the virtual team structure is complex (Hinds and Mortensen, 2005).

The level of conflict in the team increases instead of reduces, especially when the discordance is expressed via written communication, such as emails according to Simons and Peterson (2000). Research points out that a shared-context moderates task and collaborative conflict because it smooths out the effect of team dispersion. The effect is more important on tasks when there is less emotional conflict. Shared identity seems to be more cohesive in that case and moderates interpersonal conflicts (Hinds and Mortensen, 2005).

Affective conflict appears to be more detrimental to group performance as it creates an unfavourable atmosphere and a high level of tension between the virtual teammates resulting in emotional reactions. It fosters anxiety and hostility, and consumes time and energy, which leaves the virtual team behind in its activities and mission. Paradoxically, the virtual teams with high levels of friendship usually show higher levels of affective conflict. But because this kind of team is built on trust and the expression of emotion is accepted, these virtual team members are able to solve the conflict more successfully than those from teams that experience low levels of friendships (Hinds and Mortensen, 2005).

The choice of response to affective conflict strongly affects the team dynamic (Ayoko et al., 2012). In conflicting situations, an adapted process should be adopted to repair trust and affective relationships, clearing the source and responsibility for the concerned conflict. Apologies for the trust violation presented soon after the conflict is one way to demonstrate willingness to continue collaboration. Mediators or facilitators may also contribute to effectively motivate virtual team members to try trust-building processes again. These facilitators encourage teammates to establish relationships through common agreement, especially because they understand the team leadership's role and appear in a neutral position (Muethel et al., 2012b).

Affective conflict might be more moderate in virtual teams than in conventional teams and easier to avoid, because the geographical distribution of the virtual team members reduces the opportunity to meet and/or to directly communicate. On the other hand, when paired teammates from different cultures succeed in working effciently together, they contribute to break down cultural stereotypes. They also demonstrate that communication barriers can be overcome (Malhotra et al., 2007).

Process conflict does not seem to contribute to any positive performance with the virtual team. It creates inefficiencies that lead to confusion about responsibilities and resources (Hinds and Bailey, 2003). More studies and research will contribute to an increased understanding on the impact of process conflict on virtual team functioning.

The dimensions of cognitive absorption are essential to be considered when analysing the effiect of conflict on virtual teams according to Rutkowski et al. (2007). Defined as 'a state of mental concentration' (Dictionary, 2000), or 'a state of deep involvement' (Zhang et al., 2006), cognitive absorption encompasses focused immersion and temporal dissociation. It modifies the level of performance and interpersonal conflict within a virtual team. High levels of focused immersion, and low levels of temporal dissociation result in increased performance and lower levels of interpersonal conflict (Rutkowski et al., 2007).

8.3.5 Leadership and Conflict Management

The virtual team manager plays a key role to implement and apply an effective conflict resolution approach. This approach is essential and differs according to the adopted conflict management behaviours, as identified by Montoya-Weiss et al. (2001):

- **Avoidance of conflict management behaviour:** the manager does not involve himself/herself in the conflict management. He/she holds an ambivalent style and avoids confronting the concerned parties, resulting in the absence of willingness to solve the conflict. It is expected to negatively influence the virtual team performance. Imposing intermediate tasks, reviews, and time limits may moderate this negative effect.
- **Accommodation conflict management behaviour:** one party tries to transfer all the benefit of the issue to the other party. The manager shows a passive involvement in resolving the conflict without any critical assessment. Review of team viewpoints, revisions, and agreement should reduce the negative effect of that behaviour.
- **Competition conflict management behaviour:** each party pursues his/her own interest without consideration of others with the use of power and domination. One virtual team member with sufficient authority imposes a diagnosis on the group, or a majority of the

members that agree about the diagnosis of a problem. This behaviour may resolve conflict because team members may consider competition as increased participation which, in that case, presents a positive effect on virtual team performance.

- **Collaboration conflict management behaviour:** identifies and achieves outcomes that integrate the interests of all parties involved (openness) and focus on tasks, goals, increased participation and increased quality. Collaboration conflict management positively influences virtual team performance but temporal coordination has no moderating effect. Resolution should target a long-term solution.
- **Compromise conflict management behaviour:** the manager shows intermediate concern for himself/herself and the others. Insuffcient or ineffective interaction will reduce the team outcome quality, which might be moderate through structured work processes, and temporal coordination using dialogue and cognitive processes to reach a consensus. Compromise conflict management behaviour has a positive effect on virtual team performance.

Academic research does not provide clear evidence on the relationship of virtual team heterogeneity and the type of conflict management to solve collaborative conflict (Paul et al., 2004b). However, Montoya-Weiss et al. (2001) explain that performing virtual teams usually choose a collaborative or competitive conflict management to solve conflict in a virtual context instead of avoidance, accommodation or compromising management. The reason is that it generates higher satisfaction at the team and individual levels. Virtual team members and managers must find ways to coordinate their activities, and manage conflict in order to maintain or increase the team performance.

Some of the different steps of team development (e.g. forming, storming, norming and performing steps) seem more favourable to conflict, as demonstrated by Ayoko et al. (2012). The storming stage is characterized by disagreement and competition and, therefore, fosters the emergence of conflict and emotional behaviours. When teams show higher difficulty to transfer from one step to the other one in their development, conflict is also expected to emerge more frequently. Friendly communication helps to decrease possibilities of conflict, but it usually occurs at the performing step of group development.

One of the critical characteristics for the virtual team managers is to be able to detect a conflict situation within virtual teams and interpret any signal that could lead to conflict. Wakefield et al. (2008) say that early detection facilitates conflict resolution. Most of the time, in virtual teams, dissensions and crisis highlight the signal of a potential conflict, and the need for integration and adapted conflict management (Maznevski and Athanassiou, 2003).

Literature on conflict detection in virtual teams is not extensive and we have not found any relevant research results. It concentrates more on the possible roles played by e-leaders to react to conflicting situations, depending on the sources and the types of conflict to be solved. Based on Quinn's (1988) model of competing leadership roles, Wakefield et al. (2008) identify the following four leadership roles that influence conflict management, which are similar to the leadership types already mentioned:

- **Monitor role:** mitigates task conflict by providing stability concerned with the internal functioning of the virtual team as it is strictly oriented to task activities.
- **Coordinator role:** gets the processes, tools and systems compatible within the virtual team and across the encountered boundaries. Such standardization may raise political or practical discussions during the process of implementation but it is recognized to reduce work process conflict (Hinds and Mortensen, 2005).
- **Mentor role:** encourages the virtual team members' development at the team and individual level by providing support, understanding and sense-making. Mentoring enables the e-leader to build relationships between virtual team members and positively influence collaborative conflicting situations.
- **Facilitator role:** develops cohesion, teamwork, participation, smoothing out the possible existing differences within the team. It facilitates the exchange of ideas and perspectives while looking for consensus and compromise. Thus, it influences the emotional or collaborative conflict.

Wakefield et al. (2008) conclude that an effective virtual team manager in conflict resolution has to be able to show various roles to manage conflict triggered by different sources and appearing under diverse situations. Those leaders also have the capacity to consequently adapt their behaviour to the nature of the conflict (Kankanhalli et al., 2007).

The method chosen to solve conflict influences the performance of the team. An integrative style looks for solutions that provide satisfaction to all participants, whereas, a distributive style imposes one person's choice on another. Integrative methods demonstrate higher levels of performance in comparison to other methods, e.g. distributive style (Paul et al., 2005). However, the researchers have not found any evidence of relationships between individual satisfaction and the type of conflict resolution management, as long as the results offer a consensual solution. Shin (2005) proposed virtual negotiation, which requires adequate competencies and mediation systems that may contribute to reaching a consensus.

Above all, virtual team managers have to show developed leadership competencies in order to reach conflict resolution, specifically if the virtual team evolves in a complex context. They should obtain all discordant sides to solve the conflict and this is more difficult to obtain in virtual teams. A healthy and open resolution is highly recommended as a result of Hinds and Bailey (2003). Spontaneous communication facilitates conflict resolution because it is associated with a shared identity and shared context, both variables in conflict resolution. However, in the virtual environment, it might be longer and more challenging to establish (Maznevski and Athanassiou, 2003). Most frequently, a collaborative resolution shows higher self-reported decision-making satisfaction (Paul et al., 2004b), decision-making quality, virtual team members' participation, and fosters the assertiveness of one side with cooperation from the other side of the group (Thomas, 1992). However, special attention is also requested in terms of communication as frequent communication may stimulate conflict (Hinds and Bailey, 2003; Friedman and Currall, 2002).

8.4 TO KEEP IN MIND: RELATIONSHIPS BETWEEN LEADERSHIP AND CONFLICT IN A VIRTUAL CONTEXT

Leadership holds a critical role in the management of virtual teams. Virtual team managers and leaders are accountable for any events or activities engaged in, by the virtual team towards team performance and team development. Being the 'sense-maker' and 'sense-giver', the virtual team leader evolves in a complex environment and has to be a manager and a leader to achieve optimum results with virtual teams. Therefore, understanding virtuality and all connected boundaries and processes is essential. It requests specific skills, personal characteristics, leadership competencies and constant adaptability. E-leaders may use various techniques with adequate styles depending on the situation they need to manage and because leadership might be perceived differently within a multicultural team.

Conflict may affect tasks, affective relationships, team and cognitive processes within a virtual team, and is usually caused by a lack of mutual understanding. The main sources of conflict come from virtuality and diversity that characterize the virtual environment. Geographical distance, diverse cultures, computer-mediated communication, and the lack of shared context interfere on team members' behaviours and lead to conflicting situations. Most of the time, those situations negatively impact team productivity and performance, depending on the level of task interdependence, collaboration, and social capital existing in the team.

Leadership and conflict are linked by the way that conflict resolution is handled by virtual team managers. They may adopt various attitudes such as avoidance, accommodation, competition, collaboration or compromise behaviours. Those behaviours need to be adapted to the conflicting situation depending on conflict sources and types, with the final goal of reaching group consensus. E-leaders play different roles in regard to the team attributes and conflict type such as: monitor, coordinator, mentor or facilitator.

8.5 CONCLUSION

This chapter demonstrates the relevance of the managerial process through two main elements as far as virtual or remote team management is concerned: leadership and conflict management. Leadership skills and aptitudes in virtual teaming share the same basic skills and aptitudes needed for conventional teams. However, the virtual and technological environment should not be underestimated as it gives higher complexity in leadership. Therefore, in addition to global business knowledge, e-leaders have to learn how to use appropriate technologies, not to simulate presence but to create virtual interactions. Therefore, 'presence' might need a deeper definition that is adapted to the virtual context because it does not mean 'physical presence' anymore but another form of presence.

When the essential competencies seem sufficient to lead conventional teams, virtual leadership requires an additional disposition and capabilities to run virtual teams efficiently and, therefore, add value to the organization. This proficiency can be learned through virtuality understanding on the various boundaries and their implication into the managerial process. The lack of leadership aptitudes and skills may lead a virtual team to failure.

Therefore, it seems essential that training and awareness of virtuality should start at the earlier stage, with students, for instance. They should be initiated and trained to virtual teamwork and its complexity during their studies. Because they are easily comfortable with technologies (Houck, 2011) this generation obtains a wider range of work possibilities within intra- or interorganizations, but it may appear to be more individualistic and more demanding in terms of personal and professional life balance.

We may also wonder whether the younger generations in the position of virtual team leaders are less inhibited in communication to go over the multicultural misunderstandings due to their communication style and, therefore, become performing virtual team leaders. It is likely that an ever-larger spectrum of younger persons will get more or less involved in virtual teaming in the near future. Therefore, more skills and competences in the critical processes of virtual teaming could emerge if awareness is developed along with their studies and professional experiences. However, research results today are not yet consistent on the effect and benefits of age, gender and culture diversity for e-leadership skills but, rather, it shows the implication of global staffing and IHRM. Further research would contribute to a deeper understanding of the managerial approach on how to foster a shared mindset and collaborative aptitudes with new generations from different cultural worlds. The idea is to see if the multicultural new generation's expectations are oriented in the same direction or how wide the gap is among diverse requirements. Comfortable with digital tools, they may, however, be more ill at ease with virtual team processes. The results are essential because they have a direct connection with conflict management, collaboration, or the willingness of virtual team members to collaborate and, therefore, with team performance and individual satisfaction. Collaboration, when ineffective, negatively influences virtual team performance more than dispersion or heterogeneity does.

The final purpose of a virtuality assessment is to measure how a virtual team leader can share and leverage the benefits of diversity within the whole team, and enhance the group towards successful performance. The more accurate and the wider knowledge on virtual teaming and the virtual context; the more efficient the leader is. These competencies facilitate conflict management and resolution as the leader gets a more precise idea of the levers to be used and their expected result or influence. Virtual leaders should prepare the team on the process issues, standards, communication and methods to address conflict before it occurs. However, more research is needed on conflict management in a virtual environment, specifically on conflict detection and identification, where few results have been found. The purpose is to understand the potential benefit and synergies that the conflict process may generate.

8.6 GUIDELINES FOR MANAGERIAL PRACTICES: MANAGERIAL PROCESSES

Managerial processes in virtual teaming may improve when the virtual team manager is aware of his/her leadership style and competencies, and the possibilities of adapting them in accordance with the context. These guidelines highlight the leadership style associated with certain competencies and facilitates the identification of a possible need for training or adaptation.

Table 8.1 Managerial processes—leadership and conflict management

Key actions	Key suggestions
Leadership Define precisely the level of management you are in charge of:	– Top level (settlement of policies and objectives). – Middle level (communicate policies and objectives, structure and lead the team). – Low level (monitor team activities and work).
Identify: – the virtuality of your team (see guideline 1); – the level of relationships in the team (socio-emotional processes, see guideline 6); and – the team capacity for integration (process, roles, assignments etc.).	
Describe your leadership style: – personality traits; – behavioural characteristics; – your position and roles in regards to the team, your environment and organization; – your personal objectives as a manager; and – your managerial style.	Sense-maker, sense-giver: (Develop team collaboration culture, lead the team to performance and to team members' satisfaction etc..) (Coordinator, director, transactional, transformational, inspirational, facilitator, emergent etc..)
Identify your characteristic capabilities and how you would: – deal with paradoxes and discontinuities; – create a global multicultural team mindset; and – develop team cohesion, collaboration and trust.	Capacities such as: Flexibility and openness to adapt your management style to the team typology and to team members.

Assess the level of your: – cultural intelligence; – emotional intelligence and stability; and – the perception of your leadership in the team. List your training needs for virtual team management.	Multicultural management, technology, communication etc.
Analyse how you communicate to your team members: – team vision; – team visibility; – team goals; and – team targets.	Through a clear cross-cultural communication, based on a cooperation process and clear role distribution.
List the key factors that you use to motivate and satisfy the members of your team:	At material, cognitive and social levels.

Conflict management

Identify the types of conflict affecting your team: Identify the source of the conflict and the reasons:	Task, process, affective or cognitive conflict? Organization, contradictory instructions (between local and distant structures), culture, integration, collaboration, repetitive technical issues etc.
Measure the impacts of the conflict on the team activities:	– discussions and improved ideas; – increased team members' dissatisfaction, anxiety and hostility; and – decreased team performance.
Choose the possible managerial behaviour to solve a conflicting situation:	– Avoidance, accommodation, competition, collaboration, compromise etc.

PART IV

Outputs: virtual teams a source of performance

Business environments always push for enhanced performance, across larger distances and involving various cultures. More virtual partnerships are involved in corporations internally and externally which increases the complexity of teamwork through virtual and intensified networks.

Chapter 9 focuses on teamwork performance, which is one aspect of virtual team performance outcomes. Whereas Chapter 10 addresses affective performance whose outcomes encompass individual satisfaction and customer satisfaction, both playing a key role in a global virtual team's performance. Customer satisfaction is a measure of the successful achievement of the team mission or tasks, and individual satisfaction is the sense of a successful process within the team. Figure IV.1 below illustrates a virtual team's outputs.

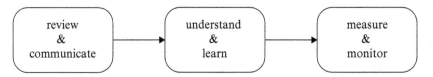

Figure IV.1   The learning cycle fostering improvement and higher performance

9 Teamwork performance in virtual teams

9.1 INTRODUCTION

Virtual teams become a conveyor of flexibility and agility, coping with increased speed and a new form of work processes. Creating or developing effective virtual teams through effcient work processes and performing team outcomes is, in reality, more difficult than expected (Duarte and Snyder, 2001). Moreover, key practices and crucial factors that are essential for virtual team performance need to be identified and set up by organizations in order to maximize their return on investment (DeRosa, 2011).

We first define the research's understanding of teamwork performance at the organization, team and individual levels, and go through the main challenges for virtual team performance. Challenges mainly consist of difficulties in evaluating performance in virtual contexts as well as the complexity of dispersion and virtuality. The relationships of team structure, sense of presence, leadership and conflict management as key drivers to teamwork performance are discussed.

9.2 DEFINITION OF VIRTUAL TEAMWORK PERFORMANCE

Virtual teamwork performance is the completion of tasks, activities and work sought for planned targets in relation to the quality of team decisions, solution acceptance, customers and team members' satisfaction with the provided outcomes (Chang et al., 2011). Work outcomes compare teamwork results to set-up objectives. They are measured against predefined targets and metrics, and represent the 'obligation' of the virtual team, its members and the team leader. Teamwork performance occurs at three levels: organizational, team and individual levels.

9.2.1   Teamwork Performance at Organizational Level

Teamwork performance at the organizational level refers to the quality of support provided by the organization and infrastructure to execute work processes. It includes policies that reward team performance. Global resources support virtual teams to reach higher levels of performance providing that companies invest in ICTs that are necessary for a virtual context. The objective is to develop organizational performance responding to the virtual environment (Townsend et al., 1998).

In their study, Thomsen et al. (2007) proposed a shift from measuring and controlling the quality management through work processes to measuring and controlling the quality of the organization that executes the work processes, introducing trade-offs between effciency and teamwork quality.

Resources and infrastructure that effectively support virtual work, including virtual culture and the most advanced and standardized technological structures, contribute to improving virtual team performance (Duarte and Snyder, 2001; Schepers et al., 2011; Glückler and Schrott, 2007). The effects of distance can be reduced at the organizational level through work-based or task-based learning, and a corresponding investment in structured processes, which reduces the negative effect of work dispersion and improves team performance (Ramasubbu et al., 2008).

To achieve teamwork performance Jawecki et al. (2011) recommend that an organization to be aware of the distance characterized by cultural differences. Virtual team members from different cultures may react with contrasting behaviours, along with various routines and motivations. Therefore, organizations should align the collaborative tools with the cultural attributes of people expected to interact together. This alignment can be used to bridge cultural and organizational contrasts, and to enhance relationships among people within the organization (Thamhain, 2011).

Performance perception might also vary among virtual team members, depending on what they value the most. Multicultural differences should be valued in a way that provides common sense to virtual team members, which differs according to culture. Jawecki et al. (2011) use the example of the process used to reward virtual team performance. In Western countries, rewarding the most creative members within a team seems a standard process, whereas it would render ill at ease team members from Eastern countries. Eastern countries would prefer to praise creativity streamlined with team expectations, rather than diverse individual creativity. Values assigned to creativity and innovation vary from one culture to another, and individualism confronts collectivism.

Thomsen et al. (2007) recommend that the organization identify the possible organizational risks that restrain virtual teams from performing efficiently. The organizations should take into account the profile of the virtual teams or, rather, the supposed profile as it may differ with possible organizational changes. Organizations should reduce or find solutions to avoid the recognized and potential risks while improving work processes to develop, and sustain performance on a continuous basis. Risk avoidance positively impacts project or work performance.

9.2.2 Teamwork Performance at Team and Individual Levels

Not all virtual teams reach the expected targets with similar enthusiasm or the same level of performance. High-performing teams may surpass the targets, and low-performing teams may not reach the objectives. Well-performing virtual teams reach their outcomes on time, to requested quantity, quality, to budget, and meet the internal and external customers' satisfaction levels.

The level of teamwork performance varies according to team capacity too. The higher the team capacity, the more possibilities available to the team to use to solve difficult problems in order to achieve the expected outcomes. Therefore, the level of team capacity directly affects team outcomes (Turel and Zhang, 2011).

Team performance is measured through work outcomes assessed on variables such as: project duration, project cost, problem-solving quality, coordination quality (including the accuracy of lead times and monitoring the team activities), decision-making quality, the state of the expected targets and type of tasks (Duarte and Snyder, 2001; Martins and Schilpzand, 2011).

Team and individual expectation is measured through the discrepancies between expected outcomes and effective outcomes. Expectation is defined as the general belief held by the virtual team members about what they will find and gain in the team concerning their job in the organization and the team, and the resources to perform their tasks, thus, generating individual satisfaction.

Virtual team members tend to believe that expectation is based on mutual agreement, which means that virtual members believe in a team's capacity of successfully working towards common goals in a virtual context (Hardin et al., 2007). Mismatch in those expectations and satisfaction levels may lead to negative behaviours and feelings or, on the contrary, may foster learning to improve the situation (Bosch-Sijtsema, 2007).

The researchers Driskell et al. (2003) remind us that team performance might be negatively affected by the perception transmitted by the virtual teamwork outcomes. If the results are lower than expected, they may slow down team engagement and even more intensively when the reason is not dependent on the team members' effort. Possible technological failures could be an example of a main barrier to achieving the expected results, which does not depend on team members' areas of expertise, but negatively affects their results. On the contrary, when team outcomes are related to improved solutions and positive progression, the transmitted perception might be positively enhanced.

Depending on the team's system of working, team performance more or less requests management implication. Some teams may function at an individual work level through individual uncoordinated efforts toward a goal (pooled task interdependence). Task interdependence is the degree to which teammates are dependent on each other to perform their tasks. In that case, they do not need specific coordination. Task interdependence positively influences team performance because it drives team members to develop collaborative and facilitative behaviours (Maynard et al., 2012).

This dynamic also occurs at the teamwork level under two forms. First, when virtual team members need efficient coordination to bridge independent efforts (e.g. sequential or reciprocal task interdependence). Second, the dynamic may develop when all team members' concerted efforts drive the team to common goals (task integration) (Nunamaker et al., 1996). Then, team performance is elevated to team innovation when virtual team members succeed in influencing team decisions through frequent leader–member internal and external communication (Gajendran and Joshi, 2012).

Confirmed by Chang (2012) such performance is favourable to creativity. In addition to the aforementioned factors, further elements contribute to innovation and they are defined as new idea generation and the commercialization of these ideas. The elements are diversity (a mix of skills, expertise, gender, age, ethnicity etc.), participative safety and task conflicts (however, not relationship conflicts). However, team longevity may moderate creativity and inspiration within the team. A long team lifespan does not act in favour of new idea generation as virtual team members may lose motivation and enthusiasm, especially if activities become repetitive.

Due to geographical dispersion, virtual team members may use electronic brainstorming, which is more productive because it presents lesser effects of production breakdown, evaluation apprehension or social loafing. An e-leader plays a critical role in monitoring, guiding, and encouraging team members as a team and as individuals, thus, avoiding social loafing.

Technological advances enable organizations and virtual team leaders to support team dynamics. Indeed, the group capacity and the technological collective effectiveness contribute to virtual team performance (Hardin et al., 2007). Technologies give them the possibility of measuring and monitoring the outcomes of the virtual teamwork performance. Team effciency can be enhanced and sustained through a learning approach that creates synergies and value to virtual teamwork (Klein et al., 2003). It also brings about a dynamic in the virtual team by fostering improvement, where outputs often become inputs (Martins and Schilpzand, 2011). The dynamic operates at the individual and teamwork level.

Thanks to appropriate skills and competencies, organizations and virtual team leaders are able to analyse and understand the teamwork results in order to consequently adapt the methods to improve teamwork processes that influence team performance. The achieved results and actions to be set up have to be continuously communicated and revised, not only in a top-down direction but also in a bottom-up one, as illustrated by Figure IV.1.

E-leaders are pushed to propose ideas and solutions and adapt further development of models that go beyond the existing frames. Thus, they obtain improved solutions, models, processes and contribute to virtual team performance. Thanks to this continuous improvement approach, technologies and adequate policies, virtual team leaders are able to identify the highest performers within the team or organization.

It also confirms the following recommendation: organizations should implement a knowledge management system (KMS) in order to develop and implement organizational training strategies to learn and formalize the experience they will be going through because of the operational teamwork. If highly performing, these organizations could offer in–house training programmes and should be able to capture the knowledge produced by the virtual team process cycle, and inject it back to the virtual team learning process (Pauleen and Corbitt, 2003).

The effective usage of knowledge management allows both the leverage of the management of the virtual team and facilitates the control of their challenges, thus, contributing to organizational performance due to explicit tools, process systems, structures and cultures at the team and individual levels (Karayaz, 2006) as long as it is monitored (Griffith et al., 2003).

The created synergies encourage the virtual team members to discuss the team-related topics and can even develop organizational citizenship behaviours (OCB). The OCB are characterized by team members whose behaviours go beyond what is expected from their job description and routine duties. They share ideas, help and develop cooperation with teammates and may perform extra duties without complaining, based on volunteering (Buentello et al., 2008).

This behaviour is designed as an 'extra-role innovative service performance' by Schepers et al. (2011) in reference to team members trying to sell extra or new services to 'customers'. Rico et al. (2011) demonstrates the relationship between OCB and team performance, taking into account the degree of task interdependence.

They find out that OCB plays a positive role on virtual team performance when tasks are interdependent and virtuality low. The framework is closer to traditional teams. When tasks are more independent, virtual team members develop reduced interpersonal relationships and it negatively impacts work motivation and team performance. On the other hand, for virtual teams with high virtuality and low task interdependency, OCB are positive facilitators for team performance but present no effect on virtual teams with high virtuality and high task interdependency.

To conclude, OCB drives virtual teams to performance, depending on the degree of virtuality and the degree of task interdependency. They may drive team members to adjust their behaviours to the work-setting accordingly. As a consequence, OCB may enhance socio-emotional processes that increase experienced social presence, a critical factor as highlighted by the researchers. When tasks request high social interactions, virtual team performance improves thanks to a technical solution providing a high degree of social presence. From a managerial point of view, mentoring strategies set to facilitate OCB could improve effective social integration. However, the researchers' study does not analyse whether or not OCB can be constant in a team, nor if ICTs could moderate or impulse OCB.

9.3 CHALLENGES FOR TEAMWORK PERFORMANCE

9.3.1 Performance Outcome Measurement

Dispersion is often used to moderate the relationship between virtual team processes and virtual team performance. One of the reasons resides in the difficulty of measuring performance when teams are dispersed through efficient global systems. Performance measurement systems are a part of a wider system that include goal settings, feedback and reward systems (Ferreira et al., 2012a).

Performance measurement systems support the companies in keeping their strategic course while virtual team members can express their perception about the companies' goal and performance requests. Therefore, adjustment to possible deviation or gaps can be identified and settled while virtual members improve their commitment to the company's strategy. Performance measures indicate the performance of the team. They may encompass three dimensions (Jarman, 2005):

- The degree to which the team outcomes meet the expected standards of quality, quantity and lead time.
- The degree to which the team processes enable the team members to work together.
- The degree to which the team experience positively influences the development and personal well-being of team members.

Measures represent metrics adapted to reward outcomes (Duarte and Snyder, 2001) but the virtual team leader has to make sure that the concerned virtual team members understand what is expected from them and from the team. Virtual team members must understand the performance objectives and the way that they are measured (Duarte and Snyder, 2001) which is a challenge due to the complexity of virtuality and virtual team boundaries (Martins and Schilpzand, 2011). Martins and Schilpzand (2011) even consider that metrics should be agreed before staffing the virtual team.

The challenges of virtual teamwork outcomes consist of consolidating the different results towards performance of the team, which is considered as one entity, whilst keeping values and sense for each member (O'Leary and Cummings, 2007). It is the reason why conventional practices and measures of teamwork outcomes, which used to efficiently operate in co-located teams, that are not suitable anymore for virtual teams. It is due to the high degree of virtuality that affects the quality of team interactions and performance, making the team dynamic more complex (Schweitzer and Duxbury, 2010; Lepsinger and DeRosa, 2010).

The main challenge between virtuality, distribution and virtual team performance management is the complexity in performance evaluation, as well as measuring the effects of virtuality on performance (Chudoba et al., 2005). Some researchers propose some directions for performance evaluation such as efficiency, profit, innovation and value creation (Furumo and Pearson, 2006; Gibson and Gibbs, 2006; Jan et al., 2005; Lu et al., 2006) but no explicit methods adapted to a multicultural environment are suggested.

Virtuality makes it difficult to measure, especially because indicators might not be understood similarly by members belonging to multicultural virtual teams. Common and coordinated work practices within a positive social environment, team structuring, clear role distribution, set priorities, adequate communication, direction and information-sharing are recognized to smoothen virtuality and its boundaries, which may contribute to a deeper understanding of measurement systems and their indicators (Chudoba et al., 2005; Karayaz, 2008; Lepsinger and DeRosa, 2010; Jawadi and Boukef Charki, 2011). One of the measures can be proactivity, looking for continuous improvement, and therefore innovative ideas to achieve performance (Atanasova and Senn, 2011).

Different tools or models facilitate measurement, such as the balanced scorecards initiated by Kaplan et al. (1996), or the Internet-based measurement model, such as virtual team competency inventory, based on three main areas: task work, teamwork and collaboration (Hertel et al., 2006). The results of the assessment may vary depending on who is determining the rating (Jarman, 2005) and the usage done. Once measured, performance needs to be maintained or improved through incentive systems.

Performance incentives can take the form of financial team-based reward systems, where rewards integrate pay systems including individual incentives, gain-sharing, profit-sharing and/or team-based rewards. Financial team-based rewards are usually calculated on a variable reward in regards to performance outcomes versus previously determined targets. The final purpose strives for even more successful teams whilst gaining the individual's satisfaction through pay satisfaction.

Therefore, in a virtual environment, virtual team managers should assess the team characteristics in order to achieve successful outcomes when introducing performance measurement and incentive policies. The virtual context amplifies the complexities of such measurement and policies because diverse variables should be taken into account, such as personal preferences or values, cultural and educational backgrounds. A mixed structure might be recommended based on the financial and affective incentive.

9.3.2 Virtuality Challenges Virtual Team Performance

Academic research often mentions virtuality and virtual characteristics, such as dispersion and heterogeneity, mainly multiculturalism and boundaries, as one of the critical challenges faced by virtual teams to reach performance (Schweitzer and Duxbury, 2010; Chudoba et al., 2005; Cramton and Webber, 2005; Karayaz, 2008). Therefore, team composition is also a key factor to consider when analysing the impact on teamwork performance; not only because of the difficulties of coordination it implies but also for the benefits in terms of creativity and data integration (Algesheimer et al., 2011). Virtuality and virtual characteristics may positively and negatively affect teamwork and team effectiveness.

As already mentioned, virtuality is based on a concept of discontinuities that include geography and lack of face-to-face meetings, time zones, organizations, cultures, work practices and technology requesting coordination. In fact, virtual teams fail in achieving goals and targets on time when dispersion and diversity are not monitored (Lu et al., 2006). And when it is monitored, virtual teams are revealed to be effcient tools because virtual team members are exposed to heterogeneous work experiences, feedback, and much more frequent networking opportunities. They bring more vantage points. Diversity, such as virtual context and time differences, affect the team climate, which may reduce creativity and fast advancement of a project, especially at the beginning of the innovation process. If we consider that creativity and a monitored innovation process increase team performance, the team climate should retain special attention in that respect. The affected team climate is favourable in conflicting situations but the situation may change over time and result in positive outcomes. Additionally, power distance plays a critical role as far as innovation is concerned. Therefore, team composition and human resources are the relevant levers to be used to smooth out the negative effects of diversity and foster virtual team performance (Winkler and Bouncken, 2011).

Research studies are confronted with the difficulties of setting or obtaining significant measures that assess virtual team performance. It is then complicated to provide an accurate analysis on the evaluation of teamwork performance in the virtual context.

9.4 KEY DRIVERS FOR VIRTUAL TEAM PERFORMANCE

9.4.1 Virtual Team Structuring

Diverse factors influence the virtual team functioning mainly related to virtuality: work group structuring, team management and virtual work principles.

Work group structuring is one of the main factors that makes virtual teams function effectively and efficiently (Andres, 2002; Liu et al., 2008). Naik and Kim (2010) suggest an analytical framework whose purpose is to explain the factors influencing the success of a virtual team. The principle of that theory called the extended adaptive structuring theory (EAST) is a focus on the structural dimensions of virtual teams that create the necessary connections between 'IT, people, tasks, organizations, and processes'. It also includes the variables of performance, such as social interaction and team outcomes embedded in team structure. Structural dimensions occur at the operational level and integrate key elements to be considered in the assessment of teamwork performance: mission analysis, team goal and strategy specifications, activity planning, technological, organizational and individual factors (Maynard et al., 2012).

Further investigations, for example, those led by Horwitz et al. (2006)

and Jawadi and Boukef Charki (2011) highlight drivers at a management level, such as team development, cross-cultural variables aimed at cultural adaptation, leadership competences, rules and quality of communication, goal-setting and role clarification, social cohesion and relationship building based on trust, designated as the most important elements that contribute to virtual team structuring (Chang et al., 2011; Gaan, 2012; Verburg et al., 2013). Their identification, assessment and adjustment are crucial for the virtual team performance (Ferreira et al., 2012b).

The mentioned drivers are not self-sufficient. They contribute effectively to virtual teamwork performance when they adhere to the following virtual work principles: alignment company strategy, internal coherence, embedded culture, management involvement, respect balance of global and local needs, and employee branding through differentiation. Virtual work principles appear more powerful than just best practices because best practices are usually efficient in the context for which they are created, and might not be valid for another context or company (Stahl et al., 2012).

We come to the conclusion that the essential criteria that lead virtual teams to teamwork performance are criteria that smoothen dispersion and heterogeneity, structure virtual team processes and those that enable the transmission of a trustful 'sense of presence' (De Leo et al., 2011).

9.4.2 Sense of Presence

As previously mentioned, sense of presence is a fundamental element in virtual team managerial processes. Perceived sense of presence in virtual conditions does not mean physical presence but the feeling of belonging to a team with other teammates and a leader, despite distance. Four dimensions are identified: feeling of membership, feelings of influence on and in the team, integration in the team, and a shared emotional mindset (Crespo et al., 2012).

The virtual team leader provides that feeling through the capability of transforming information in a way that enables team members to move towards their goal (D'Eredita and Chau, 2005). It can be engendered by co-locating virtual team members within a certain frequency to foster social cohesion and sustain virtual teaming (Baskerville and Nandhakumar, 2007) or through advanced technologies substituting face-to-face interactions (De Leo et al., 2011).

In some cases, technologies may negatively influence the virtual team members' interaction and reduce the opportunity of building social capital due to anonymity. In some other cases, anonymity conveyed by technologies and group support systems may foster a higher dynamic in the team, and increase virtual team members' participation. Anonymity encourages participants to evaluate ideas more objectively and more constructively (Nunamaker et al., 1996). The basic key driver to create perception of presence remains effective communication within the virtual context (Trzcielinski and Wypych-Zoltowska, 2008).

Comparison between co-located teams and virtual ones contributes to identifying the major impacts of 'sense of presence'. Effectiveness of face-to-face teams is compared to virtual teams with the aim of isolating any possible drivers that differ between both types of teams. Interactive styles look very similar for both face-to-face and virtual teams as far as tasks and process outcome performances are concerned. However, virtual teams perform at a lower level when it comes to outcome measures. The studies conclude on the need for a sense of presence and interactions between virtual team members and the virtual team leader that directly influence individual and customer satisfaction, which concerns affective performance, as explained in the next chapter. 'Sense of presence' directly affects task motivation. Lount et al. (2008) demonstrate that working in a virtual context does not imply loss of motivation but, on the contrary, may encourage gains in motivation when the necessary conditions for efficient virtual team processes are set up.

9.4.3 Time Allocation

Cummings and Haas (2012) identify 'time allocated to virtual teamwork' as a factor contributing to the team performance. They demonstrate that virtual team members, who allocate a higher proportion of their time to the focal virtual team to which they work for, focus their attention to that team's work. On the other hand, virtual team members, who share their time across a greater number of diverse virtual teams, disperse their attention across these teams' work. They may lose a part of their identification to their principal team. This point should draw the virtual team leaders' attention because virtual team members who share their time on multiple teams currently represent the main trend (Maynard et al., 2012).

The effect increases with geographical distance and dispersion. Geographical distance and time zone differences request more time and attention for coordination, technology adjustment, and communication. Consequently, virtual team members engaged in any given virtual team develop awareness, motivation and behaviours adapted to the requirements of that team. They allocate more time to the preparation of the team activities and, at that level, contribute to the team's effectiveness. That team becomes operational quicker because the activity preparation is strengthened and gives to the team members the capacity to set priorities and positively react to unexpected changes.

On the other hand, virtual team members committed in diverse teams are less likely to allocate time and be involved in preparing team activities, in addition to the critical and time-consuming issues of a single team. Maynard et al. (2012) identifies two working areas for those virtual members: the central and the peripheral working spheres. They illustrate the degree of the individual's involvement in the team activities, which shows that the level of implication may vary according to 'central' or 'peripheral' priorities. However, Cummings and Haas (2012) demonstrate that both cases contribute to team performance. They note that a team performs at a higher level when virtual team members allocate more time to that team due to the fact that their attention and contribution are focused on that team's work and its relevant needs. They enable knowledge integration.

Virtual team members, who allocate less time to their central or principal team and are engaged in other teams also positively contribute to the central team performance, even though they may not be willing to commit themselves fully with the main team's tasks. They enable knowledge acquisition from other teams to their local team. Both knowledge integration and knowledge acquisition increase team performance.

9.4.4 Virtual Team Composition

The virtual members' profile plays a role too. The individual with a high level of education, company experience and organizational implication tends to spend more time with a larger number of diverse virtual teams rather than concentrating their attention on one main virtual team.

Moderation comes with the fact that during the same time duration, some individuals provide a different quality of attention and thus contribute with variable levels of benefits to a team's work performance. The share of virtual team members engaged in one virtual team or several teams may influence the team performance in diverse ways.

Teamwork performance also depends on the composition and structure of the team that groups skilled persons to complete the tasks, using common working language and sharing a sufficient common goal (Davison, 1994). Increased competition across the world pushes IHRM to look for a wider range of talents from various international locations, different functional positions and different organizations (Duarte and Snyder, 2001).

Therefore, the requested level of competencies tends to increase because the organizations can afford a wider range of various talented individuals. Four critical dimensions of competencies are identified for virtual teams: human, social, political and cross-cultural (Harvey et al., 2005) with the idea to benefit from diversities in order to gain higher performance. These competencies encompass core technical or relational competencies. They require the ability to adopt the adequate individual behaviour, the capacity to integrate the organizational culture and the competencies to meet the organization's accurate need at a precise requested time.

Team composition influences both teamwork and affective outcomes. Therefore, different factors need to be considered regarding the staffing and effectiveness of virtual teams. We could add functional competencies as well. Haas (2006) demonstrates the contribution of diversity to teamwork performance when comparing cosmopolitans and locals. He concludes that cosmopolitans offer greater benefits than locals, highlighting diversity, as long as there are not too many of them otherwise it leads to constraints and difficulties of dispersion. Peters and Karren (2009) confirm that 'multiple person-teams' also meaning diversity (Nemiro, 2001) contribute to improved virtual team performance. Since diversity impacts task completion, task planning and synchronization, multicultural staffing requires learning, and training for diversity and virtuality to reach higher team performance (Martins and Schilpzand, 2011).

When virtual team members are able to understand, identify, align, and utilize all the dispersed talents of their team, they contribute to team performance, even though those parameters alone are not sufficient. Virtual team members reach a performing level when they are able to develop knowledge management and more specifically transactive memory, including knowledge specialization, task credibility and task coordination (Maynard et al., 2012).

The capability of the virtual team, including the leader and team members, to benefit or not from the multicultural composition of the team influences the teamwork performance. The researchers DiStefano and Maznevski (2000) designate the performance results linked to multicultural benefit as destroyers, equalizers and creators.

Destroyers are those who are unable to take any positive elements from the multicultural composition of the team. As a consequence, team members generate negative cultural stereotypes about their teammates, which results in destroying value rather than in creating it. The equalizer types of teams are those whose cultural diversity does not lead to difficulties in team processes. However, team members do not use their cultural differences as a performance lever because they tend to think that their teamwork process runs smoothly. Finally, creators are multicultural teams performing at a level that is higher than their expectations as far as value diversity is concerned. For instance, these teams are able to develop new products and market them within a very short time, set up remarkable cost savings in a price-competitive industry or to create new successful alliances with suppliers or customers. The key for performance within such teams is the understanding of virtual team interaction processes used as a real leverage tool.

9.4.5 Performance Management

Leadership in virtual teams plays a key role in enhancing and monitoring team performance but has a lowered possibility of compensating or influencing low-quality teamwork due to distance (Hoegl et al., 2007). Leaders of virtual teams need to understand and recognize the barriers to performance, and reach a balance between managerial skills, emergent practices, interpersonal communication and cultural factors (DeRosa, 2009). DeRosa also mentioned that managing from a distance implies some management behaviours, for example, a change management approach, team collaboration and communication facilitation with a clear objective: to indicate team goals and direction. It implies that the understanding of the virtual team's objectives and roles are shared between the team's leader and the team members for positive team performance (D'Eredita and Chau, 2005). Team objectives enable the team members to adjust their behaviour and process, identify and use the dedicated resources, and develop the adequate collaboration with their teammates (Algesheimer et al., 2011). Thus, they may tend to work with increased satisfaction. The managerial behaviours might be supported by some managerial processes, such as appreciative inquiry as demonstrated by Conkright (2011). Based on his own experience of reorganizing and managing a virtual instructional system developer group, Conkright (2011) recommends applying appreciative inquiry in the virtual team management toward team performance. The principle results in asking positive questions in order to obtain positive answers from the team members, thus, stimulating the individuals to openly discuss and share their experiences within the team.

Questions should be open and involve the participants in sharing what they believe is most crucial for the team development, what they value the most about themselves, the teamwork and the organization. It seems essential in the appreciative process to prepare the inquiry or meeting with some preliminary questions whose purpose is to catch the main team's interest. It is also important to give the tone for that inquiry while respecting a balance in information distribution, team profile, team size and teamwork culture.

The benefit of appreciative inquiry is to provide ideas and solutions for team development within the organization, from bottom-up instead of top-down. Adoption of these ideas and solutions by the team members seems more efficient and moves virtual team members into a positive approach of transformational change. Therefore, an effective leader guides his/her virtual team to success when he/she manages to allocate the adequate resources to the teamwork and processes, in terms of staffing, technology, training and budget in accordance to the organization strategy. Technological advances enable the leaders to focus on the work results since the team's deliverables can be stored, retrieved and dispatched via online systems. Similarly, the virtual team members can use and value their own contributions, as well as the team contributions, which is a factor to boost their career expectations (Nunamaker et al., 2009).

A clear process is an essential contributor to team performance in addition to effective leadership behaviours. Those behaviours present diverse possibilities such as delegation of leadership, shared leadership and a transformational or inspirational type of management as discussed in Chapter 8. Leadership affects teamwork performance but also affective outcomes at high proportions influencing team members' reactions as detailed in the next chapter. Perceived effective leadership encourages virtual team members and reinforces the team processes, which regulate team performance and team satisfaction (Wakefield et al., 2008). A clear relationship is also established with leadership effectiveness and team performance, including communication frequency and trust building (Chen et al., 2011).

9.4.6 Virtual Team Dynamic

In the previous chapter about managerial processes, we mention that research globally reports that task conflict brings a dynamic interaction in a group. A close relationship links conflict to performance and the understanding of individual expectation. A virtual team without conflicts is unlikely to reach a high level of performance (Davison, 1994). However, it cannot always be considered as positive, even though virtual teams are more often confronted with task conflict than affective conflict because they are distant and more task-focused.

When individual expectations are explicitly expressed between virtual team members and leaders, preferably in the early building phase of the team, conflict opportunities are reduced (Bosch-Sijtsema, 2007). The reason is that matching the individual expectation leads to higher individual satisfaction and productivity. Therefore, team performance increases. On the other hand, mismatched expectation negatively influences trust building within virtual teams, leading to dissatisfaction and decreased motivation. Virtual teams, in that case, perform at a lower level and this may also engender conflict.

Teamwork conflict leads to confusion and disagreements, which negatively impacts performance. Conflict resolution is more difficult to reach and takes a longer amount of time in a virtual context mainly because team cohesion is more difficult to build due to complexity, dispersion and virtuality boundaries.

Preventive measures may facilitate performance when 'the realities of business dictate their use' (Hinds and Bailey, 2003) such as adopting the most advanced technologies to smoothen the effect of distance, provided that this technology is assimilated into the daily routine (Nunamaker et al., 2009). Additional preventive measures facilitate performance including the integration of common 'best practices', information-sharing, daily team life such as a shared calendar, office politics, and main events linked to the team activities to reinforce team coordination whose influence positively affects performance (Massey et al., 2003).

9.5   TO KEEP IN MIND: COMPLEXITY TO MEASURE TEAMWORK PERFORMANCE

Teamwork performance is assessed on predefined objectives and metric measures concerning the achievement of virtual team tasks and activities, which are based on results of quality, quantity, timing and customers' satisfaction. It is, however, more complex to measure than in co-located teams and is not very accurate as far as affective performance is concerned. Teamwork performance affects all levels of an organization from the organizational to the individual level. Therefore, the quality of the needed resources and infrastructure necessary for work processes, including virtual culture and advanced technologies, are key players in virtual team effectiveness. The organization's responsibility is to sustain performance by evaluating and managing the possible risk of failure and find solutions to eradicate those risks.

Challenges for virtual team performance stand in the capability of the organization or virtual team leaders to monitor virtuality and its effects without moderating teamwork performance. The main difficulty is to find the adequate tools and indicators to assess virtual team performance, and to be able to analyse, understand, adapt, revise, improve and communicate the diverse actions, activities and team outcomes. The key drivers to teamwork performance keep a strong relationship with virtual team structuring including its processes, especially through the 'sense of presence' embedded in the team and the composition of the team, which is one factor of team complexity, and, how performance is managed in the team, taking advantages of emergent conflicts. All these factors affect work team performance along with team and individual satisfaction.

9.6 CONCLUSION

Teamwork performance in the virtual context is complex and difficult to measure even though research globally agrees that teamwork outcomes are assessed on predefined objectives and measured with metrics. The main reason for complexity is virtual team dispersion within a multicultural context as well as the involved key drivers on performance at organizational, team and individual levels. Virtual team members from various cultures demonstrate different levels of satisfaction. Therefore, the feedback of performance assessment cannot always be done with the indicators as they need to remain meaningful to all of the virtual team members. Misunderstanding within virtual teams, in addition to heterogeneity, may result in increased conflict among team members, and less effective performance of the team.

This is a reason why optimization and maintenance of communication technologies is essential along with the reliability and performance of team processes. It has been demonstrated that virtual team performance and collective technologies directly influence global team performance prediction. When effectively monitored and managed, virtual teams are considered as an effective tool to create synergies and to increase performance by creating pools of strong expertise and reduced functional diversity due to specialization. They are able to integrate the corporate network to perform a specific task and thus to meet the organizational strategy.

Virtual team performance is sustainable as long as affective performance is considered as relevant in the outcomes of virtual team task or activity processes. However, more extensive research is still needed to better understand the direct or indirect links between virtuality and performance, more specifically to see if virtuality and multicultural interconnections may benefit from cultural characteristics to increase performance and reach performance outcomes more quickly and effciently. Research could measure the impact of virtual team development and the organization's strategy oriented to the development of centres of excellence, clustering competencies within specific areas, which are integrated in their corporate network whilst using local competencies etc. Within a fast-moving and changing context, continuous adaptation in performance monitoring and measures are required.

9.7　GUIDELINES FOR MANAGERIAL PRACTICES: TEAMWORK PERFORMANCE

Measuring virtual teamwork performance is complex in a dispersed environment, therefore, the virtual team manager needs to assess teamwork performance while taking into account the team's variables. These guidelines enable the assessment of the implemented measurement system at diverse levels: at the managerial, organizational, team and individual levels. The gap between the expected virtual team objectives and the results are one of the key factors that lead to team and individual performance if properly analysed and used.

Table 9.1　Teamwork performance

Key actions	Key suggestions
At managerial level Name and analyse the system of performance measurement and list the indicators that evaluate the teamwork performance. List the defined objectives and compare them to the results achieved by the virtual team. How do you make sure that those indicators are similarly understood by all of your team members?	Metrics linked to the team activities, project cost, project duration, problem-solving quality, coordination quality, decision-making quality, lead times, type of tasks etc. The team results go over, lower or at the expected level.
At organizational level Assess the quality of the organization as a support to the team's activities: – What reduces the complexity of virtual teams? – What prevents alignment between tools, culture and virtual teaming?	Think about the possible risks for the team to perform effectively.
At team level Identify the teamwork values praised by the diverse cultures that exist within the team.	

Table 9.1   (continued)

Key actions	Key suggestions
At team level	
Identify the team capacity.	Higher coordination, team dynamic set up, conflict management etc. Team structure, team composition, clear process etc.
Name the possible managerial implications, especially to recognize and understand the possible barriers to team performance.	Learning approach to achieve performing virtual teaming and improved results.
At individual level	
List what each team member gains or misses in the team. Measure mismatch between those expectations and possible satisfaction or dissatisfaction.	
How do you reward the virtual team members?	Financial bonus (e.g. a team-based or an individual-based calculation?), individual incentives etc.
Name the possible managerial implications, especially to recognize and understand the possible barriers to individual peak performance.	– Sense of presence, incentives to participation, motivation, communication, creativity, social loafing avoidance etc. – Drive to possible adjustment (e.g. behaviours, organization, technology, time allocation, mutual understanding, training etc.)

10 Affective performance in virtual teams

10.1 INTRODUCTION

With an approach that is similar to teamwork performance, we concentrate on individual satisfaction, and start by defining what affective performance means and how it appears at the different levels of virtual teaming. We discuss the constrains of virtuality, which makes the evaluation of affective performance in virtual environment somewhat difficult. Finally, we look at the impact of relevant drivers such as trust, attitudes and interactions, leadership and the way that conflicts are resolved.

10.2 DEFINITION OF AFFECTIVE PERFORMANCE IN VIRTUAL TEAMS

Affective performance focuses on the individual's satisfaction. Individual satisfaction involves attitudes, motivation, personal values, relationships, willingness, preferences and elements valued by the individual. It relates on how a virtual team member feels about teamwork, processes and the outcomes of the teamwork. In most cases, affective performance is connected to the individual emotions, which might be excitement or anxiety, loneliness or a feeling of isolation.

Satisfaction is defined as a result, or discrepancy from, a team member's comparison of current outcomes and expected outcomes. A customers' satisfaction refers to the difference between received results and expected results of the 'contract' of which the virtual team is engaged in forms of objectives and on time achievement with the agreed quantity and quality. A customers' satisfaction depends on the group motivation to successfully fulfil its 'contract'. Indeed, the group motivation directly influences the customer service quality and employee work satisfaction (Mehandjiev and Odgers, 1999) which is measured through the quality of the solutions adopted by individuals and the group. When successful, team member's satisfaction increases, as well as the positive relationships and interactions with teammates and other stakeholders; customers' satisfaction also increases.

Algesheimer et al. (2011) refer to a combination of rational-cognitive and emotional-motivational dimensions, where the cognitive aspect is represented by shared ideas and goals and emotional side is represented by shared motivations to perform. Both cognitive and emotional motivations define an implicit or explicit agreement among virtual team members in connection to performance characterized by the affective aspect. This affective aspect is supported at the organizational level and operates at the team and individual levels.

10.2.1 Affective Performance at Organizational Level

Organizations involved in virtual teaming have the responsibility to develop a culture, policies and systems that keep virtual teams and individuals satisfied and engaged in virtual teamwork processes. International human resource management and the organization need to find ways to provide such satisfaction to virtual team members through their own processes. A human resources approach and policies may need revisions consequently due to the rapid evolution, differing motivations, and expectations of the actual younger generation, when compared to the former generation with a more traditional work position and conventional professional expectation. Mentoring programmes are recommended to overcome possible generational gaps and to develop respect among generations (Houck, 2011).

As seen previously, the virtual context and its characteristics have to be taken into account along with adequate systems of measurement. Organizations encompassing reward and recognition systems that are developed for individual and team contribution positively foster individual and functional work (Duarte and Snyder, 2001). Measures need to be adapted to the virtual environment to reach work outcomes, and also to provide value and satisfaction to each member. Therefore, organizations need to map their own virtual environment in order to support and sustain affective performance of a team or an individual.

The difficulty in measuring affective performance at the organizational level consists of setting appropriate global indicators. We have seen that, in most cases, indicators concentrate on results rather than on an individual effort when measuring team performance. As a matter of fact, distance does not enable the daily or frequent, and accurate assessment of individual commitment.

In the virtual context, team members demonstrate higher performance and motivation when the reward system is based on team-based outcomes, and when incentive distribution is based on equality principles. Equality principles means that the same amount of reward is distributed to each virtual team member regardless of their personal contribution,

whereas equity principles take into account the individual contribution in
the reward amount (Rack et al., 2011). In addition to the above consideration, the researchers raise one major point from their observations: an
individual's level of assertiveness, along with skills and capabilities, may
moderate the effect of the reward structure. A low level of assertiveness
contributes to higher individual satisfaction and performance in a reward
distribution based on equality principles, rather than on equity principles.
Equality conditions positively affect the low level of individual assertiveness because these individuals do not need to be able to defend their own
interest, or be self-confident in their personal contribution. Individual
motivation is not only attached to financial incentives but also to feelings
of pride and recognition, that are not only metric measurements. The communication of success stories or best practices posted on the intranet of
the organization can be, for example, a measure of the individual or team
affective performance. Affective satisfaction can be measured through
employee turnover, providing the rate at which employees leave the team.
Preparing virtual team leaders and members to virtual team assignments
and effectiveness is one way to enhance affective performance in virtual
teams (Rosen et al., 2006).

10.2.2 Affective Performance at Team Level

According to researchers, virtual teams reach the world-class affective
level when the concerned teams present a wide range of variables that are
typical of virtuality. Those variables comprise cultural, temporal, spatial,
social factors and components that develop a collaborative team climate
such as stimulating colleagues, attitudes, feelings and behaviours (Jan et al.,
2005; Ocker, 2005). Additionally, further elements that provide necessary
resources and appropriate tools, norms, protocols that reduce misunderstandings, and continuous assessment and learning seem necessary as well
(Nemiro, 2001).

Affective performance appears in successful virtual teams that establish
high levels of synergies and social capital within the group or organization,
and show the capacity to generate new ideas, methods, approaches, inven-
tions, or applications. They can even achieve creative performance (Jan
et al., 2005).

Chang's work (2012) confirms that result and also insists on the
importance of trust as a trigger for efficiency in a virtual team, which is
tightly linked to the collaborative climate, as for example, with e-learning.
E-learning requires a collaborative climate because it is one of the main
factors of performing learning. In that environment, it is relevant to
create a cohesive and collaborative learning community to encourage the

students to develop enough self-confidence and trust to share their work with the other online participants, take part in discussions, and exchange mutual comments on their works. At this level, social interaction and feedback incite emotional connections that create effective collaboration and effective learning community. Affective participation at this level is a conveyor of effective performance; it is here to get students involved in online exchange and achieve group satisfaction to succeed in learning together. Further factors determine virtual team members' satisfaction, such as quality of work, and work outcomes that achieve the expected targets, which implies a participative consensus in the group on the acceptance of decision (Lin et al., 2008). They show reduced performance when virtual team members are 'always co-located or always dispersed' and when inhibitors emerge such as dominance, lack of knowledge sharing, lack of mutual understanding, lack of standardization, or when time pressure, technical, and technological difficulties increase (Ocker, 2005).

In reference to those difficulties, some researchers come to the conclusion that face-to-face teams are providing a higher level of individual satisfaction than virtual teams with similar communication effectiveness (Redman and Sankar, 2005; Warkentin et al., 1997). But, virtual teams are showing effective coordination and communication, which demonstrates a higher level of satisfaction. This satisfaction is even higher when the teams are self-managed (Piccoli et al., 2004).

Multicultural self-managed teams may find difficulties to reach common norms, shared identity, structures and practices necessary to operate, and run team activities because there is no clear leader to supervise the teamwork processes. However, the accumulation of diverse cultural values along the development of the team may compensate this lack of clear leadership.

Uncertainty avoidance is also a factor that influences efficiency for those teams. As a matter of fact, virtual teams showing a low degree of uncertainty avoidance perform at a higher level than those with a high degree of uncertainty avoidance because they demonstrate a wider openness to change and, in particular, unexpected changes. The manner of functioning is confirmed when the degree of diversity in these teams is low, but it is more complex to demonstrate when the degree of diversity is high (Cheng et al., 2012).

Another point to consider is how an individual is situated within the team in regards to performance criteria. A virtual team member may belong to a team that provides a low level of performance, even though that individual demonstrates a high level of performance. Consequently, the individual's belief in collective performance decreases (Schepers et al., 2011). It may negatively impact his/her own motivation and affective performance.

The next challenge to maintaining or developing affective performance in a virtual team is to create relationships that are concrete and reliable enough to coordinate and overcome the possible cultural barriers after the forming and storming steps of team evolution. Thus, virtual team members can benefit from the cultural diversity existing in the team to potentially reach a high level of team performance. The quality level of relationships may decrease uncomfortable feelings, stress and anxiety in the team. However, the virtual team members should be cautious not to be trapped in to a process of looking for a consensus; in order to avoid possible conflict. This behaviour would negatively affect affective team performance and then therefore teamwork performance, if we consider that conflict can positively influence idea creation in a team.

10.2.3   Affective Performance at the Individual Level

Affective performance is often based on affective outcomes and relationship dimensions that generate individual dissatisfaction or satisfaction. Individual satisfaction is closely linked to the individual level of interest in the task and affective commitment (Short et al., 2005). A high amount of virtual team members who reach individual satisfaction in a team tends to increase satisfaction at the team level. Individual satisfaction is translated by the individual's positive or negative reaction to personal or team performance and the expected compensation. Satisfaction is usually expressed through emotion.

Emotion is a feeling that emerges at the individual level about a situation, result or relationships, which shows an affective implication. Emotion highlights the importance of a constant presence of the communication medium richness in the virtual environment, where the communication of individual emotions still challenges the virtual communication process; emotions can be positive or negative, such as anger or happiness. It remains relevant as far as the team dynamic and team satisfaction are concerned.

Emotions are conveyors of social information, on how to act in given situations and the way teammates assess the others' emotions. Some individuals compare their own emotions to the other virtual members' emotions and take a position on how they should feel regarding affective performance and emotion existing within the team. In that case, emotion can be 'contagious' impacting, thus, positively or negatively, the team's social dimension and affective performance.

Emotion can be transmitted not only through textual communication (like a lot of work teams do today) but also through tone or length of messages and response time, which might be slower in circumstances of disagreement or anger. Using only textual communication appears too limited to convey emotions within virtual teams, and may even lead to negative emotions (Cheshin et al., 2011). Thus, it may explain the difficulty of recognizing individual satisfaction in a virtual environment.

Congruence between actions, behaviours and textual communication is relevant to avoid transmission of negative emotions, which would affect the affective outcomes of the team. In conclusion, affective outcomes are positively influenced by the social dimensions of the virtual team, which directly affects an individual's satisfaction levels (Lin et al., 2008).

A social dimension can initiate a teammates' cooperation and encouragement, fostering a positive perception of team performance at the individual level (Schepers et al., 2011). A social dimension operates at an individual level regarding dispersion: spatial, contextual, temporal and technological (ICTs use). Dispersion is one of the main factors to influence an individual's satisfaction, as facilitator or inhibitor toward interpersonal connections and that affects 'individual virtuality'. To reduce the negative effects of dispersion at the individual level, it is optimal for individuals to get a central position in the social network of the virtual organization because it influences the interactions between teammates and colleagues.

This centrality indicates the degree of visibility and connection for an individual in a network. Individuals with adapted technology, knowledge on how to use that technology, and access to relevant information are more central in the ICT network. Consequently, key factors to reaching centrality in the social network are quality of equipment and access to ICTs, as well as the time to resources. These factors contribute to team performance and individual development and, thus, individual satisfaction within virtual teams. Centrality in the ICT network is positively related to performance because individuals are likely to communicate effciently, and use ICTs as performance levers (Arling and Subramani, 2011). Therefore, we come to the conclusion that e-leaders should encourage, train and facilitate the use of ICTs to reduce frustration, enhance individual satisfaction and, therefore, affective performance.

Increased individual satisfaction positively influences individual behaviours towards team performance (Robert and You, 2013). Individual satisfaction requires the organization, virtual team leaders, and possibly the virtual teammates to get individuals to meet their own expectations, goals and aspirations (Martins and Schilpzand, 2011). Individual satisfaction seems easier to achieve in virtual teams when virtual members have easy access to experts, higher autonomy in managing their own tasks or projects, and may organize their timing in respect to their own balance of their work and private life (Webster and Wong, 2008).

It is essential that the team members recognize the team they belong to, in order to develop membership. Individual performance is closely linked to the individual's own recognition of the virtual team identity. When this recognition is high, it results in lowered opportunities of affective conflicts, which fosters job satisfaction, and so reduces frustration and dissatisfaction (Rezgui, 2007).

As demonstrated by Pauleen (2004), frustration and dissatisfaction moderate team cohesion and negatively impact virtual team collaboration, knowledge-sharing and social capital. Frustration is an inhibitor of affective performance and may generate feelings of stress for the concerned individuals because they face a limited identification within an organization and a lack of recognition.

Individual satisfaction might be enhanced by reward systems, such as financial incentives. However, reward and recognition of individual performance may create 'internal' competition which leaves virtual teams with paradoxes, such as feelings of satisfaction and dissatisfaction, stimulation and frustration at the same time. For effective individual performance toward team performance, Samnani et al. (2013) recommend to reward idea-sharing and achieving team targets. Virtual team leaders also have to ensure that virtual team members share the same career development opportunities as the traditional team members in order to avoid frustration and dissatisfaction (Duarte and Snyder, 2006).

Another important point that affects an individual's satisfaction is the individual's 'locus of control'. Locus of control is the individual's own assessment of success, either internal or external, which has a strong relationship with job satisfaction because individuals consider decisions, actions of management, and teammates as either enabling or constraining their own performance and, thus, their satisfaction in their job. As a consequence, team leaders that understand their team members' locus of control may provide higher efficient leadership towards affective performance (Lee-Kelley, 2002).

10.3 CHALLENGES FOR AFFECTIVE PERFORMANCE

10.3.1 Complexity of Evaluation within a Virtual Context

Virtuality means a confrontation of various cultural values due to workplace mobility leading to acculturation. Acculturation is a process in which an individual, group or people, adopt or borrow cultural and social characteristics of another culture, especially the dominant one. It might result in a merging of cultures due to prolonged contacts (Farlex, 2013). But acculturation may not occur so frequently in global organizations, especially when the organization is not aware of the importance of the virtual team process, or do not anticipate and integrate virtual teamwork processes as a corporate standard way of working.

Consequently, the value given to performance indicators by individuals might differ according to cultures along with the appreciation of those indicators. When teamwork quality is not perceived on the same level by virtual team members, fewer interactions occur and this results in a decrease in affective performance. In addition to this point, a virtual team member may show lower outcomes through work process indicators but he/she may reveal strong relational skills that bind the group process and positively influence team satisfaction and performance. The evaluation of that behaviour is complex to assess in a virtual context and most of the time is not taken into account, which negatively affects individual affective performance.

In a diverse cultural environment, it is difficult to know what is valued by all the virtual team members. For example, the individualistic cultures value the individual whereas collectivist cultures give importance to the group level. Therefore, reward systems that praise individual performance, such as financial bonus tied to individual results, might be senseless for members issued from collectivist culture.

Those values might be highly influenced by the local and national cultures too. For these reasons, virtual team leaders and virtual team members need to understand the impact of national work contexts, especially when newcomers join the team or when one culture dominates others.

It is also critical to understand what possible responses individuals may need to interact in a multicultural team (Samnani et al., 2013). Newcomers might be influenced by the acculturation process regarding social networks and organization. Usually, virtual managers could analyse their degree of desire for economic rewards and relational pressures, which helps to predict their employability, advancement and income.

In that case, the selected values for evaluation provide different weight and consideration for virtual team members. The negative impact of cultural diversity may decrease thanks to improved knowledge of cultural diversity through the identification, learning and acceptance of cultural diversity.

As previously stated in the book, the team composition is one of the critical factors and should show a diverse range of complementary competences. Therefore, recruiting processes should be run in a way that individual profiles with a diverse level of cultural diversity are obtained through global job recruiting campaigns (Samnani et al., 2013).

10.4 KEY DRIVERS TO AFFECTIVE PERFORMANCE

10.4.1 Trust among Virtual Team Members

According to Gurtner et al. (2007) virtual team members show lower work satisfaction, mainly due to the difficulty of trusting other team members, the fact that it is more challenging to build and achieve within a dispersed context, and the way information is shared. Therefore, trust and information management are key drivers to improve individual satisfaction, and refer to the socio-emotional processes of virtual teams, as well as to HR policies.

Some models and studies have emerged from research studies in order to identify the essential drivers leading to sound performance. Lepsinger and DeRosa (2010) propose a model that points out the main critical factors involved in team performance. They call it the relationships, accountability, motivation, purpose and process (RAMP) model, a wink on how to 'ramp up' virtual teams to performing teams.

One element emerges from that model when considering the factors of team performance. This is the relevance of trust as a bond between the mentioned factors, essential to reduce functional diversity to performance as confirmed by Peters and Karren (2009); Furumo et al. (2009). Brahm and Kunze (2012) highlight the need for trust building at the early stages of collaboration in a virtual team, to reach team performance outcomes and effective social relationships. A trusting working environment will retain higher attention in the future because it is one of the critical factors for virtual members' satisfaction in working in a virtual context.

Barriers to trust building, as previously discussed, slow down or even freeze the socio-emotional processes of the concerned virtual team members. Therefore, they hamper the team from reaching the potentially high performance level through strong relationships with work processes and affective commitment and satisfaction (Morris et al., 2002; Powell et al., 2006). More specifically, virtual team members need to learn in order to understand virtuality and adopt the adequate behaviour, such as motivation and engagement that positively influence team cohesion and team performance (Cohen and Bailey, 1997).

Motivation, although it is difficult to measure, encourages and stimulates individuals for virtual teamwork by adopting the appropriate attitudes and interactions towards teamwork performance.

10.4.2 Attitudes and Interactions

Attitudes and interactions appear to be relevant in virtual teaming and affective performance. Although they are more difficult to learn than technical skills, effective behaviours that are recommended for virtual teaming can be taught or transmitted from other teammates' experience. Learning is one way to encourage individual motivation and develop team performance.

Organizations should be aware that clarifying and making sense of the strategic reasons for using virtual teams in the organization is essential to develop virtual team members' motivation. Virtual team members should recognize that virtual teamwork is the standard way of working, the one valued by the organization. That model should be recognized as a 'core competency' rather than a model derived from a competitive advantage, which positively influences affective performance (Davidson, 2013).

Motivation is not the only attitude that contributes to affective performance; other behaviours such as extroversion affect individual satisfaction too. Extraversion usually generates productive interactions. However, different levels of extraversion among virtual team members may appear and some of them foster a negative interactive style (Richard and Pierre, 2002).

Critical attention is also required to isolate behaviours that may have a negative impact on the group, leading to a decrease in virtual team performance and member satisfaction. It reveals the relevance for generalized interaction structures to avoid letting behavioural isolation influence virtual teams, especially teams showing high-quality relational interaction among team members, as well as high levels of information-sharing and cooperation (Cogliser et al., 2013).

Social presence, media richness and an adequate communication medium strengthen positive impact on the perceived interaction quality and, therefore, on team productivity and team process satisfaction (Andres, 2002). Interaction style affects performance on collaborative decision tasks as they directly affect communication and, thus, team performance and process outcomes.

10.4.3 Styles of Leadership

A facilitator style of leadership encourages dynamic interactions, incentives and a collaborative climate (Jawadi and Boukef Charki, 2011); it finds ways to make virtual work consistent, contributes to team members' satisfaction, and succeeds in setting up an effective evaluation and reward system assessing performance (Nunamaker et al., 2009). Effective and successful virtual team leaders demonstrate adequate and complete interpersonal and competency behaviours and succeed in engaging team members with a project, solution or desired outcome quality, within a virtual context that they understand (Martins and Schilpzand, 2011).

Leadership behaviours are able to develop high levels of relationship, gaining consideration and efficient task-management based on structured organization. They provide effective communication, which affects virtual team members' emotions and, therefore, their satisfaction or dissatisfaction, as seen above. E-leaders care about communication in a virtual context, and aim to promote individual and team satisfaction (Glückler and Schrott, 2007; Lin et al., 2008). Effective communication clearly organizes, provides visibility, communicates the work processes and strategy, and demonstrates the capacity to implement a virtual 'culture that values teamwork, communication, learning, outcome-based performance and capitalizing on diversity' (Duarte and Snyder, 2006; Powell et al., 2006). Shared leadership and individual trust facilitates the increase of individual team member satisfaction in virtual teams (Robert and You, 2013).

Virtual communication is not an issue when the quality and tone of communication is considered as relevant to the project or team activities (DeSanctis et al., 2001). In the communication process, feedback plays a key role in team performance (Martins and Schilpzand, 2011) and reveals the level of virtual team cohesion. If responsiveness is quick and reliable, the virtual team cohesion level increases. It positively affects the team performance and the individual's satisfaction. Reciprocally, the virtual team members' motivation, relationships and work levels satisfaction stimulate both feedback and group motivation (Jawadi and Boukef Charki, 2011). The virtual team leader's effectiveness can be measured through the virtual team members' participation in the team activities encouraged by his/her managerial actions (Montoya-Weiss et al., 2001). Outcomes of team activities are measured through systems that need to be 'integrated and aligned to recognize, support and reward people who work on and lead virtual teams' (Duarte and Snyder, 2006). This approach should be supported by IHRM policies to value the performance not only at the team level but also at the individual level.

Therefore, an effective leader guides his/her virtual team to success when he/she manages to allocate the adequate resources to the teamwork and processes, in terms of staffing, technology, training and budget, in accordance with the organization strategy. Technological advances enable the leaders to focus on the work results since the team's deliverables can be stored, retrieved, and dispatched via online systems. Skills in that area can be developed rather easily, while competencies in virtual teaming are more complex in terms of behavioural and relational abilities. An efficient virtual team leader cannot underestimate that point and should provide training involving all team members and stakeholders. Similarly, individuals can use and value their own contributions as well as the team contributions when they understand, and know-how to tackle virtual teaming, which is a factor to boosting their career expectations and individual satisfaction (Nunamaker et al., 2009). Efficient virtual team leaders should be aware that affective performance is strongly tied to the preparation, and readiness of individuals to work in a virtual context and it may not emerge spontaneously.

10.4.4 Types of Conflict Resolution

A rather negative relationship is established between affective conflict and performance because it generates decreased satisfaction and reduces virtual team members' engagement to the team, and organization (Hinds and Mortensen, 2005; Hinds and Bailey, 2003). Hinds and Bailey (2003) specify that the 'open expression of affective conflict' triggers a decrease in performance, as long as conflict resolution is not reached. As demonstrated by Liu et al. (2008), trust associated to a collaborative style of conflict management contributes to team satisfaction. Research suggests that a collaborative conflict management style positively affects satisfaction due to the quality and acceptance of the decision-making process, perceived decision quality and perceived participation (Paul et al., 2004b). The collaborative style of conflict management may empower virtual team members and team empowerment is recognized to increase team performance as it is strongly related to process improvement and customer satisfaction (Chang et al., 2011).

Such teams feel able to solve complex coordination issues, and quickly and efficiently remove obstacles to their activity processes without managerial approval. Their effectiveness is even greater for virtual teams that do not meet frequently (Kirkman et al., 2004), especially for teams that share leadership or those with an emergent leader.

The integrative type of resolution produces a similar impact on a group agreement (Martins and Schilpzand, 2011) unlike the avoidance and accommodation type of resolution that generates a negative effect on performance. Creating team cohesion and mutual knowledge improves team performance and reduces team conflict (Wakefield et al., 2008).

10.5 TO KEEP IN MIND: EVALUATION AND KEY DRIVERS OF AFFECTIVE PERFORMANCE

Affective performance in virtual teams focuses on an individual's satisfaction, and assesses the discrepancies between their expectations and the current situation; in terms of satisfaction regarding elements valued by the individual about both personal and professional motivation. Affective performance is linked to organizational support, recognition systems, social capital and relationships established within the virtual team.

The main critical factors influencing affective performance for virtual team members are the degree to which team members like their job, team and social relationships within the team. When positive, those factors push the individual to commitment and engagement. Virtuality and the complexity to assess individual satisfaction render the measurement of affective performance difficult. The cultural diversity and the value given to performance criteria increase that difficulty. Key drivers are, however, identified such as motivation, trust, behaviours and interactions, leadership and the way conflict is resolved.

10.6 CONCLUSION

Even though virtual teams tend to be focused on task and result, affective outcomes cannot be dissociated from the work team performance, and individual satisfaction to perform that work, even though the relationship between teamwork performance and affective performance needs further analysis (Atanasova and Senn, 2011). This chapter demonstrates the relevance of affective performance within a virtual team or an organization, but it also shows the difficulty of monitoring that performance.

Assessing and measuring individual satisfaction is limited by the virtuality boundaries and the difficulty of measuring intangible outcomes. The risk of wrong analysis and interpretation is high and may generate dissatisfaction and, thus, negatively influence performance. This is the reason why achieving a high level of affective performance in a virtual environment requires e-leaders to display high-level competencies that are not only results focused, but are also oriented to multicultural and interrelational skills and attitudes.

The difficulty remains in succeeding to manage individual expectations: to match the organizational, team and work requirements as well. When successful, virtual teams have higher opportunities to meet team performance, including job satisfaction, matching organizational commitment and customer satisfaction, and appear to be efficient tools for global organizations.

Research on individual satisfaction in virtual teams is still ongoing. One direction for further research is the analysis of the organization's willingness to provide time and resources for efficient virtual team leaders promoting affective performance. How far can those organizations respond to the economic pressures of seeking a higher competitive advantage and an improved margin, whilst setting the policy of sustainable affective performance in a virtual environment? Are those policies and strategies reserved to certain profiles of companies, such as worldwide companies?

10.7 GUIDELINES FOR MANAGERIAL PRACTICES: AFFECTIVE PERFORMANCE

Affective performance is difficult to assess because it is complex to bridge intangible outcomes to a metric system. Affective performance can be reached through team members' satisfaction and engagement at organizational, team and individual levels. Through the practical guidelines presented in Table 10.1 we can observe how the virtual team leader may find concrete results linked to affective performance of the team—based on the cognitive and emotional dimensions relating to diversity.

Table 10.1   Practical guidelines: Affective performance

Key actions	Key suggestions
At an organizational level	
– Name and analyse the policies and systems implemented in the organization whose purpose is to foster people satisfaction within that organization.	– Refer to the organization's strategy general motto, communication campaign, programmes, rules etc.
– List the global indicators that define the measurement of affective satisfaction and performance.	– Precise if they are related to individual effort.
	– Are they based on equality or equity principles?
At the team level	
– List the variables inside the team that contribute to high or low affective performance.	– The factors can be cultural, temporal, spatial, climate—related to colleagues, attitudes, feelings, rules, protocols etc.
– Assess the social capital of the team.	
– Analyse the reward and recognition systems applied in the team.	
– List the indicators and analyse how they are built up.	– How far do they impact the quality of work?

Table 10.1   (continued)

Key actions	Key suggestions
At an individual level	
– Define how each individual assesses affective performance.	– Affective performance might be defined differently by diverse cultures and persons.
– Evaluate the critical factors valued by the team members.	– Task liking, team and social relationships, motivation, trust, behaviours.
– List each individual's expectations and the current situation or result within the team.	– Measure the gap that may lead to dissatisfaction or frustration.
– Assess how each member of the team is situated within the team.	– Is the affective performance linked to one or several person or to the whole team?
Analyse how: – the individual affective performance is expressed within the team; – through which preferred communication tool (text, video etc.); and – at what response time (quality of feedbacks).	– You can determine the quality of emotional relationships, positive, or negative reactions.
– Evaluate the centrality of the individual in the team social network.	– It indicates the visibility and connection of the concerned individual and possibly his/her frustration, dissatisfaction, or possible isolation.

11 Final conclusions

This book covers the research findings on virtual teams over the last two decades. It highlights the main questions and concerns that are raised about virtual teams and their environment. Virtual teams are considered as a benefit to the economic changes across the world and they need certain awareness from organizations, managers and their team members, which is demonstrated throughout this book. Research findings converge to the same conclusion. Practising and working in or with a virtual team is not, globally, a spontaneous way of working. However, today, virtual teams involve a wide range of individuals working in a business context or not, with a higher or lower level of complexity and degree of virtuality. The economists agree that today's business world is facing a real metamorphosis. Therefore, more adaptation might be expected from individuals, leaders and organizations.

We also note that virtual teaming, as such, continuously evolves and it requests regular adaptation to its environments. For this reason, research should consider changes in economies and note the influence of emerging countries, and constraints on virtual team management. Would the emerging countries bring a new way of working and thinking together with unexpected new methods of management, thus, opening the era of 'post-globalization'? How can emerging practices and already established methods match together in a constructive, productive and sustainable evolution?

Technology development might answer the question partially. For example, on a micro level, we can already see the evolution of contacts between service providers and customers: they have become more and more virtual. In order to reduce that virtuality, companies try to give a sense of 'reality' to virtual relationships. For example, voyages-sncf.com, the web service of the French national railways, uses the services of external call centre experts to answer customer questions thanks to chat messages. The customers might not realize that this service is outsourced. We can assume that in the near future, the contacts will tend to appear in the form of avatars, through improved graphics. The idea is to reduce the distance between service providers and customers. The goal is to satisfy customer demand in a competitive, attractive and efficient way, while establishing a certain level of social links, which tend to disappear in virtual relationships. Technology incentives at the micro level can also contribute to a wider scale of technology adoption, which facilitates technology deployment at macro level such as virtual teaming.

Research findings should help explain the global economic evolution and its influence on virtual teams and/or individuals. Acceptance and deeper knowledge of possible evolutions helps people benefit from those changes. Virtual teams could be considered as a sustainable and flexible tool, with specific instructions for adequate use on a wide consultation. However, some areas do not seem feasible through virtual teams. Consultations appear unlikely without frequent face-to-face interactions. Coaching or mentoring also looks difficult. E-medical care still needs to convince the users and some professionals. Future research could help identify the areas that are critical when virtually handled. Additionally, more questions are raised on the possibilities of avoiding failures in processes and leadership. Essential levers need to be identified to foster team and individual satisfaction, which are recognized as key triggers to performance. However, they are especially difficult to set up and manage at a distance.

Virtual teaming in some specific areas might be even more complex. For this reason, research is still needed to help practitioners understand the critical mechanisms of virtual teams. Thus, academic research proposes applying more fragmented models to areas such as education. However, they usually need to be tested on a larger scale in real life or business conditions. As demonstrated in the book, socio-emotional and managerial processes are relevant factors in virtual teaming. Therefore, we recommend research to find out to which extent the organizations allocate resources and time to embedding leadership in a virtual context. It may also be relevant to check the extent to which e-leaders are ready to efficiently tackle those processes and cope with the pressure of time and performance metrics. Virtual leadership might be difficult to promote in an environment where performance figures are the major focus, allocating less room for other focuses, such as individual affective performance.

Researchers should investigate and link virtual team evolution with changes in major areas; IHRM is one of these areas. It has to deal with the younger generation and, therefore, it deals with new characteristics and different expectations than those conveyed by the conventional workforce.

The younger generation may have an impact on virtual teaming because they are familiar with technologies and volunteer to use them in cyberspaces; they may contribute to a certain level of performance, including collaborative performance. It is likely that e-working looks like a more standard way of working for the younger generation. It is then that the question is more focused on teamwork processes and the possible gap that may emerge between the 'Y' generation and the senior one. It might be accentuated by multicultural diversity, opportunities and necessities. Would this gap create a higher risk of team conflict? What about the impact on social aspects in a multicultural and geographically widespread team? How can one ensure that this younger generation meets affective performance? As an extension of this idea, employee privacy rights are not really addressed by academic research.

Today, organizations speculate on and investigate the time spent by employees surfing on the web on company time. This time may be valuable work time that is being largely used for personal activities, such as sending personal email messages and looking for private information. On the other hand, when an organization accepts personal web-surfing during work time, it may foster creative performance among employees. They might look for information linked to their tasks and activities. This actually remains an unanswered question in companies' policies. Should the access to social networks during work time be submitted to authorization and regulation? Another question is raised about social and economical areas. Do organizational policies, that develop virtual culture and work in a virtual mode, create or destroy jobs? Delocalization and relocalization offer new job opportunities due to work mobility, higher fluidity on the job market and higher visibility on the 'e-job market' across the world. However, it requests that individuals have certain characteristics to develop their self-branding and reach that level of visibility.

Research could offer an indepth analysis on the e-job market or international job market in order to inform about the current changes and new trends in needs, profiles and the movements of that market. Research should focus on job creation and destruction, and discuss how it is linked with virtual teams. The discussion could also address individual satisfaction and task profile, which emerges from the new positions. The financial aspect could also be approached and investigated. When do virtual teams become a profitable tool for organizations, taking into account the organization, implementation, coordination, and management costs of those teams? Does IHRM really take advantage of the worldwide talent resources and opportunities to diversify membership, regardless of age, culture, ethnicity, gender, handicaps, race, talents, and personal obligations? Or, do they tend to employ people in the area close to their local offices, thus, reducing the network of possible candidates? Could they manage otherwise? Finally, we note that virtual team understanding evolves due to academic research that offers practitioners some clues for using this tool with the most appropriate methods.

The approach on the functioning of virtual teams evolves: it concentrates more on intangible aspects, such as processes and performance outcomes, its roles in the economic environment, and its impact on individuals. Those areas still present a range of open questions and, consequently, there is a wide field for academic research.

PART V

Case studies

12 Case studies

CASE STUDY 1 FASHIONING VIRTUALITY: THE CASE OF ECO FASHION WORLD

The story behind ecofashionworld.com starts with four people spread across three continents. Diverse individual backgrounds, but with the same collective goals. We all believe in embracing personal style. And we are all empowered by the possibilities of change.

Today being aware of what you wear takes on a very different meaning than it once did! It begins with understanding the global repercussions that come with careless consumerism. It continues with realizing that we are all linked, from New York to New Delhi, Paris to Pakistan, Brazil to Bangladesh, and Vancouver to Vietnam, by the very strings of our garments. It evolves with recognizing that when we support eco and socially responsible fashion, we help reduce poverty and environmental damage, and support workers' rights. Our actions have an impact. Our decisions energize transformation.

The eco fashion world is moving forward! Every day a new development is made in sustainable fabrics. An innovative designer creates a super-glam, socially aware collection. A boutique devotes itself to making ethical clothing more easily available. An admired celeb dons an eco-friendly gown on the red carpet and declares the smartest style statement possible. Someone picks up her first bamboo fibre shirt or an organic pair of jeans and instantly falls in love with them. Really, every day, a new eco fashionista is born.

We do not sell anything on this site, but rather we aim to inspire you with new ideas, ideals, and information. Our goal is to keep you green, gorgeous and growing with a comprehensive guide to finding sustainable designer brands and online eco fashion stores. Search our guide by category, eco criteria, or country. Look to us for all the latest eco fashion news and reviews, events, designer Q&As, store profiles, launch updates, and interviews with our favourite ethical divas. Learn more about organizations that are involved with the eco-fashion movement. Check out our glossary for the latest terminology. Use our site as your go-to eco fashion resource.

Fashion is one of the most visible and seductive mediums there are. Arm yourself with the power of knowledge, indulge your passion for art and, suddenly, anything can happen.

How it Started

Ethical Fashion Show, October 2007. Webmaster Richard travels all the way from Vancouver with a dream: to build an online platform connecting people passionate about eco fashion. He meets videomaker Linda who is volunteering at the event and she is excited to join. So is researcher Rebecca who has been working within the field of eco fashion for several years and is now pursuing a PhD in organization theory. Upon his return Richard finds a fourth partner: healthcare worker Nicky who has been a friend for a long while. Within a month they are committed to realizing Richard's dream that has now become their shared common vision. The contours of the project are sketched.

Building Connections

The building starts. A domain name needs to be registered. Texts need to be written. A logo designed. Navigation developed. All of this happens online: the team has daily contact via email, bouncing around ideas and sharing tasks that need to be done. Once a week they meet over Skype, always designing an agenda beforehand with the most urgent things that need to be discussed, but leaving space for issues that spontaneously pop up. They bring in expertise from friends and family, but do the bulk of the work themselves, as a virtual team. In June 2008 the beta version of Eco Fashion World launches. The team celebrates remotely: Richard and Nicky in two different cities in British Columbia (BC), Canada; Linda in Paris; Rebecca in Rio de Janeiro. Although they have been meeting over Skype and exchange emails every day, Nicky, Linda and Rebecca have never met in real life. An opportunity for face-to-face contact is created when Rebecca moves back from Brazil to Europe and manages to visit Linda in Paris. Together they attend the Ethical Fashion Show, this time with brightly coloured T-shirts as reporters from Eco Fashion World. During four days they connect to many ethical fashion brands and players in the field, which results in a lot of content for the website. Richard and Nicky do the same and travel from Vancouver to Portland Fashion Week to connect with North American designers. Experiences about these events are exchanged within the team over Skype and new relations are built: the website starts to attract a larger numbers of visitors.

These face-to-face encounters give much needed new energy to the team members: after one year of having worked purely in virtual reality, it had started to become challenging to stay highly spirited. All four have busy jobs and devote their time, energy and skills whenever they can. Richard is the webmaster in charge of smooth operation of front- and back-end, including the uploading of all the website content. Nicky does most of the research and administrative tasks that need to be done. Linda is editor-in-chief responsible for all the content including daily news and the monthly magazine. Rebecca is being dubbed 'CEO', filling in all the blind spots in terms of developing the business plan, strategy, finances and marketing. She also manages external relationships as she is the most well-connected within the field of eco fashion and she does a major part of the writing: including a weekly blog. The private savings of the team members are used to pay experts from around the world: from web programmers in India, to graphic designers in Europe to contributing writers from countries as diverse as Australia, Bulgaria, South-Africa, Spain and the US. In no time a global enterprise is built: collaboration among the different individuals takes place in virtual reality. On the basis of a common passion for eco fashion, people get connected to each other and contribute their skills and ideas to the business. The team is not able to pay everyone, but manages to reward them *in natura* with eco fashion products that are sponsored by the participating brands.

By now the website comes up as number one on Google searches for 'eco fashion'. Visitor numbers and page views grow at a steep rate, and the synergy among the four partners seems to thrive on these developments. They are proud to have built such an inspiring platform in a virtual context, and the excitement about the different collaborations and global nature of the (extended) team fills them with joy and motivation.

Drain or Sustain?

One year later doubts start kicking in. Although culturally, all team members feel connected to each other, as three of them are Canadian and the fourth is from another Western country, the geographical distance between Vancouver and Europe has started to pose a psychological barrier. Often the Skype connection doesn't function well enough to have a conference call and thus they miss the opportunity to hear each other's voices clearly. Conference chats are practical as they serve as meeting minutes and can be read by those team members who had not been able to participate in the meeting. Unfortunately, the lower richness of communication and less social presence as compared to face-to-face interaction, negatively affects the productivity and performance of the team.

A result is that advertising does not generate the expected volume of income stream, and a reality check with a finance expert puts the dream into perspective. The four understand Eco Fashion World as a social enterprise that informs and inspires the growing community of eco fashionistas. They started the website first and foremost with the goal of creating a social impact, and support the transformation in the fashion industry towards the integration of more ethical practices. Whilst conventional enterprises aim to deliver a ROI, social enterprises focus on the social return on investment (SROI). The SROI is able to deliver a financial figure to social and environmental value, which is created by the enterprise. Eco Fashion World has not been designed and doesn't perform in such a way. Being one of the very first online sources for eco fashion, responses from all over the globe had always been overwhelming. People were very happy with the rich resources in terms of information and visuals, and students used the website to write their final theses about the topic. Unfortunately, one can't pay the bills by providing information and publishing beautiful images. Eco Fashion World needs to be redesigned to be able to deliver a combination of social and financial value.

The goal is clear: the site needs to become financially self-sustaining, and this causes friction with the vision of growing the community, and providing free information with which the founders started their venture. Still, the individual savings of the four partners have dried up and ideally they would like to be able to quit their regular jobs, and work full-time for the venture. They decide that the website needs to be an enterprise so as to be able to make money. In order to give material form to this economic perspective, they register the website as a 'Ltd.' in Canada for the reason that half of the team lives in BC, Canada, and three of the four partners are Canadian. Different business models are investigated and finally they decide to develop a membership system. Eco fashion brands and stores can increase their online visibility through becoming paid members of the site. For customers of these companies, the website remains freely accessible. To enable worldwide payments coming in from the different members, a PayPal account is created that will be connected to a newly opened Canadian bank account.

Shifting Priorities

With a stronger focus on generating income, other activities are put on hold. The monthly magazine doesn't attract enough visitors and is abandoned. Attempts to increase the number of newsletters decrease. From following one's passions and interests, the partners need to draw on or acquire additional sets of skills. For Linda, this quickly becomes a dead end. She realizes she no longer wants to sit on her own in front of a computer night after night. She misses the physical proximity of team colleagues and chooses to put more effort in her video work again. The lack of a sense of presence could unfortunately not be compensated for by advanced technologies that would have been able to substitute face-to-face interactions, as occurs in bigger companies. The team members lacked the resources to meet more often in real-time, which could have fostered greater social cohesion and have sustained their collaboration practices in virtual reality.

In March 2010 Linda quits her activities for Eco Fashion World. Around that time Rebecca has the opportunity to go to Canada where she meets Nicky in person for the first time. Even though it is valuable for the three partners that are left to connect in real life, the relationships don't evolve into friendships. Brainstorming over coffee about the future of the site stays superficial, and this lack of synergy negatively affects creativity and the capacity to generate new ideas. A result is that a certain feeling of well-being within the team and 'on the job' doesn't increase. Rebecca gets the chance to network in Vancouver and sees many opportunities in BC because of the region's new focus on becoming green. She feels it makes more sense to continue networking there as this is also the place where the venture is registered. Upon her departure, she hands over these valuable contacts to Richard and Nicky as it would be much more complicated to nurture such relationships from Europe. Regrettably, these connections are not followed up on, thus not creating the much-needed environment to grow the business.

In that sense, Rebecca feels that her locus of control is shifting: she is convinced that it is more logical to develop the business in Vancouver, but is not there herself to push this. The consequence is that she starts feeling restrained in being able to maximize her performance and thus satisfaction in developing the enterprise. Upon her return to Europe, she takes maternity leave to focus on her baby. Richard and Nicky are working hard to keep a steady flow of news published and get more members on board. The cohesion of the team is drastically decreasing: the geographical distance prohibits flourishing into a mature venture.

New Leadership

By January 2011 Nicky has taken up the daily management of the site. Richard's focus is on his other web ventures whilst Rebecca tries to balance the care for her child with finishing her PhD. The small revenue from memberships is just enough to allow Nicky to put some hours of work in, next to her busy job. Unfortunately, her foreseen shift to a different career doesn't work out quite well and she is on the verge of a burn-out. In March 2012 Richard receives an offer from a web trader to buy Eco Fashion World. The team discusses this option, but feels opposed to it. What if they lose control over all the content on the site? What happens to all those years of unpaid work that have gone into the project? Then Rebecca proposes to buy the other partners out for the same amount offered by the trader. Her PhD on eco fashion management has come to an end and she envisages continuing her activities in this field. It only makes sense to retain the website and breathe new life into it. With renewed energy she aims to fundraise some investment capital for the website and establish contacts in Switzerland. The goal would be to transfer the business to where she lives, so that she can better manage it, and find partners to support it. Unfortunately, the fundraising keeps on being problematic as the website mainly serves a North American audience and Swiss investors are simply not interested. Geographical distance and virtuality turn out to be a big challenge again and make it impossible for Rebecca to give the venture the necessary push.

In December 2012 they receive another offer from a potential buyer with whom they start negotiations. Then their editor, Viviane, who has been running the website since June, proposes that she take over. She doesn't have the money to buy the partners out like the investor does, but she is passionate about the website and wants to take it to the next level. Her strength is that she is not only working with the current virtual team members, from founders, to writers, to technicians, but also has her local network of people in place. Based in Florida and surrounded by supportive family members and friends, she envisages creating a local hub of people working on the website. Her sister is ready to jump in as a marketing professional and a friend can offer to host the site for free. Within a few days, she and Rebecca come to a deal that enables Viviane to take over the business, with Rebecca staying on board as an investor and shareholder. In January 2013 the Ltd. in Canada is closed, the taxes are filed and Rebecca wires the respective shares to the other founders. While they part ways, Viviane starts a fresh team: a real one this time combined with virtual reality. A new chapter begins.

Key Take-aways

There are several lessons which can be drawn from the first four years that Eco Fashion World has been up and running.

Envision the Future

From the beginning there was a lack of vision for the company. The team started off with the wish to provide information and inspiration to a wide audience of people interested in eco fashion. This mission brought about a lot of energy, but sadly did not sustain when the economic objective became more important. Safeguarding finances could have maintained the zest necessary to live and work the vision. After almost five years of experience of developing and managing the website, Viviane (supported by Rebecca) should now develop a strong vision of what the future for Eco Fashion World should look like. She would need to craft a new story that strongly visualizes what lies ahead, and will draw new people into the business that will co-create this dream.

Don't Start from Scratch

Research on social enterprise shows the struggle of seeking a balance between the social and economic aspects of the venture. Eco Fashion World is no exception as financial resources have led to people becoming worn-out, as they had to keep their paid jobs to earn a living. If a certain amount of start-up money would have been secured at the very beginning, problems to sustain the different activities could have been avoided. The issue of controlling the sourcing of such investment was the global nature of the company. Registered in Canada with contributors and visitors from all over the world did not make it easy to find (business) partners. Geographical distance played a huge role for the team members and, held them back in pursuing investor relations. With no specific location and focus, possible investors felt that reality was too virtual to put their money where their mouth was. At the start of the next phase, it would be wise to seek local support to be able to grow to the next level. The advantage is that Viviane has now registered the website in Florida where she lives, and works and sustains her networks, thus making geography less of an issue. Finding, for example, a business angel will enable her to either work full-time herself or hire someone who can work full-time and boost the number of memberships. More hours devoted to marketing, collaborations, and membership relations will certainly increase the amount of income the site can generate and thus the sustainability of the venture.

Finding Equilibrium

One could argue that the Eco Fashion World core team was a loosely coupled network consisting of four individuals who were driven by a passion for the concept. They also managed to draw in most often unpaid external labour from people just as ardent. The work processes were very informal: based on their skillsets and interests they divided the tasks, and supported each other where necessary. These processes and tasks were not specified and written down as job descriptions, but rather discussed during team meetings and renegotiated when necessary (i.e. when changes were taking place; for example, when team member Linda stepped back). In addition, outcomes and concrete deadlines were not put on paper: team members all felt a certain responsibility for the multiple tasks that they had assigned to themselves in accordance with the others. One could say that this loose way of organizing work processes did not positively affect team performance. At certain times, members perceived a lack of skill and/or time that was actually put into the website. It was impossible to measure these things as everyone worked autonomously. This casual culture was on the one hand attractive as the different individuals were free to organize their own time. On the other hand, it was possibly too loose to function optimally: there was a lack of collaboration. According to Dustdar's Caramba model (2004), it is important to determine objectives for every team member in order for everyone to understand the: 'who?', 'what?', 'when?' and 'in which context?'. Ideally, the team leader should have access to the team members' progress statuses in order to be able to measure team performance.

It would be wise if Viviane designs work processes that guide the different individuals that contribute to the development of the website. The Caramba model could be a tool to help her define and show relative importance among the tasks and activities, work processes and team members. Such a 'mapping' of the organization would reveal best practices and 'rules', and can develop a sense of awareness of the various interrelations between activities and team members. An example is the recent creation of a Facebook group that allows writers from all over the world to continuously brainstorm about topics for articles. Instead of one directional communication between the editor and writers, this social network allows writers to meet each other online, and share their ideas and inspiration leading to exciting new content. Social media presence also strengthens positive perception of the company and in that way enhances team productivity. The marketing scan of the website in the fall of 2012 showed that the Eco Fashion World is already quite successful with inbound marketing, and the use of social media. Viviane can use the suggestions for improvement to intensify the social media presence and increase recognition of what the company contributes to the field of eco fashion.

Capitalize Talent

Over the years Eco Fashion World has been an appealing platform for people to be involved with. Several gifted writers have contributed to the website, but unfortunately have not stayed on board for long. The main reason was that their efforts could not be rewarded, only occasionally *in natura* with eco fashion products. Again, financial resources play a role as they help to keep talent within the team. Viviane should focus on finding the right people to move the business forward and appropriately recompense them for their contributions. Her advantage is the virtuality of the enterprise as it doesn't matter where these individuals live: as long as they have an Internet connection, they can connect to the mission and play their own role as a force that materializes that dream. In that sense, one could argue that the website brings together a variety of talented individuals that, despite their physical locations, each contribute to the higher performance of the team. Distance doesn't matter to a virtual team and can even be seen as a big advantage.

Building the Right Team

As Viviane is now the sole captain (with Rebecca as her sparring partner) it might be easier to navigate choices of which people to bring on board. Working as a team of four founding partners had many advantages in terms of dividing the work, but the group had been formed in a rather random way. Richard had basically brought together people who wanted to start the venture with him, not because they had certain skillsets necessary to build a successful venture. The heterogeneity within the team allowed everyone to do what they wanted to do, but they did not promote a real group identity. Maybe building such an identity would have been essential particularly because of the virtuality of the team. There certainly was a sense of belonging in that all team members felt great commitment to and responsibility for the website. Notably, its commitment to social and relational values remained until the very end. Even when the partners were tired and ready to sell the website, they favoured handing it over to Viviane (and Rebecca) instead of a foreign investor while he was offering double the amount. For them, the mission of the website was more important than the money they would make by selling-out. They believed Viviane could carry this mission forward and was thus meant to become the new person in the driving seat.

With the aim to take Eco Fashion World to the next level, it would do her good if she hires a finance person who helps her to make Eco Fashion World a viable business enterprise. She already works with an editor who is doing marketing-related activities and her sister can take on the role of marketer: aiming to increase the visibility of the website. Instead of relying on people who are not experienced in carrying out important tasks, she can set the skills criteria for new staff higher—which will likely lead to better outcomes. Whilst building her new team, it would make sense to properly introduce every new team member to the team, and clearly communicate what kind of profile and which skills that person brings to the team. When expectations are transparent and objectives are defined in a straightforward way, this will serve the development of trust building and cohesion within the team. It will also help to quickly integrate new team members, as an individual's main motivation to identify oneself with a group is self-enhancement and the reduction of uncertainty. It definitely makes sense if she can find these people closer to home to increase synergy instead of having to work with them again relying on virtual reality. Working from different time zones has proven beneficial in terms of how quickly things could be accomplished (e.g. Indian programmers could deliver as soon as Richard would wake up as they were doing their job during his 'night'). Nevertheless, to have face-to-face meetings once in a while can make a huge difference in the amount of motivation and dedication to the company.

Facilitating Workflow

Another way to capitalize on talents, aside from making them feel part of a community and proper payment, is to accommodate their desire for a balanced life. A virtual work environment can give enormous flexibility, but can also cause an inability to disconnect. It is all too easy after a busy workday in a paid job to go online and spend a few more hours ticking away. Or to simply not be able to draw borders between professional and private life, which can lead to burn-out. Especially entrepreneurs who are passionate about their (social) mission tend to forget about taking care of themselves. One could argue that this is a characteristic of enterprise in general, but specifically of virtual enterprise. Entrepreneurs often work around the clock and time differences (that are particularly common in virtual enterprises) only enhance the need to work a 24-hour day. For example, Rebecca and Linda usually had a full day of work behind them, when they would meet co-founders Richard and Nicky for a Skype meeting at 6pm. As the latter two were in Vancouver (a nine-hour time difference to Europe) they only started their workday at 9am. This negatively impacted on Linda's social life, as she was unable to meet with her friends in the evening. For Rebecca, it took precious time away from her, that could have been spent with her family.

Eco Fashion World is a fabulous playground for talent that doesn't want to, or simply can't confine itself to a 9–5 job scope. People can work on the website 24 hours a day, from wherever they are, no matter how much time they have. From previous experience, Viviane could inspire contributors to do what is right for them without over-doing it. She and her husband run several enterprises, and have just welcomed their first child, thus they have first-hand experience in balancing business and private life. They also know what it means to run a virtual business having built an online fashion store. As such, Viviane can accommodate others to manage a similar equilibrium, which will only enhance the workflow among team members.

Transforming Relations

It is expected that a stronger internal synergy among individuals involved in Eco Fashion World will have its impact on external forces. If Viviane can rely on a great team of unique contributors that generate quality content, it will attract more visitors to the website. This will make it easier to attract advertisers and new members that see the value of becoming involved with the company's website. It will also increase the chances of finding investors who are willing to support growth. With competition becoming tougher, it would do her good if Viviane positions the website more strongly as the most comprehensive and well-established resource on eco-fashion in the world. If she can convey her passion for the business to her new team, Eco Fashion World certainly has an excellent opportunity to transform into a virtual success.

Conclusions from the Authors

In summary, this case study offers an example of how virtuality can be fashioned in a social enterprise. We have learned that e-enterprises, whether they have social goals or not, need to have a clear vision and mission. In addition, e-enterprises just like virtual teams, require specific manage-ment processes to develop performance outcomes. We have seen that performance heavily relies on having a shared vision, internal and external relationships, creativity, trust, communication and collaboration, team dispersion (and cohesion), individual and group identity, recognition (e.g. through a social media presence and an interaction with 'customers') and on clear role assignment and goal-setting. The virtuality of Eco Fashion World and its social mission, increase the complexity of these management processes: sustainability is a real challenge. A consequence of the lack of management processes is that it is difficult to build social capital. To create team cohesion and team spirit, and to establish interpersonal relationships inside a virtual team requires a lot of attention. Strong awareness of the importance of social capital and creative approaches to enhance connec-tions among team members will increase efficient collaboration and team performance. Drawing in and keeping skilled people is crucial, and will become easier when these processes are specifically fashioned for virtuality.

Virtuality can be a playground for innovative working processes such as 'crowd-brainstorming'. It can facilitate capitalizing on talent and support a flexible lifestyle. At the same time, it can become a trap, as people tend to overstretch their working hours thereby infringing the balance between professional and private life. Virtual teaming can easily lead to personal isolation and consequently decrease the individual satisfaction, one of the essential factors in affective performance. Monitoring virtuality and its boundaries associated to passion is a crucial trigger in reaching successful outcomes of an e-social enterprise and, as a result, team member and customer satisfaction within a virtual environment. In the context of this book, we can conclude that even small virtual teams need to be managed, taking into account the specificities of working in virtual teams, including the context and the different personalities and skills of team members. The best practices, derived from the literature and taken as a guideline to analyse the case described in this chapter, can help small enterprises to critically reflect on how they can improve their performance and contribute to fashioning a more sustainable future. This case is interesting because it analyses some of the virtual team issues of a very small activity compared to a big company as, for example, in Case study 3, Thomson Reuters.

CASE STUDY 2 RESTRUCTURING INTRODUCES A NEW WAY OF WORKING: THE CASE OF EKS

Context

The company Eks is a family-run group, one of the six biggest companies in the world, and manufactures valves. It employs 2500 people located mainly in Europe and Asia, and has a turnover of 500 million euros consolidated. Eks is headquartered in Europe from where sales are organized, but the production operates in Shenzhen, China.

Six years ago, the company adopted a new strategic orientation with the aim to become a global player with more simple and rationalized structures for higher efficiency, flexibility and competitiveness. To support that strategy, Eks settled a lower-cost policy and reduced the number of production units, namely kept those operating with reduced labour costs. Eks decreased the capacity from 12 to four units. Each unit had to focus on specialties. In addition, Eks bought 100 per cent of Hydros' shares and merged. Both companies were formerly partially competitors, at least for some market segments.

Hydros, a German company, presented a more profitable position on the market and a larger network of production units distributed in 13 different facilities located in: Europe (11 units), Asia (one unit) and Africa (one unit). Employing the idea of simple structures and rationalization, Eks decided to close all Hydros' facilities, except the unit located in Shenzhen, China. The Shenzhen unit is 1000km away from the already extant Eks plant and completes the company's production range. Hydros' know-how and equipment were transferred to Eks, and its sales organization was consolidated to the different, pre-existing Eks' offices located in Europe and Asia.

Eks' structure was reduced on two main divisions: one in China and one in Europe. The Chinese division was composed of two units, one inherited from the merger. The European division centralized activities such as production, European logistics, invoicing for Europe and some overseas markets. However, these activities were not all located in the same area. Thus, 700km separated the invoicing department and the logistics centre. Sales management based in Europe covered 12 different sales offices situated in different countries. Five of them and four R&D offces were distributed throughout Europe, but had no senior manager to lead the division.

Distance appeared to be an issue that could become quickly a real difficulty, or even a barrier to efficient interactions. It could jeopardize Eks' expansion toward globalization. Shortly after the merger and restructuring, it appeared to top management that virtual work would be the answer to overcome distance, especially for sales and R&D departments. To support the activity expansion, globalization and distance, an ERP system, SAP, was implemented in all units.

The new organization and the new technologies affected the managers' area of operation. Before the change, each manager had to operate within the same unit. After the change, the managers' responsibility covered at least four different locations. Most of the managers were not used and not prepared to work on a wider activity zone that includes multicultural stakeholders. They were not prepared either to work within virtual teams. This situation led the employees to a feeling of isolation: due to distance and lack of both support and objectives.

Virtual Teams

Eks did not have a clear strategy when and how to deploy virtual teams. Eks used virtuality to adapt their working process to the new structure after the merger. Virtual teams offered the possibility to travel less and therefore to decrease travel costs. The company's leaders considered that collaboration among distant divisions or departments could be spontaneously created and developed through virtual connections.

The difficulty to integrate the new working environment was accentuated by the structural change. In fact, top managers wanted to control the change management process, and communicated information little by little to avoid any internal upheaval. Despite lowered information flow, some managers succeeded in keeping their team members motivated, and cooled-down rumours. Others could not prevent concerns and therefore retained a certain tension within their teams.

However, top management underestimated the need for preparation, discussion and communication about the new ways of working, including adoption of adequate behaviours. Top management did not consider the fact that virtual teams differ in key processes from co-located teams, mainly in the way they should be managed. The lack of preparation took place even in technical aspects. The IT system was not stable and not efficient enough to support virtual teaming.

In fact, developing the awareness of virtuality and its constraints would have been a great help for people involved in virtual teaming. Specific training would have encouraged people and improved competences, and personal skills such as autonomy, for instance. A lot of colleagues were not able to work independently in a virtual environment. Confronted with the lack of direct authority or hierarchy, they had problems to efficiently report working or relational issues. Some teams were also confronted with inexperienced leaders to virtual teaming, who became less motivated and did not master English well enough. They found themselves in an uncomfortable position.

The language barrier, computer-mediated tools and organizational change created a disturbing situation for individuals, generating sometimes resistance to the new managerial approach. For example, the Hydros working language used to be German. Then, the employees had to use English, which appeared to be difficult for some of them. English spoken by European and Chinese people might be hard to understand due to the accent differences, and thus lead to misunderstandings.

Feelings of frustration emerged amongst the employees. Even those showing a long working experience in the company could not recognize the initial values deployed by the group. They became destabilized and demotivated. They could not find anymore a sense to their current tasks and became lost in the virtual way of working. Until now highly committed, some colleagues left on sick leave, burnt-out, openly discriminated against and blamed Asian colleagues. This tumultuous situation, highlights the fact that change management, in general, and more precisely when it is implemented in virtuality, needs to be supported by top management. The human resource management function and technological infrastructure implementation are particularly concerned. Otherwise, the possible benefits of virtual teaming can be quickly reduced to a painful and expensive experience.

Virtual teams became permanent teams, and not temporary teams assigned to short-term tasks. All teams' activities were dependent upon each other but were not well-planned. Consequently, conflicts intensified between the European and Asian centres, and partly internally amongst the European teams. Instead, of creating a team mindset performing towards common goals and outcomes, top executives who are also the company leaders sometimes developed competition among teams. They did not consider the relevance of social and interpersonal relationships within virtual teams, and, among diverse virtual teams. Nevertheless, the social aspect is relevant because it is one way to bridge the different team players together. It happened that the lack of social binding led to a form of mistrust among the different stakeholders.

Working in virtual teams with new colleagues created unexpected challenges too, such as relationship building, coordination, mutual understanding, knowledge and know-how sharing, communication, and technology adaptation. In addition, no specific actions or managerial processes took into account that the new teams issued from the restructuring should also be integrated.

Therefore, the lack of attention regarding virtual teaming and individuals resulted in a leakage of know-how. Some talented colleagues left the company and competitors hired others. The integration issues were particularly critical due to cultural heterogeneity between Europe and Asia, this requiring specific management.

Rather soon, within that framework, difficulties of communication among departments emerged thus creating tension and conflicts. Those difficulties appeared to be more critical because they occurred in a continual change period generating bad moods among colleagues and misunderstandings, mainly due to a lack of managerial communication. The climate deteriorated generating individual dissatisfaction.

Focused on financial results, top managers underestimated or neglected the impact of a company's organizational support for virtual teaming. Virtual team leadership, a relevant factor for virtual team success, was almost non-existent. Virtual team leaders did not develop a collaborative team mindset or team common goals, and did not care about strategic communication. They did not assess the possible impacts. Consequently, some of the virtual teams were dismantled.

The impact not only affected internal organization but also on the external side, more critical for the company's image. Clients started to complain about a lowered quality of services, longer delivery times and product quality problems. The whole process cycle lengthened. Employees and clients could not accept the company's decision about transfer and offshoring of know-how to Asia.

Conclusions from the Authors

Eks had to face different major steps in the implementation of its strategy: company absorption, change management and a new way of working. The upheaval shook the whole organization at management, team and individual level. Surprisingly, the company leaders did not pay specific attention to the virtual environment and its constraints. They focused more on the financial aspects and neglected communication. Both, in addition to other factors, are necessary, though, to successfully perform change management within the virtual context.

The company leaders thought that virtual teaming through internal competition could solve problems. However, they ignored the necessary preparation for both virtual team managers and virtual team members, especially requisite in the company because working virtually was not a current practice. They also ignored the larger diversity that managers had to face from now on, with more demanding: technological infrastructure, multicultural and organizational practices.

Infrastructure was not ready: the IT system could not support the company's new requirements. This point is especially relevant during tough times, as it emphasizes the difficulties and dissatisfaction. Restructuring lasted too long a time and no official objectives were settled or communicated. People did not understand the final purpose of this important turmoil, even though some improvements could be remarkable. For example, colleagues issued from Hydros, joined Eks' organization bringing thus additional new expertise and new knowledge that could be shared. After a certain time, internal logistics flow improved and lead-time shortened.

However, organizational and multicultural complexity added to virtuality made all the organizational changes even more problematic. All of these elements lead to demotivation. The learning from that experience is that developing and adopting virtual teamwork requires strategic preparation including: training, technology deployment and people care, especially if it is implemented in a complex and changing situation.

Virtual teaming cannot solve organizational problems, if it is not well-managed. Executive management has to design an implementation program that points out the benefits and contributions that virtual teams bring to an organization.

CASE STUDY 3 HUMAN RESOURCES—A REAL FACILITATOR TO VIRTUAL TEAM (VT) MANAGEMENT: THE CASE OF THOMSON REUTERS

Pierre Rosius, HR Director at Thomson Reuters, agreed to explain the context and the challenges to which the group was confronted when implementing a new operating model across the whole Markets Division. He describes the model and the reasons why the group chose its implementation as well as the stakes the group faced at a global level. More precisely, he points out how Thomson Reuters addressed the impacts of such a change and how those challenges were tackled both with external customers and employees, whilst facing the implementation of virtual teams (VTs). When analysing the consequences of the new organization, Pierre Rosius measures the weight of 'real life' within such a change. Finally, he details the learning he retained from this experience, sharing with us his perception and practice as a local HR Director supporting the evolving structure. As a real facilitator involved in this change management, Pierre Rosius concludes by pointing out why the achieved results did not exactly match what the company intended to reach.

From Sales to Human Resources

Pierre Rosius graduated in 1983 from the ICN Business School in France in the sales management area. Soon after, he started his career as a sales manager at Sovac, a financing group lending equipment loans to companies. Then, he moved to Volvo France as a financial adviser in charge of the car dealer network in western France. Eager to get higher responsibilities at Volvo, Pierre Rosius was appointed to the position of Product Marketing leader. He focused on the French market and on the relationships with the Dutch and Swedish plants as far as procurement was concerned. After round ten years of valued professional experience, Pierre Rosius joined Reuters, a famous international news agency, headquartered in London. Reuters provided the latest intelligent information for businesses and professionals on various areas such as science, finance, medicine, media, accountability and legal domain. For 20 years, Pierre has been carrying on his career in charge of different relevant management jobs such as Director of Sales Administration, Key Account Manager and Global Project Manager. In 2008 matters took a new turn for Pierre Rosius and for the company. Reuters Group PLC was acquired by Thomson Corporation, a Canadian information provider, and became Thomson Reuters reaching thus the status of one of the leading information providers across the world. As for Pierre Rosius, 2008 offered him the opportunity to move his professional career towards human resources, an area for which he had genuine enthusiasm. Besides his job at Thomson Reuters, Pierre Rosius holds since 2006 an official mediator certification taken at the Faculté de Sciences Sociales et Economiques. His mediator position and his significant experiences as a practitioner and manager, as well as his involvement in diverse associations, were seen as a real asset to access the HR function. First, he took the position of HR Business Partner taking care of Sales and Clients Services employees, and then became HR Director of the French branch dealing with 400 employees.

Thomson Reuters

One of the leaders in the international professional information field, Thomson Reuters delivers an essential insight to its customers in the following sectors: Finance & Risk, Legal, Tax & Accounting, Intellectual Property Sciences and Media markets. The information provider combines industry expertise with innovative technology to deliver quickly and efficiently critical information to leading decision-makers in the concerned industries. Thus, professionals get the knowledge to act. Thomson Reuters operates as the world's most trusted news organization and hires round 60,000 employees across more than 100 countries.

The merger of 2008 enabled Thomson Reuters to access about one-third of the financial data market. It could directly compete with Bloomberg Group, considered as the leader specializing in financial data. Headquartered in New York, Thomson Reuters was reaching revenues approaching 12.5 billion dollars in 2011, with high performance from their Legal, Tax & Accounting, and Intellectual Property and Science businesses. Their shares were listed on the Toronto Stock Exchange (TSX: TRI) and the New York Stock Exchange (NYSE: TRI). In France, Thomson Reuters is implemented in Paris, Clichy and Puteaux La Defense, where, still in 2008, 500 employees worked for the Financial & Risk, Editorial, Intellectual Property Sciences and R&D areas. More than 80 of them were managers. Half of the managers lead teams, composed from ten to 20 members, spread over several countries, even sometimes over several continents. As a matter of fact, more than 50 per cent of the French employees were reporting to a manager based abroad, which showed the complexity of the organizational configuration. Based on this network, some dedicated local face-to-face front-line team members were dealing with clients and held different positions such as account managers, client trainers, markets sales specialists, sales administration and technical account managers. The organization was relying on local managers and one country representative. The local managers could hold the position of sales managers, client training team leaders or technical account managers. The country representative was heading a region, for instance, France that included also Benelux. Regarding the financial aspects, each country controlled its consolidated budget, including all businesses. P&L accounts referred to the country level as well. Only a few major clients were grouped into one 'global' department, the so-called Focus Group Accounts. This was the case, for instance, of the French global banks headquartered in France. Next to the acquisition, in 2009, Thomson Reuters decided to reshape the whole Sales and Client Service organization which belongs to the Markets Division. The centric idea focused on being better aligned to customers' needs and business.

New Operation Model

The decision for the implementation of a new operation model (NOM) took place in the context of globalization where investment banking, trading and professional investors were globalizing their businesses whilst acquiring higher specialization. It sounded naturally fair to Thomson Reuters to address the appropriate responses to those challenges through an adequate structure, pushed by a tight economical environment across the world. The change affected about 400 people worldwide, out of which 250 were in France. The NOM was planned to roll out roughly over 18 months between the kick-off and the completion due date in September 2010. As a result of this new model, the Sales and Client Service organization was split in to four business segments whose focus concentrated on customers' satisfaction. They consisted of Globals, then Major Accounts that are the top domestic customers ranked just after the Globals in terms of size and activities, and finally Trading and Investment. Four cross-segmented channels are created: Direct, dealing with the remote client management, Solution, taking care of the complex customized/mixed Sales and Client Service (including the Sales Administration) and the Client Technical Services. Each channel could serve any segment, which embedded NOM into a matrix system. On top of that organization, one senior site representative was appointed for legal purposes. He/she was usually the most experienced senior manager in the country who did not supervise any local managers. Those local managers reported to their business line i.e. channel or segment. Budget and P&L became virtualized and consolidated at least at the regional level, EMEA, US or Asia, which showed Thomson Reuters' willingness to centralize Finance. Countries only report on their costs and revenues.

Impacts of the Changes

The reconfiguration of the Sales and Client Service implied various impacts within the corporation, first at an individual level, then at an organizational structural level and HR level. At individual level, team members had to demonstrate the capacity to deal with the change requested by NOM. More specifically they had to adopt and get adapted to the recent transformation and to work within a matrix model that required new, deeper or additional skills. The new global teams had to be able to manage global customers who represented the most important clients. This type of task assumed a capacity to run negotiations at a global level and to report the revenue globally.

At the organizational level, Thomson Reuters gave a different dimension in the role and job distribution. Verticals replaced geographies. It meant that, from now on, the local face-to-face resources had to manage clients segmented per specific business or product range.

Practically, this required a move to sale generalists such as client trainers or markets sales into new roles, becoming thus client or sales specialists. Conversely, depending on the potential of local markets, a specialist may cover wider geographical areas to embrace the whole potential of a specific business across a region. This new 'vertical' organization implied a real specialization as per jobs, in responsibility and development of professional competencies. In addition to the job redistribution, Thomson Reuters set up some central organizations to remotely manage smaller clients and to develop online platforms to offer services for end-user training, called the 'Knowledge Network'. People who used to work locally had to eventually move into these central teams whose main centre was located in Geneva for Europe. Finally, the new scene of the organization towards clients got aligned with a Direct Network, remote teams dealing with customers, Globals, in charge of top-ranked customers, and more traditional face-to-face teams, but always spread over wide areas that could count with several countries.

At HR level, the observation was rather clear. There was an obvious need to raise the bar in professional skills which looked a must when it came to address the expert part of the business. Aware of the impact on individuals and the organizational structure, HR had to adapt its own strategy and work for the development of new reflexes, competencies embedded in the appropriate culture. Their support appeared to be essential in the efficiency of NOM in particular to overcome real challenges.

Main Challenges Fostered by the New Operation Model

Such transformations generated challenges for Thomson Reuters to ensure a full and efficient implementation of NOM in order to reach the expected performance. Those challenges concerned, in particular, the technical part of the business structure, HR sphere and technologies.

One of the first demanding tasks consisted of building up a solid customer base in each segment. The difficulty came from the fact that some clients were not so much segmented in their business, particularly in European markets. Therefore, the choice and selection of adequate criteria were critical. To approach as close as possible pertinent results, criteria were settled and reviewed with the countries' managers before the effective switch to NOM. Once the segmentation system was ready, the corporation had to adapt the internal processes to the new structure in order to finalize the whole work process. For instance, they adapted the reporting line changes and the authorization level redefined for the concerned managers in regards to the newly involved staff in the new-built organization. This process could not work without the support and the help of HR expertise.

To start with, HR mapped all of the impacted staff by the 'switch' date. In the case of Paris, the process concerned about 200 persons. Among the key issues, the essential effort concentrated on keeping the front-line staff engaged and focused on their daily tasks all along the process while 'losing' a minimum of people. Therefore, the internal communication policy was monitored in order to balance the information content, giving enough detailed information but not too much on sensitive points. As a result of efficient communication, indeed in France, few people left or were dismissed. However, pressure was aroused from the local constraints such as information, consultation and discussion with the local work councils. At the same time, the project had to be completed by the due date while avoiding too much gap in handovers within accounts, and minimizing customers' disruption. External communication appeared to be relevant as well, in the way that customers received the information on changes.

Human resources faced also another issue in terms of training because the transformation of the organization implied, as already mentioned, to 'raise the bar' as high as possible in terms of competencies. Training meant coaching and preparing the managers on new cultural and geographical challenges that they were facing. Beyond the need for stronger expertise due to the now-requested specialization, most of the new roles needed higher capability. Capabilities in flexibility and communication, in interpersonal competencies such as building relationships, personal organization and self-discipline to fulfil the constraints linked to virtual management. The reason lay in the fact that the involved managers were working in a more open and multicultural environment than before NOM. For that reason, HR deployed Global Virtual Team workshops, engaged in cross teamwork with basic guidance. The idea aimed to keep the dispersed teams functioning and achieve the success of NOM. The training process operated as per the following steps. First, it seemed relevant to explain and clarify the new roles required within the new operating model. Second, the different managers assessed all of the staff affected by the new roles, based on the overlap between old and new roles as well as regarding the identified skills. Consequently, resources were redeployed across geographies when required by the model. The distribution took also into account the fact that some small locations were closed. Of course, a regular communication supported the phases of structuring through quarterly newsletters from senior management. Third, the main challenge in NOM implementation was linked to technologies. The new model was highly reliant on technology: the importance of which increased as ever. In concrete terms, Thomson Reuters had to invest in a delivery network capacity such as a new Adobe reader including video, video conference, virtual presence and WebEx. WebEx is a web conferencing solution which allowed file combination and presentation sharing voice, video and new virtual meeting spaces. 'Meet anywhere, with anyone and get more done.' Investments meant also the acquisition of mobile devices for all people in order to support more flexible ways of working. Those people could then load APIs on their smart phones and became easily accessible and operational. The possibility to work at home turned into a reality. Investments were not over. The corporation had to enhance the central database and reporting capability through systems such as customer relationship management (CRM) and sales force tools associating thus transversal processes. Technology deployment did not seem to be a real problem among the staff, as far as technology adoption was concerned. The reason lied in the fact that the group was already largely immersed in new technologies. In spite of that immersion, some training sessions on communication technologies were organized to increase people's skills on technological 'know-how' when working with global virtual teams, as well as to intensify technological assimilation. This assimilation would help managers to carry this technological knowledge down to their team members. The ICTs facilitated here the work processes, the communication and virtuality, a nascent boundary within the development of the division. The technology difficulties arose more with the rigidity of the existing system and the coming procedures imposed by globalization. Those procedures were pretty much connected to the authorization matrix system and the reporting system. Since Thomson Reuters wanted to ensure the success of NOM, they engaged huge investments into new capabilities and technology.

Consequences of the New Operation Model

The implementation of such a new structure inside a division presented some consequences at both external and internal levels. First, of all for the clients, then for the managers, and their teams, eventually for HR that needed a response to them.

As a result of NOM, most of the customers got their usual contact changed at Thomson Reuters. They also had to understand the group's new organization: the networking approach implied by the fact that specialists intervened beyond the account manager, depending on the type of projects or opportunities. The main customer's contact remained though the account manager. But in some cases, their new account manager was based in a different country which meant that customers started a discussion with people whose culture and native language differed. One could note, however, that in financial markets most of the correspondences and meetings occurred in English which reduced the impact of different languages because the customers used to speak that international language. Finally, and surely more sensitively, many of the small- and mid-size customers experienced a much bigger change as they had to switch from face-to-face relationships within Thomson Reuters' teams to remote support pool or a dedicated contact named Direct Network. They became confronted with the virtual environment most probably without proper preparation. On the other hand, similarly to the customers, the managers had to grasp a new situation with direct reports and relationships across countries and from multiple cultures. Because most of them discovered remote management, they had to be supported to engage their team in a model which required higher autonomy, accountability and trust. Many of the new appointed managers, as well as the managers dealing with extended territories, started to travel. Their aim was to introduce themselves to all people who now reported to them. They also saw the importance of fostering team spirit and establishing interpersonal and social relationships as an incentive to enhance trust within their team. It became rapidly obvious though that most of subsequent management activities had to be handled remotely, for cost reasons but also to keep the effectiveness of the model. Culture looked relevant at this step and clearly interfered in the managerial process. Managing in a virtual mode was revealed to be much easier in Anglo-Saxon culture, e.g. USA, UK and the Nordic countries, in comparison to the Latin ones, e.g. France or Italy. In addition to the cultural diversity, the communication style appeared also to be sensitive with and among people who did not necessarily understand oral and written messages in the same way. The Latin people showed their preference for an implicit mode of communication where personal and face-to-face relationships played an important role, and therefore were less comfortable with virtual management. Managers had to develop a certain awareness about that aspect on culture and communication in order to adapt their own leadership style. Furthermore, higher pressures arose from a practical difficulty for some of the managers willing to keep a balance between their working and personal life. In fact, managing teams over countries required more travels to cover wider geographical areas. Accessible 'all the time, everywhere' increased the individual pressure, in addition to the research for an efficient personal organization interfering with diverse time zones.

Such challenges imposed by NOM pushed the business sponsors and HR to jointly create or develop several activities, not anymore to prepare the managers but to support them in their actions. In reality, the remote managers in the change process were facing from now on new boundaries. The business sponsors and HR offered them information packs on local social rules and labour regulations as support. Communication on the matter intensified through the promotion of the group's 'cultural wizard' website. The purpose of that website, whose access was delivered against an internal password, aimed to build a cultural and virtual intelligence. This 'Cultural Guide to the World'[1] intended to provide the 'essential information to help you to understand, work and succeed in this diverse world'.[2] The target was to create people's awareness on various boundaries linked to virtuality. To be more precise, they had to realize that working within a virtual environment meant dealing with diversity: in particular social and cultural diversities. For instance, authority, power distance and levels of responsibilities can differ from culture to culture. Each culture sees the world under its own angle and therefore acts accordingly, even though globalization pushes to standardization of the processes. The business sponsors and HR decided to set up 'Global Virtual Team Management' workshops for the concerned managers to provide them with the knowledge and tools to act efficiently in the virtual organization. The content of those workshops consisted of exposing managers to managerial processes with the aim of building essential relationships, maintaining engagement and managing performance. Thus, they offered the possibility to identify logistical skills to help managers to interact across time zones. They also proposed practical tips to run effective online meetings. The HR function considered as essential that their managers understood and felt at ease with critical elements of virtual processes such as engagement in new challenges and new ways of empowering people. The workshop programmes encompassed a sequence of modules. First, a proposed 'definition of a virtual team' and second, the explanation of the differences between 'traditional team skills' versus 'global virtual team skills'. The critical areas when leading or managing a virtual team were strengthened in order to 'get the most out of your team', the 'real life' challenges and advantages brought by virtual teams, including the cultural dimension 'how to cope and behave with cultural diversity'. Finally, practical exercises through test scenarios engaged the managers in questioning themselves on: 'What will you do if?', 'What is hard and why?' The workshops focused on how virtuality resonated to the managers versus their former more traditional professional experience, in order to create the awareness of new managerial behaviours and processes. The last module consisted of 'coaching mindset' programmes about the possible leadership styles, behaviours and the new forms of management. To be more precise, the managers were trained in the process of virtual delegation, and inspirational roles with the aim to inspire and lead their team to performing outcomes within virtual boundaries. In the same way, they learnt how to behave with initiative, decision-making and risk-taking. The main benefits expected by Thomson Reuters were to get managers aware of how to adjust themselves to virtual management. Most especially, they expected managers to know how to build trust in inter- and intra-teams with clients and staff, to use accurate and appropriate communication within a virtual context, and to adopt the specific technological know-how required to handle properly the updated tools.

Reality in the Virtual Context: Life Challenges and Advantages

If theory told the organization how to proceed, reality showed that turning it into practice entailed the emerging of some more-difficult-than-forecasted barriers, but also enabled the capture of advantages. To start with, guiding and motivating people was revealed to be a real challenge, but could open a wider framework and increased motivation levels. Developing a leadership adapted to virtual team management required high expertise to foster the appropriate behaviours from the concerned managers.

Reality rapidly 'jumped' into the model and programmes implementation. The staff had to quickly capture the newly designed organization: more 'focused' but also much more complex than the previous one. In fact, it appeared always challenging at a senior level to nurture a communication flow that timely addressed the progress of the whole project while managing also simultaneously individual concerns and expectations which necessarily arose sooner than later. As soon as you initiate such a major reshaping in an organizational structure, each individual suddenly focuses on their own personal case, and wonders how far the change will affect their own individual case. But many people rapidly realized some of the benefits of the change. They identified the possibility to move to more open and multicultural locations thanks to higher skills and business alignment beyond geographical considerations. They recognized the opportunity to access a wider diversity due to the composition of the teams opened to mixed people from multiple countries, cultures and languages. Generally, their level in English was raised too. The increasing globalization engaged many people to contribute beyond their personal boundaries, providing them with new fun in their work and finally higher individual satisfaction. The creation of central virtual teams though, named Direct Network and supposed to grow rapidly through the staff transfer from different locations, did not really work well. Mobility could not be easily manageable. Human resources were concerned by the fact that people fell in a situation where they could not find a new role. Critical in small locations, it happened in Luxemburg and Belgium or any locations where the local office closed as a result of restructuring. Their business got transferred to remote support teams settled in Monaco. In such a case, people had to consider moving to another location, which did not arouse enthusiasm.

The middle managers (as well as their own concerns) had to manage the expectations of their subordinates as part of the assessment and mapping exercise to the new roles. The main difficulties arose with the combination of team members' empowerment, and the management of difficult and tight situations, despite processes in place. Those processes aimed to lead the different teams to performing outcomes through 'objectives setting' online with the group strategy. The review of those objectives occurred regularly mid-year and at year-end. They were essential in team leadership but were not enough to empower people. Reality meant also that building up so many new teams within a 'big bang' switch really shook the organization both externally and internally. It disturbed the business, put on hold some corporate programmes and questioned the corporate values versus the latest priorities and constraints. The most critical step was in building trust and bridging the troubled processes within the matrix and a complex organization. Trust building required a certain level of stability in management and teams in order to become sustainable on the mid- and long-term. Reality was a bit different which increased the difficulty to reach a satisfied level of trust. Therefore, values on people appeared to be key features even though always challenging to feed while shaking the whole organization. Communication remained a significant lever which required higher accuracy from the remote managers in their communication process, and appeared challenging for some of them. Precise communications in a virtual context should become a source of efficiency and productivity by shortening online meetings, establishing rapid and efficient synthesis, reducing travel (and only not employing them when virtuality became a barrier). Reality reminded the group that moving to a 'new world' within an accurate timeframe implied unexpected barriers, even though theory and processes towards virtuality might be clear. Practice was more challenging. The lessons learnt from NOM were a mix of difficulties and benefits: virtuality did not seem too well associated to complexity, as pointed out by Thomson Reuters' clients. On top of that, it required appropriate managerial processes and could not skip a strict cost control.

Confronted also with increasingly higher complexities, the clients required from Thomson Reuters a local presence, essential for them in an industry that moved towards more complicated solutions also. The demanding financial markets as a result of globalization pushed to more regulations and segmentation. Finally, the effectiveness of NOM was questioned with regard to too much fragmentation. Some clients claimed that they could not understand the organization's way of operating. In addition, they had too many contacts within the group, which did not contribute to more clarity. Virtuality through remote management, dispersed teams and virtual organization originally sounded like an answer to globalization. However, according to Pierre Rosius, the virtual approach cannot fit to any situation without a prepared-on-purpose organization. The preparation in question includes organizational structure associated to various processes such as communication, knowledge, trust building, work process, technological and managerial processes. If globalization enabled best practices sharing and mutual learning from experience, it additionally necessitated a developed awareness of virtually. This awareness implied the capture of boundaries linked to virtuality that encompassed geographical and temporal, social and cultural as well as organizational diversities. Diversity appealed for specific processes more critical than for conventional team management.

Pierre Rosius could clearly note that managerial processes differed from the traditional ones. Team building and remote management remained much more difficult and sensitive in virtual world, even if wide efforts in communication were deployed. If the managerial processes were not monitored, the risk was to develop individualism, and balance adversely 'control' against 'positive influence', whereas theory requested rather a transformational or inspirational type of management. The team manager played in the latter case a role of mentor or facilitator. For many managers, it was additionally difficult to capture their team mindset and their readiness to collaborate, while keeping at the same time 'discipline' around regular online meetings, effective agenda and tasks completion.

Thomson Reuters learned also that virtual organization meant costs. The financial impact became an issue, specifically concerning travel expenses. In theory virtual management should reduce travel costs. But there were always requirements for traveling motivated by a tight commercial negotiation to close or a meeting expected to be uneasy with a team member. Because geographies were extended, the travel expenses became finally inflationist, so not going to the right direction. Finally, Thomson Reuters realized that they had to revisit NOM. The revision of the model aimed to give back more autonomy and responsiveness to the local level, and thus contribute to a most cost-effective structure. Apart from diverse difficulties, the company has gained considerable benefits from that experience that nobody wanted to lose. Above all, diversity became a reality across the teams who understood and grasped the various positive and performing elements. Diversity also supported creativity, and was a real incentive for challenge and innovation. This looked absolutely necessary in an environment pushed to reach always more innovative and competitive advantages. Nevertheless, it was difficult to evaluate the level of creativity obtained thanks to NOM. Several successes issued from NOM could be identified though, noticeably the design and implementation of global relevant solutions through global processes and procedures that eventually reached consistency. Likewise, knowledge, more precisely the transfer of knowledge, was clearly recognized as a key resource. Many new internal learning programs were developed for and during NOM. This knowledge has remained active and project management has continued to benefit from an increasing share of practices, avoiding thus 'to reinvent the wheel'.

Conclusion from the Authors

This story relates Pierre Rosius' perception of the NOM period of change. Thomson Reuters' senior management may likely see things a bit differently, according to their individual profile, experience and aspirations. Pierre Rosius can sum up the case through three major points, relevant to remember in such a global restructuring. First, there is no unique model. Any organization requires some fine-tuned balance between a global approach and a local initiative. For instance, global change means that the new model had to get adapted to some of Thomson Reuters' top global customers and at the same time had to leave room for local initiative. The purpose aims to take care of regional customs and local regulations but also to keep people engaged and motivated. Empowering staff comes as a second relevant point in Pierre Rosius' summing up. People empowerment requires a minimum of confidence in proximity management, which is the middle level of management, responsible for decision-making, budget, costs accountability and proactivity with clients. The first level of management plays an essential role not only to implement but to adapt a model to local realities and make it sustainable, which requires responsibility and power, both pillars of the necessary authority. Finally, the third point observed by Pierre Rosius, concerns the teams. The teams are the best way to address complexity and should remain the key component in any organizational model. In our complex world things cannot be done separately. Everybody needs a network of competences around him or her, a network in expertise, in communication and trust. So teams need to be at the heart of the organizational structure analysis, of the socio-emotional, technological and managerial processes. Team performance needs to be addressed as well, more specifically the team outcomes and the individual satisfaction. The approach to virtuality, as mentioned by Pierre Rosius, takes at this level its greatest relevance.

ENDNOTES

1. Available at: thomsonreuters.culturewizard.com (accessed 14 March 2016).
2. Available at: thomsonreuters.culturewizard.com (accessed 14 March 2016).

CASE STUDY 4   E-LEARNING—CHALLENGES AND OPPORTUNITIES: THE CASE OF CHLOÉ

Chloé is currently preparing a Master's degree in Teaching at the University of Quebec (Canada) at Trois-Rivières. Chloé has subscribed to a newly implemented online programme intending to virtually train and graduate students who aim to teach in middle schools at Quebec. Very keen on history, Chloé's objective is to succeed in receiving this Master's degree to be able to legally teach history, geography and civics in the area of Quebec. E-learning enables Chloé to study in her field of preference without bearing the constraints of distance, accommodation and transport costs, as she lives far away from the university.

E-learning, however, may request a different approach than traditional learning in class for students, and also for teachers. Chloé shares her experience and thoughts about that approach and virtual way of working.

The Learning Environment: Virtual Context and Adapted Equipment

Online teaching, online courses and distant collaboration constitute the context of the programme. Indeed, courses are provided through virtual classrooms where students who share the same courses are virtually grouped together via a web platform.

The university presents that online programme as a real opportunity for students to easily access interesting and dynamic courses at any time via an Internet connection. Classes occur at the end of the day, from 6:30pm to 9:30pm, to give higher flexibility of access to teachers who already work during the daytime and have enrolled on this programme in order to pass the exam, compulsory to teach in Quebec for ten years now. Students need to go to the university only once or twice per session, where they meet face-to-face teachers and other students of the same group. The university offers the possibility to take the exams in the area where the students live in dedicated facilities. Finally, very few face-to-face contacts link students with teachers but a professional team is available to assist students for their administrative and practical questions via Internet or phone connections. The idea is to compensate a possible feeling of 'loneliness' and to facilitate the approach to that virtual world. Student group size is limited too, there is 15 people maximum to constitute the group. That limit enables the teachers and participants to easily monitor connections and thus reduces the possible lost time for technical issues that may emerge within that virtual context.

Prerequisites constrain students to get the adapted technology and equipment. A computer that operates with Windows, Internet access with sufficient speed, computer screen with a certain resolution (1024×768 minimum) and web browser such as Google Chrome or Internet Explorer v.9, and software, e.g. Flash and Acrobat Reader. The university cannot ensure a complete compatibility with Mac computers. Therefore, students are considered as responsible for getting the correct computer and software to avoid any compatibility issues during exams. Teachers and students come into virtual contact, joining thus the same web platform through Via technology. Via, a worldwide Taiwanese corporation, provides advanced technological access to information, education, entertainment and commercial resources as well as cost-effective solutions to develop networking. Additional tools exist to create wider links among course materials, practices and relationships among students, such as a course portal, student portal, discussion forum, available videos, demonstrations, questionnaires and short tests.

First, Get Registered . . . via the Internet

First, students need to be registered through the student portal, accessing directly the homepage of the university website. There, they can fulfil all transactions requested by the administration such as course enrolment and payments. When their enrolment to a course is confirmed, the students receive by email the course planning and schedule. Starting from this point, the students have access to all documents necessary for the courses prepared by the teacher and available online. Thus, directly from their portal, students can get a syllabus of courses, PowerPoint presentations, video and website links, advised readings etc.

For each course, the students receive a Via invitation per mail in their university mailbox, where they are kindly requested to connect to the course platform. When connected, students select the concerned course and join a virtual classroom where they can see the teacher, each other participant and a white board.

Teachers present their courses and may accept filming of the course which students can later watch as many times as they want. It is really convenient to clarify some notions, especially when personal notes are not totally complete or clear enough, or to go deeper in a topic addressed in a virtual class.

In virtual class: many options exist and challenges too. Nearly every-thing is possible in our virtual classes, at least if we compare them to traditional face-to-face courses. Students can 'raise their hand' to ask question by clicking on a tab. The teacher can use the white board and each participant can simultaneously answer the question. The instructor can show the PowerPoint on the white board whilst asking the students to log on to a given website. It is not a problem for him to divide the group into subgroups and ask students to work together for a certain period. The teacher can even request a student to lead the group, for example, during oral individual presentations. The teacher can deactivate the students' camera but never the teacher's one. The diversity of possible options is really impressive. However, it requires from the teacher a high level of technical knowledge which all teachers do not have. Preparation to be able to monitor technical issues should be improved. Even though teachers get specific training, it might not be adequate, especially for the senior generation. I can remark from my experience that senior teachers encounter greater difficulties or questions related to those technical options, or show a less intuitive usage than students. I think that teachers should get efficient training to teach online and to monitor, reduce and hopefully avoid technical difficulties relating to the virtual environment. The lack of preparation and the fact that teachers are not trained in virtual technologies presents a serious issue in my case. For example, it is very likely to encounter noisy feedback in the communications, or breakdowns in connections, thus increasing the connection time before starting the course. Some participants may suddenly 'disappear' from the network during the class. We lose some time too when some teachers look for the adequate option among all the possibilities offered by the platform. As a matter of fact, the platform options do not usually create problems with students. As group leaders, teachers should give clear instructions from the very first course, providing details that facilitate virtual communication. For example, they should remind the students to mute their microphone or even to check beforehand the level of tone. It would avoid the painful repetitive: 'we can't hear you' and thus it would save time. Thus, clear instructions on how to run virtual meetings or classes could efficiently facilitate the teaching and learning process.

What about Virtual Pedagogy?

E-learning is not confronted to technical difficulties only but also to the way a course is taught in a virtual environment. I think that pedagogy or the way the course is taught should be adapted to the virtual context. According to my experience, the dynamism of online courses may rapidly decrease, which is intensified by the reduced contacts characterized by online courses. Some teachers, those who feel the most comfortable with the platform, propose workshops and various interactive activities which create social relationships between students and a learning climate. We better know each other, which encourages greater participation.

Some other teachers provide traditional lectures, interrupted sometimes by questions. Those courses appear to be long and boring, as they could be similarly also in traditional face-to-face course. However, the fact that we try to concentrate in front of a screen enhances this aspect. I even faced the case where a teacher was just reading her teaching notes which cannot be accepted in virtual conditions. The reason is that students' motivation decreases rapidly, especially if this way of teaching is often repeated.

I deduct that if students can feel isolated in front of their screen, teachers might show similar feelings, especially if they usually teach in face-to-face situations. Teaching in face-to-face situations offers frequent opportunities to see if students understand, think, are about to participate, or if they are bored. Thus, the teacher can adapt the course accordingly, which might become more challenging in virtual courses.

Distance Does Not Prevent Social Relationships

Once a semester and for each course, all students have to go to the University to physically attend the course. It is a real opportunity to meet teachers and other students of the same group face-to-face, and create or maintain social contacts. It is really pleasant.

In order to maintain or intensify social contacts within the group, a social network (Facebook) is available to foster communication among students and solve logistical questions. For example, it is one way to exchange our course notes, to agree on meeting dates on Skype or to arrange car-sharing. It is also an easy means to share personal and professional comments, share our work experience, discuss about education, recommend pertinent websites, and develop mutual aid in document research etc.

This student group is very pleasant and the social network reveals it to be an effective means to be closer with each other and know each other from a different angle since that social network is largely open. That network compensates easily the lack of social human relationships, even though it remains a virtual network.

What I've Learned from E-learning

Technological barriers, pedagogy in a virtual context, and a social web-based relationship with teammates illustrates my experience of e-learning, and has some real advantages. First, the time saved by *quasi* non-existent transport to university due to online courses, in addition to a diversity of tools and services such as the online library. From my home office, I access documents available in the university library database. The fact that teachers save and share documents and course contents offers the possibility to deeper analyse some of the topics.

Replacing physical distance by virtual access becomes very convenient and even more attractive when you need a long bicycle ride in the cold and rain to reach the university! Online courses offer the possibility to run other activities, to compensate for some health issues, and are one way to balance student life and private life, for those who are concerned. A higher number of students can also join educational programmes which they might not be able to do otherwise.

Conclusions from the Authors

From Chloé's experience, we understand that e-learning demonstrates very similar characteristics and issues as those encountered with virtual team management which implies a required infrastructure for virtuality, adapted technology and equipment, adequate behaviours and methods.

First, external infrastructure should be ready to link internal (university) and external (students) stakeholders. University infrastructure needs to have the capacity to provide information, a registration system, and an online database which requires anticipation in the university strategy regarding the development of its educational offer. This point is relevant as it represents a competitive advantage and differentiation in comparison to some other universities.

The internal process necessitates efficiency too, in order to sustain the competitive advantage and to provide high levels of education and service. Technology, a key factor in the process, needs to be available, efficient, understood, and adopted to run online courses within the planned timeframe. Students have to be aware that virtual leaning in this case requires adequate equipment: computer and software. Virtuality issues should be taken into account in order to bridge far-away students with the university services. The exposed situation is very similar to recommendations suggested to virtual team leaders and members. Stakeholders should learn how to e-learn or e-teach and adopt the adequate behaviours that facilitate distant teamworking. As for online meetings and virtual teaming, the process might not be a spontaneous way of working for both students and teachers. Reduced group size tends to limit the complexity of team management.

Chloé underlines that preparation to virtual teaching brings a real benefit when effective. Therefore, training to develop capacity to work virtually, to adopt the right behaviours and pedagogy for the virtual environment, and to raise awareness of virtuality boundaries remains essential. The exchange of best practices contributes to an improved performance as well as clear instructions that should be shared by all stakeholders.

We also note that the developed process uses different means to create a sense of presence, highlighted by some regular even though not frequent face-to-face meetings between students and teachers. The quality of technology and the way communication is delivered remains one of the main challenges in a virtual course, as long as the tools associated to that technology and communication run efficiently and serve virtual teamwork.

Finally, adaptation is required in terms of behaviours and pedagogy to get them aligned not only with the virtual mode of teaching but also with the expectations of the student generation. That young generation may require a highly interactive and animated course presentation which should be confirmed by further research.

References

Ackoff, R. L. (2010). From data to wisdom. *Journal of Applied Systems Analysis*, 16: 3–9.

Adler, T., Black, J. A. and Loveland, J. P. (2003). Complex systems: boundary-spanning training techniques. *Journal of European Industrial Training*, 27(2/3/4): 111–124.

Agrawal, N. M., Khatri, N. and Srinivasan, R. (2012). Managing growth: Human resource management challenges facing the Indian software industry. *Journal of World Business*, 47(2): 159–166.

Ahn, H. J., Lee, H. J., Cho, K. and Park, S. J. (2005). Utilizing knowledge context in virtual collaborative work. *Decision Support Systems*, 39(4): 563–582.

Ahuja, M. K. and Carley, K. M. (1998). Network structure in virtual organizations. *Organization Science*, 10(6): 741–757.

Ahuja, M. K., Galletta, D. F. and Carley, K. M. (2003). Individual centrality and performance in virtual R&D groups: An empirical study. *Management Science*, 49(1): 21–38.

Ahuja, M. K. and Galvin, J. E. (2003). Socialization in virtual groups. *Journal of Management*, 29(2): 161–185.

Aiken, M. and Vanjani, M. (1997). A comparison of synchronous and virtual legislative session groups faced with an idea generation task. *Information & Management*, 33(1): 25–31.

Al-Ani, B., Horspool, A. and Bligh, M. C. (2011). Collaborating with 'virtual strangers': Towards developing a framework for leadership in distributed teams. *Leadership*, 7(3): 219–249.

Alavi, M. and Tiwana, A. (2002). Knowledge integration in virtual teams: The potential role of kms. *Journal of the American Society for Information Science and Technology*, 53(12): 1029–1037.

Algesheimer, R., Dholakia, U. M. and Gurau, C. (2011). Virtual team performance in a highly competitive environment. *Group & Organization Management*, 36(2): 161–190.

Altschuller, S. and Benbunan-Fich, R. (2008). In search of trust for newly formed virtual disaster recovery teams. *International Journal of Technology, Policy and Management*, 8(4): 383–400.

Amant, K. S. and Zemliansky, P. (2008). *Handbook of research* on virtual workplaces and the new nature of business practices. IGI Global.

Amrit, C. and Van Hillegersberg, J. (2008). Detecting coordination problems in collaborative software development environments. *Information Systems Management*, 25(1): 57–70.

Anawati, D. and Craig, A. (2006). Behavioral adaptation within cross-cultural virtual teams. *IEEE Transactions on Professional Communication*, 49(1): 44–56.

Anderson, A. H., McEwan, R., Bal, J. and Carletta, J. (2007). Virtual team meetings: An analysis of communication and context. *Computers in Human Behavior*, 23(5): 2558–2580.

Andres, H. P. (2002). A comparison of face-to-face and virtual software development teams. *Team Performance Management*, 8(1/2): 39–48.

Andres, H. P. (2006). The impact of communication medium on virtual team group process. *Information Resources Management Journal (IRMJ)*, 19(2): 1–17.

Apgar, M. IV (1998). The alternative workplace: changing where and how people work. *Harvard Business Review*, 76(3): 121–136.

Arling, P. A. and Subramani, M. (2011). The effect of virtuality on individual network centrality and performance in on-going, distributed teams. *International Journal of Internet and Enterprise Management*, 7(4): 325–348.

Arnison, L. and Miller, P. (2002). Virtual teams: a virtue for the conventional team. *Journal of Workplace Learning*, 14(4): 166–173.

Ashforth, B. E. and Mael, F. (1989). Social identity theory and the organization. *Academy of Management Review*, 14(1): 20–39.

Atanasova, Y. and Senn, C. (2011). Global customer team design: dimensions, determinants, and performance outcomes. *Industrial Marketing Management*, 40(2): 278–289.

Au, Y. and Marks, A. (2012). Virtual teams are literally and metaphorically invisible: Forging identity in culturally diverse virtual teams. *Employee Relations*, 34(3): 271–287.

Avery, G. C. (2004). *Understanding leadership: Paradigms and cases*. Sage.

Avolio, B. J. and Kahai, S. S. (2003). Adding the 'e' to e-leadership: How it may impact your leadership. *Organizational Dynamics*, 31(4): 325–338.

Ayoko, O. B., Konrad, A. M. and Boyle, M. V. (2012). Online work: Managing conflict and emotions for performance in virtual teams. *European Management Journal*, 30(2): 156–174.

Babar, M. A., Kitchenham, B., Zhu, L., Gorton, I. and Jeffery, R. (2006). An empirical study of groupware support for distributed software architecture evaluation process. *Journal of Systems and Software*, 79(7): 912–925.

Badrinarayanan, V., Madhavaram, S. and Granot, E. (2011). Global virtual sales teams (GVSTS): A conceptual framework of the influence of intellectual and social capital on effectiveness. *Journal of Personal Selling and Sales Management*, 31(3): 311–324.

Bafoutsou, G. and Mentzas, G. (2002). Review and functional classification of collaborative systems. *International Journal of Information Management*, 22(4): 281–305.

Bailey, D. E., Leonardi, P. M. and Barley, S. R. (2012). The lure of the virtual. *Organization Science*, 23(5): 1485–1504.

Baïna, K., Charoy, F., Godart, C., Grigori, D., Hadri, S. E., Skaf, H., Akifuji, S., Sakaguchi, T., Seki, Y. and Yoshioka, M. (2004). Corvette: a cooperative workflow for virtual teams coordination. *International Journal of Networking and Virtual Organisations*, 2(3): 232–245.

Bajwa, D. S., Lewis, L. F., Pervan, G. and Lai, V. S. (2005). The adoption and use of collaboration information technologies: International comparisons. *Journal of Information Technology*, 20(2): 130–140.

Baker, G. (2002). The effects of synchronous collaborative technologies on decision making: A study of virtual teams. *Information Resources Management Journal (IRMJ)*, 15(4): 79–93.

Bal, J. and Foster, P. (2000). Managing the virtual team and controlling effectiveness. *International Journal of Production Research*, 38(17): 4019–4032.

Barczak, G. and McDonough, E. F. (2003). Leading global product development teams. *Research Technology Management*, 46(6): 14–18.

Barczak, G., McDonough, E. F. and Athanassiou, N. (2006). So you want to be a global project leader? *Research-Technology Management*, 49(3): 28–35.

Bartel-Radic, A. (2006). Intercultural learning in global teams. *Management International Review*, 46(6): 647–678.

Baskerville, R. and Nandhakumar, J. (2007). Activating and perpetuating virtual teams: Now that we're mobile, where do we go? *IEEE Transactions on Professional Communication*, 50(1): 17–34.

Bazarova, N., Walther, J. B. and McLeod, P. L. (2012). Minority influence and virtual groups: A comparison of four theories of minority influence. *Communication Research*, 39(3): 295–316.

Beise, C. M., Niederman, F. and Mattord, H. (2004). IT project managers' perceptions and use of virtual team technologies. *Information Resources Management Journal (IRMJ)*, 17(4): 73–88.

Bélanger, F. and Watson-Manheim, M. B. (2006). Virtual teams and multiple media: Structuring media use to attain strategic goals. *Group Decision and Negotiation*, 15(4): 299–321.

Bell, B. S. and Kozlowski, S. W. (2002). A typology of virtual teams implications for effective leadership. *Group & Organization Management*, 27(1): 14–49.

Beranek, P. M. and Martz, B. (2005). Making virtual teams more effective: improving relational links. *Team Performance Management*, 11(5/6): 200–213.

Bergenti, F., Poggi, A. and Somacher, M. (2002). A collaborative platform for fixed and mobile networks. *Communications of the ACM*, 45(11): 39–44.

Bergiel, B. J., Bergiel, E. B. and Balsmeier, P. W. (2006). The reality of virtual teams. In *Competition Forum*, Vol 4: 427. American Society for Competitiveness.

Berry, G. R. (2011). Enhancing effectiveness on virtual teams understanding why traditional team skills are insufficient. *Journal of Business Communication*, 48(2): 186–206.

Bertels, H. M., Kleinschmidt, E. J. and Koen, P. A. (2011). Communities of practice versus organizational climate: Which one matters more to dispersed collaboration in the front end of innovation? *Journal of Product Innovation Management*, 28(5): 757–772.

Bjørn, P. and Ngwenyama, O. (2009). Virtual team collaboration: building shared meaning, resolving breakdowns and creating translucence. *Information Systems Journal*, 19(3): 227–253.

Blaskovich, J. L. (2008). Exploring the effect of distance: an experimental investigation of virtual collaboration, social loafing, and group decisions. *Journal of Information Systems*, 22(1): 27–46.

Boddy, D., Boonstra, A. and Kennedy, G. (2005). *Managing information systems [electronic resource]: an organisational perspective*. Pearson Education.

Borenstein, N. S. (1996). Perils and pitfalls of practical cybercommerce. *Communications of the ACM*, 39(6): 36–44.

Bosch, O. and Zhang, Y. (2010). Does virtual team composition matter? Trait and problem-solving configuration effects on team performance. *Behaviour & Information Technology*, 29(4): 363–375.

Bosch-Sijtsema, P. (2007). The impact of individual expectations and expectation conflicts on virtual teams. *Group & Organization Management*, 32(3): 358–388.

Bosch-Sijtsema, P. M., Fruchter, R., Vartiainen, M. and Ruohomäki, V. (2011). A framework to analyze knowledge work in distributed teams. *Group & Organization Management*, 36(3): 275–307.

Bourhis, A., Dubé, L. and Jacob, R. (2005). The success of virtual communities of practice: The leadership factor. *The Electronic Journal of Knowledge Management*, 3(1): 23–34.

Boutellier, R., Gassmann, O., Macho, H. and Roux, M. (1998).

Management of dispersed product development teams: The role of information technologies. *R&D Management*, 28(1): 13–25.

Bradner, E., Mark, G. and Hertel, T. D. (2005). Team size and technology fit: Participation, awareness, and rapport in distributed teams. *IEEE Transactions on Professional Communication*, 48(1): 68–77.

Brahm, T. and Kunze, F. (2012). The role of trust climate in virtual teams. *Journal of Managerial Psychology*, 27(6): 595–614.

Bravo, C., Duque, R. and Gallardo, J. (2013). A groupware system to support collaborative programming: design and experiences. *The Journal of Systems and Software*, 86(7): 1759–1771.

Breitenöder, A. F. (2009). *Knowledge sharing in cross-cultural virtual teams: A study based on the grounded theory method*. Diplomica Verlag.

Breu, K. and Hemingway, C. J. (2004). Making organisations virtual: the hidden cost of distributed teams. *Journal of Information Technology*, 19(3): 191–202.

Brewer, P. (2008a). Cross-cultural transfer of knowledge: A special case anomaly. *Cross Cultural Management: An International Journal*, 15(2): 131–143.

Brewer, P. E. (2008b). Gains and losses in the rhetoric of virtual workplaces. *Handbook of research on virtual workplaces and the new nature of business practices*. IGI Global.

Britannica, E. (2013). *Encyclopedia Britannica Online*.

Brooks, N. (2006). Understanding IT outsourcing and its potential effects on IT workers and their environment. *Journal of Computer Information Systems*, 46(4): 46–53.

Brown, H. G., Poole, M. S., and Rodgers, T. L. (2004). Interpersonal traits, complementarity, and trust in virtual collaboration. *Journal of Management Information Systems*, 20(4): 115–138.

Brunelle, E. (2009). E-leadership. *Gestion*, 34(2): 10–20.

Buentello, O., Jung, J. and Sun, J. (2008). Exploring the casual relationships between organizational citizenship behavior, total quality management & performance. In *SWDSI Proceedings*, Decision Science Institute.

Burlea, A. S. (2007). The communication process in virtual teams. *Informatica Economica*, 11(1): 113–116.

Cahlik, T. (2000). Search for fundamental articles in economics. *Scientometrics*, 49(3): 389–402.

Cahlik, T. and Jirina, M. (2006). Law of cumulative advantages in the evolution of scientific fields. *Scientometrics*, 66(3): 441–449.

Caldwell, B. S., Palmer III, R. C. and Cuevas, H. M. (2008). Information alignment and task coordination in organizations: an 'information clutch' metaphor. *Information Systems Management*, 25(1): 33–44.

Callon, M., Courtial, J.-P. and Laville, F. (1991). Co-word analysis as a tool

for describing the network of interactions between basic and technological research: The case of polymer chemistry. *Scientometrics*, 22(1):
155–205.

Callon, M., Law, J. and Rip, A. (1986). *Mapping the dynamics of science
and technology*. Springer.

Cao, W., Xu, L., Liang, L. and Chaudhry, S. S. (2012). The impact of team
task and job engagement on the transfer of tacit knowledge in e-business
virtual teams. *Information Technology and Management*, 13(4): 333–340.

Carte, T. A., Chidambaram, L. and Becker, A. (2006). Emergent leadership in self-managed virtual teams. *Group Decision and Negotiation*,
15(4): 323–343.

Cascio, W. F. (2000). Managing a virtual workplace. *The Academy of
Management Executive*, 14(3): 81–90.

Chan, K. C. and Chung, L. M. (2002). Integrating process and project
management for multi-site software development. *Annals of software
engineering*, 14(1–4): 115–143.

Chang, H. (2012). The development of a learning community in an elearn-
ing environment. *International Journal of Pedagogies and Learning*, 7(2):
154–161.

Chang, H. H., Chuang, S.-S. and Chao, S. H. (2011). Determinants of
cultural adaptation, communication quality, and trust in virtual teams'
performance. *Total Quality Management*, 22(3): 305–329.

Chen, C. C., Wu, J., Ma, M. and Knight, M. B. (2011). Enhancing virtual
learning team performance: A leadership perspective. *Human Systems
Management*, 30(4): 215–228.

Cheng, C.-Y., Chua, R. Y., Morris, M. W. and Lee, L. (2012). Finding the
right mix: How the composition of self-managing multicultural teams'
cultural value orientation influences performance over time. *Journal of
Organizational Behavior*, 33(3): 389–411.

Cheshin, A., Rafaeli, A. and Bos, N. (2011). Anger and happiness in virtual
teams: Emotional influences of text and behavior on others' affect in
the absence of non-verbal cues. *Organizational Behavior and Human
Decision Processes*, 116(1): 2–16.

Chinowsky, P. S. and Rojas, E. M. (2003). Virtual teams: Guide to successful implementation. *Journal of Management in Engineering*, 19(3):
98–106.

Chudoba, K. M., Wynn, E., Lu, M. and Watson-Manheim, M. B. (2005).
How virtual are we? Measuring virtuality and understanding its impact
in a global organization. *Information Systems Journal*, 15(4): 279–306.

Coat, F. and Favier, M. (2000). *La réalité de la virtualité: Le cas des équipes
virtuelles*. CERAG, UMR, CNRS.

Cogburn, D. L. and Levinson, N. S. (2003). US–Africa virtual collaboration in globalization studies: Success factors for complex, cross-national learning teams. *International Studies Perspectives*, 4(1): 34–51.

Cogliser, C. C., Gardner, W. L., Gavin, M. B. and Broberg, J. C. (2012). Big five personality factors and leader emergence in virtual teams relationships with team trustworthiness, member performance contributions, and team performance. *Group & Organization Management*, 37(6): 752–784.

Cogliser, C. C., Gardner, W., Trank, C. Q., Gavin, M., Halbesleben, J. and Seers, A. (2013). Not all group exchange structures are created equal: effects of forms and levels of exchange on work outcomes in virtual teams. *Journal of Leadership & Organizational Studies*, 20(2): 242–251.

Cohen, S. G. and Bailey, D. E. (1997). What makes teams work: Group effectiveness research from the shop floor to the executive suite. *Journal of Management*, 23(3): 239–290.

Conkright, T. A. (2011). Improving performance and organization value through a virtual appreciative inquiry summit. *Performance Improvement*, 50(6): 31–37.

Connaughton, S. L. and Shuffler, M. (2007). Multinational and multicultural distributed teams: a review and future agenda. *Small Group Research*, 38(3): 387–412.

Conner, M. and Finnemore, P. (2003). Living in the new age: using collaborative digital technology to deliver health care improvement. *International Journal of Health Care Quality Assurance*, 16(2): 77–86.

Coppola, N. W., Hiltz, S. R. and Rotter, N. G. (2004). Building trust in virtual teams. *IEEE Transactions on Professional Communication*, 47(2): 95–104.

Cottrell, T. (2011). Great profits from great teams. *The Bottom Line: Managing Library Finances*, 24(4): 221–226.

Coulter, N., Monarch, I. and Konda, S. (1998). Software engineering as seen through its research literature: A study in co-word analysis. *Journal of the American Society for Information Science*, 49(13): 1206–1223.

Coulter, N., Monarch, I., Konda, S. and Carr, M. (1995). Ada and the evolution of software engineering. In *Proceedings of the Conference on TRI-Ada'95: Ada's role in global markets: solutions for a changing complex world*, 56–71. ACM.

Coulter, N., Monarch, I., Konda, S. and Carr, M. (1996). *An evolutionary perspective of software engineering research through co-word analysis*. Technical report, DTIC Document.

Cramton, C. D. (2001). The mutual knowledge problem and its consequences for dispersed collaboration. *Organization Science*, 12(3): 346–371.

Cramton, C. D. (2002). Finding common ground in dispersed collaboration. *Organizational Dynamics*, 30(4): 356–367.

Cramton, C. D. and Webber, S. S. (2005). Relationships among geographic dispersion, team processes, and effectiveness in software development work teams. *Journal of Business Research*, 58(6): 758–765.

Crespo, F. A., Pedamallu, C. S., Özdamar, L. and Weber, G. W. (2012). Contribution to the collaborative work in virtual organization – a case study. *Organizacija*, 45(5): 228–235.

Cummings, J. N. (2011). Geography is alive and well in virtual teams. *Communications of the ACM*, 54(8): 24–26.

Cummings, J. N. and Haas, M. R. (2012). So many teams, so little time: Time allocated matters in geographically dispersed teams. *Journal of Organizational Behavior*, 33(3): 316–341.

Curseu, P. L., Schalk, R., and Wessel, I. (2008). How do virtual teams process information? A literature review and implications for management. *Journal of Managerial Psychology*, 23(6): 628–652.

Daassi, M. and Favier, M. (2007). Le nouveau défi des équipes virtuelles: construire et maintenir une connaissance mutuelle. *Systèmes d'information et Management*, 3(12): 3, 30.

Daim, T. U., Ha, A., Reutiman, S., Hughes, B., Pathak, U., Bynum, W. and Bhatla, A. (2012). Exploring the communication breakdown in global virtual teams. *International Journal of Project Management*, 30(2): 199–212.

Daneshgar, F., Rabhi, F., Molli, P., Loria, F., Ray, P., Skaf-Molli, H. and Godart, C. (2004). Knowledge sharing infrastructure and methods for virtual enterprises. *E-collaborations and Virtual Organizations*, 1–28.

Davenport, T. H. and Pearlson, K. (1998). Two cheers for the virtual office. *Sloan Management Review*, 39: 51–66.

David, G. C., Chand, D., Newell, S., and Resende-Santos, J. (2008). Integrated collaboration across distributed sites: the perils of process and the promise of practice. *Journal of Information Technology*, 23(1): 44–54.

Davidow, W. H. and Malone, M. S. (1992). *The virtual corporation: Structuring and revitalizing the corporation for the 21st century.* HarperCollins Publishers.

Davidson, P. L. (2013). Why do many firms still miss the competitive advantage of virtual teams? In *Technology Management in the IT Driven Services (PICMET), 2013 Proceedings of PICMET*, 13: 1697–1708. IEEE.

Davis, D. D. (2004). The Tao of leadership in virtual teams. *Organizational Dynamics*, 33(1): 47–62.

Davison, R. and De Vreede, G.-J. (2001). Global applications of collaborative technology: Introduction. *Communications of the ACM*, 44(12): 68–70.

Davison, S. C. (1994). Creating a high performance international team. *Journal of Management Development*, 13(2): 81–90.

De Dreu, C. K. and Weingart, L. R. (2003). Task versus relationship conflict, team performance, and team member satisfaction: a meta-analysis. *Journal of Applied Psychology*, 88(4): 741–749.

de Jong, R., Schalk, R. and Curseu, P. L. (2008). Virtual communicating, conflicts and performance in teams. *Team Performance Management*, 14(7/8): 364–380.

De Leo, G., Goodman, K. S., Radici, E., Secrhist, S. R. and Mastaglio, T. W. (2011). Level of presence in team-building activities: Gaming component in virtual environments. *arXiv preprint arXiv: 1105.6020*.

De Lucia, A., Fasano, F., Scanniello, G. and Tortora, G. (2007). Enhancing collaborative synchronous UML modelling with fine-grained versioning of software artefacts. *Journal of Visual Languages & Computing*, 18(5): 492–503.

DeLuca, D. and Valacich, J. S. (2006). Virtual teams in and out of synchronicity. *Information Technology & People*, 19(4): 323–344.

Dennis, A. R., Fuller, R. M. and Valacich, J. S. (2008). Media, tasks, and communication processes: A theory of media synchronicity. *MIS Quarterly*, 32(3): 575–600.

Dennis, A. R., Robert, L. P., Curtis, A. M., Kowalczyk, S. T. and Hasty, B. K. (2012). Research note. Trust is in the eye of the beholder: A vignette study of post-event behavioral controls' effects on individual trust in virtual teams. *Information Systems Research*, 23(2): 546–558.

Denton, D. K. (2006). Using intranets to make virtual teams effective. *Team Performance Management*, 12(7/8): 253–257.

D'Eredita, M. A. and Chau, C. (2005). Coaching from afar: How ubiquitous information technology was used to develop a successful semi-virtual team. *Electronic Journal of Knowledge Management*, 3(2): 65–74.

DeRosa, D. (2009). Virtual success: The keys to effectiveness in leading from a distance. *Leadership in Action*, 28(6): 9–11.

DeRosa, D. (2011). Industry perspective: Collaborating from a distance. *International Journal of e-Collaboration (IJeC)*, 7(3): 43–54.

DeRosa, D. M., Smith, C. L. and Hantula, D. A. (2007). The medium matters: Mining the long-promised merit of group interaction in creative idea generation tasks in a meta-analysis of the electronic group brainstorming literature. *Computers in Human Behavior*, 23(3): 1549–1581.

DeSanctis, G., Wright, M. and Jiang, L. (2001). Building a global learning community. *Communications of the ACM*, 44(12): 80–82.

Dictionaries (2012). *The Oxford English Dictionary*. Available at: http://www.oxforddictionaries.com. (Accessed 17 March 2016.)

Dictionary (2000). *The American Heritage Dictionary of the English Language*. Houghton Mifflin Harcourt, Thumb Indexed edition.

Dictionary (2009). London: Collins, 2000, virtual.

Dictionary (2012a). Businessdictionary. Available at: http://www.britan nica.com/EBchecked/topic/551478/social-structure. (Accessed 17 March 2016.)

Dictionary (2012b). Longman English Dictionary Online. Available at: http://www.ldoceonline.com/. (Accessed 17 March 2016.)

Ding, Y., Chowdhury, G. G. and Foo, S. (2001). Bibliometric cartography of information retrieval research by using co-word analysis. *Information Processing & Management*, 37(6): 817–842.

DiStefano, J. J. and Maznevski, M. L. (2000). Creating value with diverse teams in global management. *Organizational Dynamics*, 29(1): 45–63.

Dixon, K. R. and Panteli, N. (2010). From virtual teams to virtuality in teams. *Human Relations*, 63(8): 1177–1197.

Doolen, T. L., Hacker, M. E. and Van Aken, E. M. (2003). The impact of organizational context on work team effectiveness: A study of production team. *IEEE Transactions on Engineering Management*, 50(3): 285–296.

Driskell, J. E., Hogan, R. and Salas, E. (1987). Personality and group performance. In *Group processes and intergroup relations*, 91–112. Sage.

Driskell, J. E., Radtke, P. H. and Salas, E. (2003). Virtual teams: Effects of technological mediation on team performance. *Group Dynamics: Theory, Research, and Practice*, 7(4): 297.

Duarte, D. and Snyder, N. (2001). *Mastering virtual teams*, 2nd edn. Wiley & Sons.

Duarte, D. and Snyder, N. (2006). *Mastering virtual teams: Strategies, tools, and technologies that succeed*. Jossey-Bass.

Dubé, L. and Paré, G. (2001). Global virtual teams. *Communications of the ACM*, 44(12): 71–73.

Dubé, L. and Robey, D. (2009). Surviving the paradoxes of virtual teamwork. *Information Systems Journal*, 19(1): 3–30.

Dubinskas, F. A. and Hargreaves, A. (1993). Virtual organizations: Computer conferencing and organizational design. *Journal of Organizational Computing and Electronic Commerce*, 3(4): 389–416.

Duffy, V. G. and Salvendy, G. (1997). Prediction of effectiveness of concurrent engineering in electronics manufacturing in the US. *Human Factors and Ergonomics in Manufacturing & Service Industries*, 7(4): 351–373.

DuFrene, D. D. and Lehman, C. M. (2010). *Building high-performance teams*. Cengage Learning.

Dustdar, S. (2004). Caramba: a process-aware collaboration system supporting ad hoc and collaborative processes in virtual teams. *Distributed and Parallel Databases*, 15(1): 45–66.

Ebrahim, N. A., Ahmed, S. and Taha, Z. (2009). Virtual teams: a literature review. *Australian Journal of Basic & Applied Sciences*, 3(3).

Edwards, A. A. and Wilson, J. R. (2004). *Implementing virtual teams: A guide to organizational and human factors*. Gower Publishing, Ltd.

Eissa, G., Fox, C., Webster, B. D. and Kim, J. (2012). A framework for leader effectiveness in virtual teams. *Journal of Leadership, Accountability and Ethics*, 9(2): 11–22.

El-Tayeh, A., Gil, N. and Freeman, J. (2008). A methodology to evaluate the usability of digital socialization in 'virtual' engineering design. *Research in Engineering Design*, 19(1): 29–45.

Ensley, M. D., Pearson, A. and Pearce, C. L. (2003). Top management team process, shared leadership, and new venture performance: a theoretical model and research agenda. *Human Resource Management Review*, 13(2): 329–346.

Eom, S. B. and Lee, C. K. (1999). Virtual teams: An information age opportunity for mobilizing hidden manpower. *SAM Advanced Management Journal*, 64: 12–15.

Espinosa, J. A. and Carmel, E. (2003). The impact of time separation on coordination in global software teams: a conceptual foundation. *Software Process: Improvement and Practice*, 8(4): 249–266.

Espinosa, J., Cummings, J. N. and Pickering, C. (2012). Time separation, coordination, and performance in technical teams. *IEEE Transactions on Engineering Management*, 59(1): 91–103.

Etienne, W., MacDermott, R. A. and Snyder, W. M. (2002). *Cultivating communities of practice: A guide to managing knowledge*. Harvard Business Press.

Farlex, I. (2013). *The free dictionary*. Available at: http://www.thefreedictionary.com/. (Accessed 17 March 2016.)

Favier, M. and Coat, F. (2002). L'influence des contextes organisationnels sur les équipes virtuelles. *Revue de gestion des ressources humaines*, 44: 44–62.

Feghali, T. and El-Den, J. (2008). Knowledge transformation among virtually-cooperating group members. *Journal of Knowledge Management*, 12(1): 92–105.

Ferreira, P. G. S., de Lima, E. P. and da Costa, S. E. G. (2012a). Developing a methodology for assessing virtual teams' performance perception. *International Journal of Productivity and Performance Management*, 61(7): 710–729.

Ferreira, P. G. S., de Lima, E. P. and da Costa, S. E. G. (2012b). Perception of virtual team's performance: A multinational exercise. *International Journal of Production Economics*.

Ferris, S. P. and Godar, S. H. (2006). *Teaching and learning with virtual teams*. Information Science Publishing.

Ferris, S. P. and Minielli, M. C. (2004). Technology and virtual teams. *Virtual and Collaborative Teams*, 193.

Fiol, C. M. and O'Connor, E. J. (2005). Identification in face-to-face, hybrid, and pure virtual teams: Untangling the contradictions. *Organization Science*, 16(1): 19–32.

Fiore, S. M., McDaniel, R. and Jentsch, F. (2009). Narrative-based collaboration systems for distributed teams: Nine research questions for information managers. *Information Systems Management*, 26(1): 28–38.

Flammia, M., Cleary, Y. and Slattery, D. M. (2010). Leadership roles, socioemotional communication strategies, and technology use of Irish and US students in virtual teams. *IEEE Transactions on Professional Communication*, 53(2): 89–101.

Flanagan, T. A. and Runde, C. E. (2008). Hidden potential: Embracing conflict can pay off for teams. *Leadership in Action*, 28(2): 8–12.

Fong, M. W. (2005). *E-collaborations and virtual organizations*. IGI Global.

Fontaine, G. (2002). Teams in Teleland: working effectively in geographically dispersed teams in the Asia Pacific. *Team Performance Management*, 8(5/6): 122–133.

Forgie, J. (2011). Working effectively in a matrix: Building and sustaining cooperation. *International Journal of E-Collaboration*, 61–70.

Franssila, H., Okkonen, J., Savolainen, R. and Talja, S. (2012). The formation of coordinative knowledge practices in distributed work: towards an explanatory model. *Journal of Knowledge Management*, 16(4): 650–665.

Friedman, J. P. (2000). *Dictionary of Business Terms*. Barron's Educational Series, Inc.

Friedman, R. and Currall, S. (2002). E-mail escalation: Dispute exacerbating elements of electronic communication. In *IACM 15th Annual Conference*.

Friedman, T. (2005). *The world is flat*. Farrar, Straus and Giroux.

Furst, S., Blackburn, R. and Rosen, B. (1999). Virtual team effectiveness: a proposed research agenda. *Information Systems Journal*, 9(4): 249–269.

Furumo, K. and Pearson, J. M. (2006). An empirical investigation of how trust, cohesion, and performance vary in virtual and face-to-face teams. In *System Sciences, 2006. HICSS'06. Proceedings of the 39th Annual Hawaii International Conference on*, Vol 1: 26c. IEEE.

Furumo, K., de Pillis, E. and Green, D. (2009). Personality influences trust differently in virtual and face-to-face teams. *International Journal of Human Resources Development and Management*, 9(1): 36–58.

Gaan, N. (2012). Collaborative tools and virtual team effectiveness: an inductively derived approach in India's software sector. *Decision*, 39(1): 5–27.

Gajendran, R. S. and Joshi, A. (2012). Innovation in globally distributed teams: The role of LMX, communication frequency, and member influence on team decisions. *Journal of Applied Psychology*, 97(6): 1252.

Gareis, E. (2006). Virtual teams: A comparison of online communication channels. *Journal of Language for International Business*, 17(2): 6.

Gassmann, O. and Zedtwitz, M. (2003). Trends and determinants of managing virtual R&D teams. *R&D Management*, 33(3): 243–262.

Gerke, S. K. (2006). If I cannot see them, how can I lead them? *Industrial and Commercial Training*, 38(2): 102–105.

Germain, M.-L. (2011). Developing trust in virtual teams. *Performance Improvement Quarterly*, 24(3): 29–54.

Gibson, C. B. and Cohen, S. G. (2003). *Virtual teams that work: Creating conditions for virtual team effectiveness*. Wiley.com.

Gibson, C. B. and Gibbs, J. L. (2006). Unpacking the concept of virtuality: The effects of geographic dispersion, electronic dependence, dynamic structure, and national diversity on team innovation. *Administrative Science Quarterly*, 51(3): 451–495.

Gignac, F. (2005). *Building successful virtual teams*. Artech House.

Gillam, C. and Oppenheim, C. (2006). Review article: Reviewing the impact of virtual teams in the information age. *Journal of Information Science*, 32(2): 160–175.

Giuffrida, R. and Dittrich, Y. (2013). Empirical studies on the use of social software in global software development – a systematic mapping study. *Information and Software Technology*, 55(7): 1143–1164.

Glückler, J. and Schrott, G. (2007). Leadership and performance in virtual teams: Exploring brokerage in electronic communication. *International Journal of e-Collaboration (IJeC)*, 3(3): 31–52.

Gluesing, J., Alcordo, T., Baba, M., Britt, D., Wagner, K. H., McKether, W., Monplaisir, L., Ratner, H. and Riopelle, K. (2003). The development of global virtual teams. *Creating conditions for effective virtual teams*, 353–380.

Goel, L., Junglas, I., Ives, B. and Johnson, N. (2012). Decision-making *in socio* and *in situ*: Facilitation in virtual worlds. *Decision Support Systems*, 52(2): 342–352.

Graham, A. (1995). Collaborating virtually in the global workplace: practical ideas to measure your global team effectiveness. *Home page online*. Available at: http://www.linkageinc.com/thinking/linkageleader/Documents/AndrewGrahamCollaborating

Grant, R. M. (1996). Toward a knowledge-based theory of the firm. *Strategic Management Journal*, 17: 109–122.

Greenberg, P. S., Greenberg, R. H., and Antonucci, Y. L. (2007). Creating and sustaining trust in virtual teams. *Business Horizons*, 50(4): 325–333.

Gressgard, L. J. (2011). Virtual team collaboration and innovation in organizations. *Team Performance Management*, 17(1/2): 102–119.

Griffith, T. L., Meader, D., and Pauleen, D. (2004). *Prelude to virtual groups: Leadership and technology in semi-virtual groups*. IGI Global.

Griffith, T. L. and Neale, M. A. (2001). Information processing in traditional, hybrid, and virtual teams: From nascent knowledge to transactive memory. *Research in Organizational Behavior*, 23: 379–421.

Griffith, T. L., Sawyer, J. E. and Neale, M. A. (2003). Virtualness and knowledge in teams: Managing the love triangle of organizations, individuals, and information technology. *MIS Quarterly*, 265–287.

Grosse, C. U. (2010). Global corporate virtual teams. *Virtual Teamwork*, 193.

Grundy, J. and Ginger, J. (1998). Global teams for the millennium. *Management Decision*, 36(1): 31–33.

Gupta, A., Crk, I. and Bondade, R. (2011). Leveraging temporal and spatial separations with the 24-hour knowledge factory paradigm. *Information Systems Frontiers*, 13(3): 397–405.

Gurtner, A., Kolbe, M. and Boos, M. (2007). Satisfaction in virtual teams in organizations. *The Electronic Journal for Virtual Organizations and Networks*, 9: 9–29.

Haas, M. R. (2006). Acquiring and applying knowledge in transnational teams: The roles of cosmopolitans and locals. *Organization Science*, 17(3): 367–384.

Hagen, M. R. (1999). Teams expand into cyberspace: creating, leading and learning from virtual teams. *Quality Progress*, 32(6): 90–93.

Hakonen, M. and Lipponen, J. (2007). Antecedents and consequences of identification with virtual teams: Structural characteristics and justice concerns. *The Journal of E-working*, 1: 137–153.

Hambley, L. A., O'Neill, T. A. and Kline, T. J. (2007). Virtual team leadership: The effects of leadership style and communication medium on team interaction styles and outcomes. *Organizational Behavior and Human Decision Processes*, 103(1): 1–20.

Hammond, J., Koubek, R. J. and Harvey, C. M. (2001). Distributed collaboration for engineering design: a review and reappraisal. *Human Factors and Ergonomics in Manufacturing*, 11(1): 35–52.

Handy, C. (1995). Trust and the virtual organization. *Harvard Business Review*, 73(3): 40–48.

Hanisch, B., Lindner, F., Mueller, A. and Wald, A. (2009). Knowledge management in project environments. *Journal of Knowledge Management*, 13(4): 148–160.

Hardin, A. M., Fuller, M. A. and Davison, R. M. (2007). I know I can, but can we? Culture and efficacy beliefs in global virtual teams. *Small Group Research*, 38(1): 130–155.

Harvey, M., Novicevic, M. M. and Garrison, G. (2005). Global virtual teams: a human resource capital architecture. *The International Journal of Human Resource Management*, 16(9): 1583–1599.

Harvey, M. G. and Griffith, D. A. (2007). The role of globalization, time acceleration, and virtual global teams in fostering successful global product launches. *Journal of Product Innovation Management*, 24(5): 486–501.

Hassan, E. (2005). The evolution of the knowledge structure of fuel cells. *Scientometrics*, 62(2): 223–238.

Henry, J. E. and Hartzler, M. (1997). Virtual teams: Today's reality, today's challenge. *Quality Progress*, 30(5): 108–109.

Henttonen, K. and Blomqvist, K. (2005). Managing distance in a global virtual team: the evolution of trust through technology-mediated relational communication. *Strategic Change*, 14(2): 107–119.

Hernandez, J. M. D. C. and Santos, C. C. D. (2010). Development based trust: Proposing and validating a new trust measurement model for buyer-seller relationships. *BAR: Brazilian Administration Review*, 7(2): 172–197.

Hertel, G., Geister, S. and Konradt, U. (2005). Managing virtual teams: A review of current empirical research. *Human Resource Management Review*, 15(1): 69–95.

Hertel, G., Konradt, U. and Voss, K. (2006). Competencies for virtual teamwork: Development and validation of a web-based selection tool for members of distributed teams. *European Journal of Work and Organizational Psychology*, 15(4): 477–504.

Hinds, P. J. and Bailey, D. E. (2003). Out of sight, out of sync: Understanding conflict in distributed teams. *Organization Science*, 14(6): 615–632.

Hinds, P. J. and Mortensen, M. (2005). Understanding conflict in geographically distributed teams: The moderating effects of shared identity, shared context, and spontaneous communication. *Organization Science*, 16(3): 290–307.

Hoefling, T. (2003). *Working virtually: managing people for successful virtual teams and organizations*. Stylus Pub Llc.

Hoefling, T. (2008). The three-fold path of expanding emotional bandwidth in virtual teams. In *The handbook of high performance virtual teams: A toolkit for collaborating across boundaries*, 87. IGI Global.

Hoegl, M., Ernst, H. and Proserpio, L. (2007). How teamwork matters more as team member dispersion increases. *Journal of Product Innovation Management*, 24(2): 156–165.

Hofstede, G. (1980). *Culture's consequences: Comparing values, behaviors, institutions and organizations across nations*. Sage.

Hofstede, G., Hofstede, G. J. and Minkov, M. (1991). *Cultures and organizations: Software of the mind*, Vol 2. McGraw-Hill.

Hong, J. F. and Vai, S. (2008). Knowledge-sharing in cross-functional virtual teams. *Journal of General Management*, 34(2): 21–37.

Horvath, I. and Rusak, Z. (2001). Collaborative shape conceptualization in virtual design environments. *Communications of the ACM*, 44(12): 59–63.

Horwitz, F. M., Bravington, D. and Silvis, U. (2006). The promise of virtual teams: identifying key factors in effectiveness and failure. *Journal of European Industrial Training*, 30(6): 472–494.

Hosmer, L. T. (1995). Trust: The connecting link between organizational theory and philosophical ethics. *Academy of Management Review*, 20(2): 379–403.

Houck, C. (2011). Multigenerational and virtual: How do we build a mentoring program for today's workforce? *Performance Improvement*, 50(2): 25–30.

Howard, G. (1983). Frames of mind: The theory of multiple intelligences. *NY: Basics*.

Hunsaker, P. L. and Hunsaker, J. S. (2008). Virtual teams: a leader's guide. *Team Performance Management*, 14(1/2): 86–101.

Iandoli, L., Quinto, I., De Liddo, A. and Shum, S. B. (2012). A debate dashboard to enhance online knowledge sharing. *VINE*, 42(1): 67–93.

Iles, P. and Feng, Y. (2011). Distributed leadership, knowledge and information management and team performance in Chinese and Western groups. *Journal of Technology Management in China*, 6(1): 26–42.

Im, H.-G., Yates, J. and Orlikowski, W. (2005). Temporal coordination through communication: using genres in a virtual start-up organization. *Information Technology & People*, 18(2): 89–119.

Ismail, A. M., Reza, R. and Mahdi, S. (2012). Analysis of the relationship between cultural intelligence and transformational leadership (the case of managers at the trade office). *International Journal of Business and Social Science*, 3(14): 252–261.

Jain, V. and Singh, R. (2013). A framework to study level of comfort between employees of local and foreign cultures in multinational firms. *International Journal of Business and Management*, 8(4): 104.

James, M. and Ward, K. (2001). Leading a multinational team of change agents at Glaxo Wellcome (now Glaxo Smithkline). *Journal of Change Management*, 2(2): 148–159.

Jan, K., Leenders, R.A.J. and van Engelen, J. M. (2005). Keeping virtual R&D teams creative. *Research-Technology Management*, 48(2): 13–16.

Jarman, R. (2005). When success isn't everything – case studies of two virtual teams. *Group Decision and Negotiation*, 14(4): 333–354.

Jarvenpaa, S. L. and Ives, B. (1994). The global network organization of the future: Information management opportunities and challenges. *Journal of Management Information Systems*, 10(4): 25–57.

Jarvenpaa, S. L. and Keating, E. (2011). Hallowed grounds: the role of cultural values, practices, and institutions in TMS in an offshored complex engineering services project. *IEEE Transactions on Engineering Management*, 58(4): 786–798.

Jarvenpaa, S. L., Knoll, K. and Leidner, D. E. (1998). Is anybody out there? Antecedents of trust in global virtual teams. *Journal of Management Information Systems*, 4(4): 29–64.

Jarvenpaa, S. L. and Leidner, D. E. (1999). Communication and trust in global virtual teams. *Organization of Science*, 10(6): 791–815.

Jarvenpaa, S. L., Shaw, T. R., and Staples, D. S. (2004). Toward contextualized theories of trust: The role of trust in global virtual teams. *Information Systems Research*, 15(3): 250–267.

Jawadi, N. and Boukef Charki, N. (2011). Niveaux de virtualité et performance des équipes: Proposition d'une approche multidimensionnelle d'évaluation. *Systèmes d'Information & Management*, 16(4): 37–72.

Jawecki, G., Füller, J. and Gebauer, J. (2011). A comparison of creative behaviours in online communities across cultures. *Creativity and Innovation Management*, 20(3): 144–156.

Jessup, L. M. and Robey, D. (2002). The relevance of social issues in ubiquitous computing environments. *Communications of the ACM*, 45(12): 88–91.

Johnson, P., Heimann, V. and O'Neill, K. (2001). The 'wonderland' of virtual teams. *Journal of Workplace Learning*, 13(1): 24–30.

Jones, B. L., Cramton, C. D., Gauvin, S. and Scott, D. (1999). Virtual learning environment: preparing for the knowledge age work in the 21st century. *Decision Line*, 3–6.

Joshi, A., Labianca, G. and Caligiuri, P. M. (2003). Getting along long distance: Understanding conflict in a multinational team through network analysis. *Journal of World Business*, 37(4): 277–284.

Joshi, A., Lazarova, M. B. and Liao, H. (2009). Getting everyone on board: The role of inspirational leadership in geographically dispersed teams. *Organization Science*, 20(1): 240–252.

Joy-Matthews, J. and Gladstone, B. (2000). Extending the group: A strategy for virtual team formation. *Industrial and Commercial Training*, 32(1): 24–29.

Kahai, S. S., Huang, R. and Jestice, R. J. (2012). Interaction effect of leadership and communication media on feedback positivity in virtual teams. *Group & Organization Management*, 37(6): 716–751.

Kahn, A. and Ahmad, W. (2012). Leader's interpersonal skills and its effectiveness at different levels of management. *International Journal of Business and Social Science*, 3(4): 290–299.

Kankanhalli, A., Tan, B. C. and Wei, K. K. (2007). Conflict and performance in global virtual teams. *Journal of Management Information Systems*, 23(3): 237–274.

Kaplan, R., Kaplan, R. S. and Norton, D. P. (1996). *The balanced scorecard: translating strategy into action*. Harvard Business Press.

Karayaz, G. (2006). *A dyadic composition to foster virtual team effectiveness: An experimental study*, Vol 67. Old Dominion University.

Karayaz, G. (2008). Utilizing knowledge management for effective virtual teams. *The Business Review, Cambridge*, 10(1): 294–300.

Katzenbach, J. R. and Smith, D. K. (1992). *The wisdom of teams: Creating the high-performance organization*. Harvard Business Press.

Kauppila, O. P., Rajala, R. and Jyrämä, A. (2011). Knowledge sharing through virtual teams across borders and boundaries. *Management Learning*, 42(4): 395–418.

Kayworth, T. R. and Leidner, D. E. (2002). Leadership effectiveness in global virtual teams. *Journal of Management Information Systems*, 18(3): 7–40.

Khan, A. and Woosley, J. (2012). Global knowledge management (KM) strategies and the challenges across boundaries. *International Journal of Business and Social Science*, 3(4): 110.

Kimball, L. (1997). Managing virtual teams. In text of speech given at Team Strategies Conference, sponsored by Federated Press, Toronto, Canada.

King, C. (2007). Building trust in global virtual teams: An innovative training model. *Training and Management Development Methods*, 21(3): 315–320.

Kirkman, B. L. and Mathieu, J. E. (2005). The dimensions and antecedents of team virtuality. *Journal of Management*, 31(5): 700–718.

Kirkman, B. L., Rosen, B., Gibson, C. B., Tesluk, P. E. and McPherson, S. O. (2002). Five challenges to virtual team success: lessons from Sabre, Inc. *The Academy of Management Executive*, 16(3): 67–79.

Kirkman, B. L., Rosen, B., Tesluk, P. E. and Gibson, C. B. (2004). The impact of team empowerment on virtual team performance: The moderating role of face-to-face interaction. *Academy of Management Journal*, 47(2): 175–192.

Klein, J., Kleinhanns, A., Gibson, C. and Cohen, S. (2003). Closing the time gap in virtual teams. *Creating conditions for effective virtual teams*, 381–399.

Klimkeit, D. (2013). Organizational context and collaboration on international projects: The case of a professional service firm. *International Journal of Project Management*, 31(3): 366–377.

Ko, K. K., To, C. K., Zhang, Z., Ngai, E. W. and Chan, T. L. (2011). Analytic collaboration in virtual innovation projects. *Journal of Business Research*, 64(12): 1327–1334.

Kock, N. F. (2009). *Virtual Team Leadership and Collaborative Engineering Advancements: Contemporary Issues and Implications*. Information Science Reference.

Konradt, U. and Hoch, J. E. (2007). A work roles and leadership functions of managers in virtual teams. *International Journal of e-Collaboration (IJeC)*, 3(2): 16–35.

Kossler, M. E. and Prestridge, S. (2003). Going the distance: The challenges of leading a dispersed team. *Leadership in Action*, 23(5): 3–6.

Kotlarsky, J., Oshri, I. and Willcocks, L. P. (2007). Social ties in globally distributed software teams: beyond face-to-face meetings. *Journal of Global Information Technology Management*, 10(4): 7–34.

Larbi, N. E. and Springfield, S. (2004). When no one's home: Being a writer on remote project teams. *Technical Communication*, 51(1): 102–108.

Larsen, K. R. and McInerney, C. R. (2002). Preparing to work in the virtual organization. *Information & Management*, 39(6): 445–456.

Larsen, T. J. and Levine, L. (2005). Searching for management information systems: coherence and change in the discipline. *Information Systems Journal*, 15(4): 357–381.

Latapie, H. and Tran, V. (2007). Subculture formation, evolution and conflict between regional teams in virtual organizations. *The Business Review, Cambridge*, 7(2): 189–193.

Lau, E. K. (2007). The use of an online discussion forum for case sharing in business education. *International Journal of Learning Technology*, 3(1): 18–31.

Lee, B. and Jeong, Y.-I. (2008). Mapping Korea's national R&D domain of robot technology by using the co-word analysis. *Scientometrics*, 77(1): 3–19.

Lee, G., DeLone, W. and Espinosa, J. A. (2006). Ambidextrous coping strategies in globally distributed software development projects. *Communications of the ACM*, 49(10): 35–40.

Lee, W. H. (2008). How to identify emerging research fields using scientometrics: An example in the field of information security. *Scientometrics*, 76(3): 503–525.

Lee, Y.-s. (2011a). Creating and managing global organizational teams. *Journal of Global Business Issues*, 5(1): 73–77.

Lee, Y.-s. (2011b). Distinguishing between leaders and leadership in global business. *Journal of Global Business Management*, 7(1): 1–7.

Lee-Kelley, L. (2002). Situational leadership: Managing the virtual project team. *Journal of Management Development*, 21(6): 461–476.

Lee-Kelley, L., Crossman, A., and Cannings, A. (2004). A social interaction approach to managing the invisibles of virtual teams. *Industrial Management & Data Systems*, 104(8): 650–657.

Lee-Kelley, L. and Sankey, T. (2008). Global virtual teams for value creation and project success: A case study. *International Journal of Project Management*, 26(1): 51–62.

Leinonen, P. and Bluemink, J. (2008). The distributed team members' explanations of knowledge they assume to be shared. *Journal of Workplace Learning*, 20(1): 38–53.

Leinonen, P. and Jarvela, S. (2006). Facilitating interpersonal evaluation of knowledge in a context of distributed team collaboration. *British Journal of Educational Technology*, 37(6): 897–916.

Lepsinger, R. and DeRosa, D. (2010). *Virtual team success: A practical guide for working and leading from a distance.* John Wiley & Sons.

Levasseur, R. E. (2012). People skills: leading virtual teams—A change management perspective. *Interfaces*, 42(2): 213–216.

Levina, N. and Vaast, E. (2008). Innovating or doing as told? Status differences and overlapping boundaries in offshore collaboration. *MIS Quarterly*, 32(2): 307–332.

Li, W. and Qiu, Z. (2006). State-of-the-art technologies and methodologies for collaborative product development systems. *International Journal of Production Research*, 44(13): 2525–2559.

Limburg, D. and Jackson, P. J. (2007). Teleworkflow: supporting remote control with workflow management systems. *New Technology, Work and Employment*, 22(2): 146–167.

Limburg, D. and Jackson, P. J. (2011). Information systems supporting remote control: An evaluation framework. *Journal of Organisational Transformation & Social Change*, 8(2): 143–161.

Lin, C., Standing, C. and Liu, Y.-C. (2008). A model to develop effective virtual teams. *Decision Support Systems*, 45(4): 1031–1045.

Ling, Y.-H. and Jaw, B.-S. (2011). Entrepreneurial leadership, human capital management and global competitiveness: an empirical study of Taiwanese MNCs. *Journal of Chinese Human Resources Management*, 2(2): 117–135.

Lipnack, J. (1997). *Virtual teams: Reaching across space, time, and organizations with technology.* Jeffrey Stamps.

Liu, D.-R., Lin, C.-W. and Chen, H.-F. (2013). Discovering role-based virtual knowledge flows for organizational knowledge support. *Decision Support Systems*, 55(1): 12–30.

Liu, X., Magjuka, R. J. and Lee, S.-H. (2008). An examination of the relationship among structure, trust, and conflict management styles in virtual teams. *Performance Improvement Quarterly*, 21(1): 77–93.

Liu, Y. C. and Li, F. (2012). Exploration of social capital and knowledge sharing: An empirical study on student virtual teams. *International Journal of Distance Education Technologies (IJDET)*, 10(2): 17–38.

Lojeski, K. S. and Reilly, R. R. (2008). *Uniting the virtual workforce: Transforming leadership and innovation in the globally integrated enterprise*, Vol 2. John Wiley & Sons.

London, M. (2013). Generative team learning in Web 2.0 environments. *The Journal of Management Development*, 32(1): 73–95.

Lount, R. B., Park, E. S., Kerr, N. L., Messé, L. A. and Seok, D.-H. (2008). Evaluation concerns and the Köhler effect: The impact of physical presence on motivation gains. *Small Group Research*, 39(6): 795–812.

Lowry, P. B., Roberts, T. L., Romano, N. C., Cheney, P. D. and Hightower, R. T. (2006). The impact of group size and social presence on small-group communication does computer-mediated communication make a difference? *Small Group Research*, 37(6): 631–661.

Lu, M., Watson-Manheim, M. B., Chudoba, K. M. and Wynn, E. (2006). Virtuality and team performance: Understanding the impact of variety of practices. *Journal of Global Information Technology Management*, 9(1): 4–23.

Lurey, J. S. and Raisinghani, M. S. (2001). An empirical study of best practices in virtual teams. *Information & Management*, 38(8): 523–544.

Majchrzak, A., Rice, R. E., Malhotra, A., King, N. and Ba, S. (2000). Technology adaption: the case of a computer-supported inter-organizational virtual team. *MIS Quarterly*, 24(4): 569–600.

Malhotra, A. and Majchrzak, A. (2004). Enabling knowledge creation in far-flung teams: best practices for IT support and knowledge sharing. *Journal of Knowledge Management*, 8(4): 75–88.

Malhotra, A. and Majchrzak, A. (2005). Virtual workspace technologies. *MIT Sloan Management Review*, 46(2): 11–14.

Malhotra, A., Majchrzak, A., Carman, R. and Lott, V. (2001). Radical innovation without collocation: A case study at Boeing-Rocketdyne. *MIS Quarterly*, 229–249.

Malhotra, A., Majchrzak, A. and Rosen, B. (2007). Leading virtual teams. *The Academy of Management Perspectives*, 21(1): 60–70.

Martins, L. L., Gilson, L. L. and Maynard, M. T. (2004). Virtual teams: What do we know and where do we go from here? *Journal of Management*, 30(6): 805–835.

Martins, L. L. and Schilpzand, M. C. (2011). Global virtual teams: Key developments, research gaps, and future directions. *Research in Personnel and Human Resources Management*, 30: 1–72.

Massey, A. P. and Montoya-Weiss, M. M. (2006). Unraveling the temporal fabric of knowledge conversion: A model of media selection and use. *MIS Quarterly*, 99–114.

Massey, A. P., Montoya-Weiss, M. M. and Hung, Y.-T. (2003). Because time matters: Temporal coordination in global virtual project teams. *Journal of Management Information Systems*, 19(4): 129–156.

Maynard, M. T., Mathieu, J. E., Rapp, T. L. and Gilson, L. L. (2012). Something(s) old and something(s) new: Modeling drivers of global virtual team effectiveness. *Journal of Organizational Behavior*, 33(3): 342–365.

Maznevski, M. L. and Athanassiou, N. A. (2003). Designing the knowledge-management infrastructure for virtual teams: Building and using social networks and social capital. *Virtual teams that work: Creating conditions for virtual team effectiveness*, 196–213.

Maznevski, M. L. and DiStefano, J. J. (2000). Global leaders are team players: Developing global leaders through membership on global teams. *Human Resource Management*, 39(2–3): 195–208.

Mazze, R. (2008). Creating the virtual team. *Disease Management & Health Outcomes*, 16(3): 145–153.

McCord, A. and Boone, M. D. (2008). Technologies and services in support of virtual workplaces. In *Handbook of research on virtual workplaces and the new nature of business practices*. IGI Global.

McFadzean, E. and McKenzie, J. (2001). Facilitating virtual learning groups: A practical approach. *Journal of Management Development*, 20(6): 470–494.

McNab, A. L., Basoglu, K. A., Sarker, S. and Yu, Y. (2012). Evolution of cognitive trust in distributed software development teams: a punctuated equilibrium model. *Electronic Markets*, 22(1): 21–36.

McNair, L. D., Paretti, M. C. and Kakar, A. (2008). Case study of prior knowledge: Expectations and identity constructions in interdisciplinary, cross-cultural virtual collaboration. *International Journal of Engineering Education*, 24(2): 386–399.

McNamara, K., Dennis, A. R. and Carte, T. A. (2008). It's the thought that counts: The mediating effects of information processing in virtual team decision making. *Information Systems Management*, 25(1): 20–32.

Mehandjiev, N. and Odgers, B. (1999). AMBA: Agent-supported visual interactive control for distributed team building and empowerment. *BT Technology Journal*, 17(4): 72–77.

Mesmer-Magnus, J. R., DeChurch, L. A., Jimenez-Rodriguez, M., Wildman, J. and Shuffler, M. (2011). A meta-analytic investigation of virtuality and information sharing in teams. *Organizational Behavior and Human Decision Processes*, 115(2): 214–225.

Mewton, L., Ware, J. and Grantham, C. (2005). A question of leadership: Which skills and competencies will be most critical for leaders as the workplace continues to evolve? *Leadership in Action*, 24(6): 14–15.

Michaelides, R., Morton, S. C., Michaelides, Z., Lyons, A. C. and Liu, W. (2013). Collaboration networks and collaboration tools: a match for SMEs? *International Journal of Production Research*, 51(7): 2034–2048.

Michaux, V. (2005). Performance des processus de coordination a distance: une approche exploratoire. *Système d'Information et Management*, 10(3): 69–91.

Mihhailova, G. (2007). Virtual teams – just a theoretical concept or a widely used practice? *The Business Review Cambridge*, 7(1): 186–192.

Mihhailova, G., Oun, K. and Turk, K. (2011). Virtual work usage and challenges in different service sector branches. *Baltic Journal of Management*, 6(3): 342–356.

Miles, R. E. and Snow, C. C. (1986). Organizations: new concepts for new forms. *California Management Review*, 10(6): 62–73.

Mockaitis, A. I., Rose, E. L. and Zettinig, P. (2012). The power of individual cultural values in global virtual teams. *International Journal of Cross Cultural Management*, 12(2): 193–210.

Mohrman, S. A. (1999). The contexts of geographically dispersed teams and networks. *Trends in Organizational Behavior*, 6: 63–80.

Mohrman, S. A., Klein, J. A. and Finegold, D. (2003). Managing the global new product development network. *Virtual Teams That Work*, 37.

Monalisa, M., Daim, T., Mirani, F., Dash, P., Khamis, R. and Bhusari, V. (2008). Managing global design teams. *Research-Technology Management*, 51(4): 48–59.

Montel-Dumont, O. (2009). *Travail, emploi, chômage*. La Documentation Française.

Montoya, M. M., Massey, A. P. and Lockwood, N. S. (2011). 3D collaborative virtual environments: exploring the link between collaborative behaviors and team performance. *Decision Sciences*, 42(2): 451–476.

Montoya-Weiss, M. M., Massey, A. P. and Song, M. (2001). Getting it together: Temporal coordination and conflict management in global virtual teams. *Academy of Management Journal*, 44(6): 1251–1262.

Moran, L. (2005). Invited reaction: Virtual team culture and the amplification of team boundary permeability on performance. *Human Resource Development Quarterly*, 16(4): 459–463.

Morris, S. (2008). Virtual team working: making it happen. *Industrial and Commercial Training*, 40(3): 129–133.

Morris, S. A., Marshall, T. E. and Rainer Jr, R. K. (2002). Impact of user satisfaction and trust on virtual team members. *Information Resources Management Journal (IRMJ)*, 15(2): 22–30.

Morris, S. A. and McManus, D. J. (2002). Information infrastructure centrality in the agile organization. *Information Systems Management*, 19(4): 8–12.

Mortensen, M. and Hinds, P. J. (2001). Conflict and shared identity in geographically distributed teams. *International Journal of Conflict Management*, 12(3): 212–238.

Mtshali, P. Q. and Korrapati, R. (2000). An xml-based group decision support system for enhanced collaboration. *Academy of Information and Management Sciences Journal*, 3(1): 63.

Muethel, M., Gehrlein, S. and Hoegl, M. (2012a). Socio-demographic factors and shared leadership behaviors in dispersed teams: Implications for human resource management. *Human Resource Management*, 51(4): 525–548.

Muethel, M., Siebdrat, F. and Hoegl, M. (2012b). When do we really need interpersonal trust in globally dispersed new product development teams? *R&D Management*, 42(1): 31–46.

Mukherjee, D., Hanlon, S. C., Kedia, B. L. and Srivastava, P. (2012a). Organizational identification among global virtual team members: The role of individualism-collectivism and uncertainty avoidance. *Cross Cultural Management: An International Journal*, 19(4): 526–545.

Mukherjee, D., Lahiri, S., Mukherjee, D. and Billing, T. K. (2012b). Leading virtual teams: how do social, cognitive, and behavioral capabilities matter? *Management Decision*, 50(2): 273–290.

Mullin, R. (1996). Managing the outsourced enterprise. *Journal of Business Strategy*, 17(4): 28–36.

Munkvold, B. E. (2005). Experiences from global e-collaboration: Contextual influences on technology adoption and use. *IEEE Transactions on Professional Communication*, 48(1): 78–86.

Naik, N. and Kim, D. (2010). An extended adaptive structuration theory framework for determinants of virtual team success.

Nandhakumar, J. and Baskerville, R. (2006). Durability of online teamworking: patterns of trust. *Information Technology & People*, 19(4): 371–389.

Nedelko, Z. (2008). The role and importance of groupware for teamwork. *The Business Review, Cambridge*, 10(1): 211–217.

Neff, M. W. and Corley, E. A. (2009). 35 years and 160,000 articles: A bibliometric exploration of the evolution of ecology. *Scientometrics*, 80(3): 657–682.

Nemiro, J. (2001). Connection in creative virtual teams. *Journal of Behavioral and Applied Management*, 3(2): 92–112.

Nemiro, J. (2004). *Creativity in virtual teams: Key components for success*, Vol 6. John Wiley & Sons.

Nemiro, J., Beyerlein, M. M., Bradley, L. and Beyerlein, S. (2008). *The handbook of high performance virtual teams: A toolkit for collaborating across boundaries*. John Wiley & Sons.

Nevo, D. and Wand, Y. (2005). Organizational memory information systems: a transactive memory approach. *Decision Support Systems*, 39(4): 549–562.

Newell, S., David, G. and Chand, D. (2007). An analysis of trust among globally distributed work teams in an organizational setting. *Knowledge and Process Management*, 14(3): 158–168.

Nicholson, D. B., Sarker, S., Sarker, S. and Valacich, J. S. (2007). Determinants of effective leadership in information systems development teams: An exploratory study of face-to-face and virtual contexts. *Journal of Information Technology Theory and Application (JITTA)*, 8(4): 5.

Niederman, F. and Tan, F. B. (2011). Managing global IT teams: Considering cultural dynamics. *Communications of the ACM*, 54(4): 24–27.

Norel, P. (2009). *L'histoire économique globale*. Seuil.

Nosek, J. and Mandviwalla, M. (1996). Mobile group support technologies for any-time, any-place team support. *Information Technology & People*, 9(4): 58–70.

Nunamaker Jr, J. F., Briggs, R. O., Mittleman, D. D., Vogel, D. R. and Balthazard, P. A. (1996). Lessons from a dozen years of group support systems research: a discussion of lab and field findings. *Journal of Management Information Systems*, 13(3): 163–207.

Nunamaker Jr, J. F., Reinig, B. A. and Briggs, R. O. (2009). Principles for effective virtual teamwork. *Communications of the ACM*, 52(4): 113–117.

Nyström, C. A. and Asproth, V. (2013). Virtual teams support for technical communication? *Journal of Organisational Transformation & Social Change*, 10(1): 64–80.

Ocker, R. J. (2005). Influences on creativity in asynchronous virtual teams: a qualitative analysis of experimental teams. *Professional Communication, IEEE Transactions on*, 48(1): 22–39.

Olaniran, B. and Edgell, D. (2008). Cultural implications of collaborative information technologies (CITS) in international online collaborations and global virtual teams. In *The handbook of research on virtual workplaces and the new nature of business practices*, 120–129. IGI Global.

O'Leary, M. B. and Cummings, J. N. (2007). The spatial, temporal, and configurational characteristics of geographic dispersion in teams. *MIS Quarterly*, 31(3): 433–452.

O'Leary, M. B. and Mortensen, M. (2010). Go (con) figure: Subgroups, imbalance, and isolates in geographically dispersed teams. *Organization Science*, 21(1): 115–131.

Olson, G. M. and Olson, J. S. (2000). Distance matters. *Human–Computer Interaction*, 15(2): 139–178.

Olson, J. and Olson, L. (2012). Virtual team trust: task, communication and sequence. *Team Performance Management*, 18(5/6): 256–276.

Olson-Buchanan, J. B., Rechner, P. L., Sanchez, R. J. and Schmidtke, J. M. (2007). Utilizing virtual teams in a management principles course. *Education+ Training*, 49(5): 408–423.

Oshri, I., Kotlarsky, J. and Willcocks, L. P. (2007). Global software development: Exploring socialization and face-to-face meetings in distributed strategic projects. *The Journal of Strategic Information Systems*, 16(1): 25–49.

Oshri, I., Kotlarsky, J. and Willcocks, L. (2008). Missing links: building critical social ties for global collaborative teamwork. *Communications of the ACM*, 51(4): 76–81.

Oyedele, A. and Minor, M. S. (2011). Customer typology: 3D virtual world. *Journal of Research in Interactive Marketing*, 5(1): 29–49.

Pandey, S. and Sharma, R. (2011). Organization development interventions for prospectors: A theoretical framework and its empirical validation. *Global Business & Management Research*, 3(1).

Panteli, N. and Davison, R. M. (2005). The role of subgroups in the communication patterns of global virtual teams. *IEEE Transactions on Professional Communication*, 48(2): 191–200.

Panteli, N. and Duncan, E. (2004). Trust and temporary virtual teams: Alternative explanations and dramaturgical relationships. *Information Technology & People*, 17(4): 423–441.

Paretti, M. C. and McNair, L. D. (2008). Communication in global virtual activity systems. In *Handbook of research on virtual workplaces and the new nature of business practices*, 24–38. IGI Global.

Paul, S., Samarah, I. M., Seetharaman, P. and Mykytyn Jr, P. P. (2004a).

An empirical investigation of collaborative conflict management style in group support system-based global virtual teams. *Journal of Management Information Systems*, 21(3): 185–222.

Paul, S., Seetharaman, P., Samarah, I. and Mykytyn, P. P. (2004b). Impact of heterogeneity and collaborative conflict management style on the performance of synchronous global virtual teams. *Information & Management*, 41(3): 303–321.

Paul, S., Seetharaman, P., Samarah, I. and Mykytyn, P. (2005). Understanding conflict in virtual teams: An experimental investigation using content analysis. In *System Sciences, 2005. HICSS'05. Proceedings of the 38th Annual Hawaii International Conference*, 44a. IEEE.

Pauleen, D. (2004). *Virtual teams: Projects, protocols and processes*. IGI Global.

Pauleen, D. and Corbitt, B. J. (2003). Using knowledge management processes to develop and implement organizational training strategies for virtual teams: An action learning approach. In *PACIS*, 49.

Pauleen, D. J. (2003a). An inductively derived model of leader-initiated relationship building with virtual team members. *Journal of Management Information Systems*, 20(3): 227–256.

Pauleen, D. J. (2003b). Leadership in a global virtual team: an action learning approach. *Leadership & Organization Development Journal*, 24(3): 153–162.

Pauleen, D. J. and Yoong, P. (2001). Relationship building and the use of ICT in boundary-crossing virtual teams: a facilitator's perspective. *Journal of Information Technology*, 16(4): 205–220.

Pawar, K. S. and Sharifi, S. (1997). Physical or virtual team collocation: Does it matter? *International Journal of Production Economics*, 52(3): 283–290.

Pazos, P. (2012). Conflict management and effectiveness in virtual teams. *Team Performance Management*, 18(7/8): 401–417.

Persson, J. S. and Mathiassen, L. (2010). A process for managing risks in distributed teams. *IEEE Software*, 27(1): 20–29.

Peters, L. and Karren, R. J. (2009). An examination of the roles of trust and functional diversity on virtual team performance ratings. *Group & Organization Management*, 34(4): 479–504.

Peters, L. M. and Manz, C. C. (2007). Identifying antecedents of virtual team collaboration. *Team Performance Management*, 13(3/4): 117–129.

Piccoli, G. and Ives, B. (2003). Trust and the unintended effects of behavior control in virtual teams. *MIS Quarterly*, 365–395.

Piccoli, G., Powell, A. and Ives, B. (2004). Virtual teams: team control structure, work processes, and team effectiveness. *Information Technology & People*, 17(4): 359–379.

Pinjani, P. and Palvia, P. (2013). Trust and knowledge sharing in diverse global virtual teams. *Information & Management*.

Pless, N. M., Maak, T. and Stahl, G. K. (2011). Developing responsible global leaders through international service-learning programs: The ulysses experience. *Academy of Management Learning & Education*, 10(2): 237–260.

Pliskin, N. (1997). The telecommuting paradox. *Information Technology & People*, 10(2): 164–172.

Polzer, J. T., Crisp, C. B., Jarvenpaa, S. L. and Kim, J. W. (2006). Extending the faultline model to geographically dispersed teams: How co-located subgroups can impair group functioning. *Academy of Management Journal*, 49(4): 679–692.

Poppe, E., Brown, R. A., Recker, J. C. and Johnson, D. M. (2013). Improving remote collaborative process modelling using embodiment in 3D virtual environments. In *Conferences in Research and Practice in Information Technology*. Australian Computer Society Inc.

Porter, M. E. (2008). *On competition*. Harvard Business Press.

Powell, A., Galvin, J. and Piccoli, G. (2006). Antecedents to team member commitment from near and far: A comparison between co-located and virtual teams. *Information Technology & People*, 19(4): 299–322.

Powell, A., Piccoli, G. and Ives, B. (2004). Virtual teams: a review of current literature and directions for future research. *ACM Sigmis Database*, 35(1): 6–36.

Quinn, R. E. (1988). *Beyond rational management: mastering the paradoxes and competing demands of high performance*. Jossey-Bass.

Qureshi, S., Liu, M. and Vogel, D. (2006). The effects of electronic collaboration in distributed project management. *Group Decision and Negotiation*, 15(1): 55–75.

Qureshi, S. and Vogel, D. (2001). Adaptiveness in virtual teams: Organisational challenges and research directions. *Group Decision and Negotiation*, 10(1): 27–46.

Rack, O., Ellwart, T., Hertel, G. and Konradt, U. (2011). Team-based rewards in computer-mediated groups. *Journal of Managerial Psychology*, 26(5): 419–438.

Rad, P. F. and Levin, G. (2003). *Achieving project management success using virtual teams*. J. Ross Publishing.

Radoiu, D. (2007). Application development with virtual teams: Models and metrics. In *Enterprise Interoperability II*, 853–864. Springer.

Rafii, F. (1995). How important is physical collocation to product development success? *Business Horizons*, 38(1): 78–84.

Ramasubbu, N., Krishnan, M. S. and Kompalli, P. (2005). Leveraging global resources: A process maturity framework for managing distributed development. *IEEE Software*, 22(3): 80–86.

Ramasubbu, N., Mithas, S., Krishnan, M. S. and Kemerer, C. F. (2008). Work dispersion, process-based learning, and offshore software development performance. *MIS Quarterly*, 437–458.

Rasmussen, L. B. and Wangel, A. (2007). Work in the virtual enterprise creating identities, building trust, and sharing knowledge. *AI & Society*, 21(1–2): 184–199.

Rasters, G., Vissers, G. and Dankbaar, B. (2002). An inside look rich communication through lean media in a virtual research team. *Small Group Research*, 33(6): 718–754.

Ratcheva, V. and Vyakarnam, S. (2001). Exploring team formation processes in virtual partnerships. *Integrated Manufacturing Systems*, 12(7): 512–523.

Redman, C. A. and Sankar, C. S. (2005). Results of an experiment comparing the analysis of Chick-fil-A case study by virtual teams versus face-to-face teams. *Journal of STEM Education: Innovations and Research*, 4(1).

Reed, A. H. and Knight, L. V. (2010). Effect of a virtual project team environment on communication-related project risk. *International Journal of Project Management*, 28(5): 422–427.

Remidez Jr, H., Stam, A. and Laffey, J. M. (2007). Web-based template-driven communication support systems: using shadow netWorkspace to support trust development in virtual teams. *International Journal of e-Collaboration (IJeC)*, 3(1): 65–73.

Rentsch, J. R., Mello, A. L. and Delise, L. A. (2010). Collaboration and meaning analysis process in intense problem solving teams. *Theoretical Issues in Ergonomics Science*, 11(4): 287–303.

Reza, B., Ali, A. and James, T. L. (2006). A study of communication and coordination in collaborative software development. *Journal of Global Information Technology Management*, 9(1): 44–61.

Rezgui, Y. (2007). Exploring virtual team-working effectiveness in the construction sector. *Interacting with Computers*, 19(1): 96–112.

Rice, D. J., Davidson, B. D., Dannenhoffer, J. F. and Gay, G. K. (2007). Improving the effectiveness of virtual teams by adapting team processes. *Computer Supported Cooperative Work (CSCW)*, 16(6): 567–594.

Richard, E. P. and Pierre, A. B. (2002). Understanding human interactions and performance in the virtual team. *JITTA: Journal of Information Technology Theory & Application*, 4(1): 1.

Rico, R., Bachrach, D. G., Sanchez-Manzanares, M. and Collins, B. J. (2011). The interactive effects of person-focused citizenship behaviour, task interdependence, and virtuality on team performance. *European Journal of Work and Organizational Psychology*, 20(5): 700–726.

Rico, R. and Cohen, S. G. (2005). Effects of task interdependence and type of communication on performance in virtual teams. *Journal of Managerial Psychology*, 20(3/4): 261–274.

Riemer, K. and Vehring, N. (2012). Virtual or vague? A literature review exposing conceptual differences in defining virtual organizations in IS research. *Electronic Markets*, 22(4): 267–282.

Ritke-Jones, W. F. (2008). Using cyberspace to promote transformative learning experiences and consequently democracy in the workplace. In *Handbook of research on virtual workplaces and the new nature of business practices*. IGI Global.

Robert, K., Charles, S., Chan Alice, P., Brian, B. and Anne, H. (1999). Coordination and virtualization: The role of electronic networks and personal relationships. *Organization Science*, 10(6): 722–740.

Robert, L. and You, S. (2013). Are you satisfied yet? Shared leadership, trust and individual satisfaction in virtual teams. *iConference 2013 Proceedings*, 461–466.

Robert, L. P., Denis, A. R. and Hung, Y.-T. C. (2009). Individual swift trust and knowledge-based trust in face-to-face and virtual team members. *Journal of Management Information Systems*, 26(2): 241–279.

Roberts, T. L., Lowry, P. B. and Sweeney, P. D. (2006). An evaluation of the impact of social presence through group size and the use of collaborative software on group member. *IEEE Transactions on Professional Communication*, 49(1): 28–43.

Rockett, L., Valor, J., Miller, P. and Naude, P. (1998). Technology and virtual teams: using globally distributed groups in MBA learning. *Campus-Wide Information Systems*, 15(5): 174–182.

Rockmann, K. W., Pratt, M. G. and Northcraft, G. B. (2007). Divided loyalties determinants of identification in inter-organizational teams. *Small Group Research*, 38(6): 727–751.

Rodriguez, J. P., Ebert, C. and Vizcaino, A. (2010). Technologies and tools for distributed teams. *IEEE Software*, 27(5): 10–14.

Rodriguez, V., Janssens, F., Debackere, K. and De Moor, B. (2007). Do material transfer agreements affect the choice of research agendas? The case of biotechnology in Belgium. *Scientometrics*, 71(2): 239–269.

Roebuck, D. B. and Britt A. C. (2002). Virtual teaming has come to stay: guidelines and strategies for success. *Southern Business Review*, 28(1): 29–39.

Rolstadas, A. (2013). Experience from continuing education using e-learning. *Journal of Intelligent Manufacturing*, 24(3): 511–516.

Rosen, B., Furst, S. and Blackburn, R. (2006). Training for virtual teams: An investigation of current practices and future needs. *Human Resource Management*, 45(2): 229–247.

Rosen, B., Furst, S. and Blackburn, R. (2007). Overcoming barriers to knowledge sharing in virtual teams. *Organizational Dynamics*, 36(3): 259–273.

Rosenberg, C. (2005). EMEA-US culture clash: resolving diversity issues through reflective evaluated action learning. *Industrial and Commercial Training*, 37(6): 304–308.

Rosenberg, D. and Kumar, J. (2011). Leading global UX teams. *Interactions*, 18(6): 36–39.

Roy, S. R. (2012). Digital mystery: the skills needed for effective virtual leadership. *International Journal of e-collaboration*, 8(3): 56–66.

Roy, U. (1998). Preparing engineers for a future with collaborative technology. *Computer Applications in Engineering Education*, 6(2): 99–104.

Rutkowski, A.-F., Saunders, C., Vogel, D., and Van Genuchten, M. (2007). 'Is it already 4am in your time zone?' Focus immersion and temporal dissociation in virtual teams. *Small Group Research*, 38(1): 98–129.

Rutkowski, A.-F., Vogel, D. R., Van Genuchten, M., Bemelmans, T. M. and Favier, M. (2002). E-collaboration: The reality of virtuality. *IEEE Transactions on Professional Communication*, 45(4): 219–230.

Sadowski-Rasters, G., Duysters, G. and Sadowski, B. M. (2006). *Communication and cooperation in the virtual workplace: Teamwork in computer-mediated-communication*. Edward Elgar Publishing.

Salazar, A., Hackney, R. and Howells, J. (2003). The strategic impact of Internet technology in biotechnology and pharmaceutical firms: insights from a knowledge management perspective. *Information Technology and Management*, 4(2–3): 289–301.

Salton, G. and McGill, M. J. (1983). *Introduction to modern information retrieval*. McGraw-Hill.

Samnani, A.-K., Boekhorst, J. A. and Harrison, J. A. (2013). The acculturation process: Antecedents, strategies, and outcomes. *Journal of Occupational and Organizational Psychology*, 86(2): 166–183.

Sarker, S., Nicholson, D. and Joshi, K. (2005). Knowledge transfer in virtual systems development teams: An exploratory study of four key enablers. *IEEE Transactions on Professional Communication*, 48(2): 201–218.

Sarker, S. and Sahay, S. (2003). Understanding virtual team development: An interpretive study. *Journal for the Association for Information Systems*, 4(1): 1–38.

Sarker, S. and Sahay, S. (2004). Implications of space and time for distributed work: an interpretive study of US–Norwegian systems development teams. *European Journal of Information Systems*, 13(1): 3–20.

Sarker, S. and Schneider, C. (2009). Seeing remote team members as leaders: A study of US–Scandinavian teams. *IEEE Transactions on Professional Communication*, 52(1): 75–94.

Sarker, S., Valacich, J. S. and Sarker, S. (2003). Virtual team trust: instrument development and validation in an IS educational environment. *Information Resources Management Journal (IRMJ)*, 16(2): 35–55.

Saunders, C. S., Rutkowski, A.-F., Van Genuchten, M., Vogel, D. and Orrego, J. M. (2011). Virtual space and place: Theory and test. *MIS Quarterly*, 35(4): 1079–1098.

Schepers, J., De Jong, A., de Ruyter, K. and Wetzels, M. (2011). Fields of gold perceived efficacy in virtual teams of field service employees. *Journal of Service Research*, 14(3): 372–389.

Schiller, S. Z. and Mandviwalla, M. (2007). Virtual team research: an analysis of theory use and a framework for theory appropriation. *Small Group Research*, 38(1): 12–59.

Schlenkrich, L. and Upfold, C. (2009). A guideline for virtual team managers: The key to effective social interaction and communication. *The Electronic Journal of Information Systems*, 12(1): 109–118.

Schmidt, J. B., Montoya-Weiss, M. M. and Massey, A. P. (2001). New product development decision-making effectiveness: Comparing individuals, face-to-face teams, and virtual teams. *Decision Sciences*, 32(4): 575–600.

Schweitzer, L. and Duxbury, L. (2010). Conceptualizing and measuring the virtuality of teams. *Information Systems Journal*, 20(3): 267–295.

Scullion, H. and Collings, D. G. (2006). Alternative forms of international assignments. *Global Staffing*, 159–173.

Senge, P. M. (1990). *The fifth discipline: The art & practice of the learning organization*. Random House Digital, Inc.

Shachaf, P. (2005). Bridging cultural diversity through. *Journal of Global Information Technology Management*, 8(2): 46–60.

Sharp, J. H. and Ryan, S. D. (2011). Global agile team configuration. *Journal of Strategic Innovation and Sustainability*, 7(1): 120–134.

Shim, J. P., Warkentin, M., Courtney, J. F., Power, D. J., Sharda, R. and Carlsson, C. (2002). Past, present, and future of decision support technology. *Decision Support Systems*, 33(2): 111–126.

Shin, Y. (2004). A person–environment fit model for virtual organizations. *Journal of Management*, 30(5): 725–743.

Shin, Y. (2005). Conflict resolution in virtual teams. *Organizational Dynamics*, 34(4): 331–345.

Short, J., Piccoli, G., Powell, A. and Ives, B. (2005). Investigating multilevel relationships in information systems research: an application to virtual teams research using hierarchial linear modeling. *Journal of Information Technology Theory and Application (JITTA)*, 7(3): 1–26.

Simons, T. L. and Peterson, R. S. (2000). Task conflict and relationship conflict in top management teams: the pivotal role of intragroup trust. *Journal of Applied Psychology*, 85(1): 102.

Sivunen, A. and Valo, M. (2006). Team leaders' technology choice in virtual teams. *IEEE Transactions on Professional Communication*, 49(1): 57–68.

Smith, P. B. (2002). Culture's consequences: something old and something new. *Human Relations*, 55(1): 119–135.

Smith, P. G. and Blanck, E. L. (2002). From experience: leading dispersed teams. *Journal of Product Innovation Management*, 19(4): 294–304.

Sole, D. and Edmondson, A. (2002). Situated knowledge and learning in dispersed teams. *British Journal of Management*, 13(S2): S17–S34.

Sparrow, P. R. (2000). New employee behaviours, work designs and forms of work organization: what is in store for the future of work? *Journal of Managerial Psychology*, 15(3): 202–218.

Stahl, G., Björkman, I., Farndale, E., Morris, S. S., Paauwe, J., Stiles, P., Trevor, J. and Wright, P. (2012). Six principles of effective global talent management. *Sloan Management Review*, 53(2): 25–42.

Staples, D. S. and Webster, J. (2008). Exploring the effects of trust, task interdependence and virtualness on knowledge sharing in teams. *Information Systems Journal*, 18(6): 617–640.

Sternitzke, C. and Bergmann, I. (2009). Similarity measures for document mapping: A comparative study on the level of an individual scientist. *Scientometrics*, 78(1): 113–130.

Stough, S., Eom, S., and Buckenmyer, J. (2000). Virtual teaming: a strategy for moving your organization into the new millennium. *Industrial Management & Data Systems*, 100(8): 370–378.

Sultanow, E., Weber, E. and Cox, S. (2011). A semantic e-collaboration approach to enable awareness in globally distributed organizations. *Interdisciplinary Applications of Electronic Collaboration Approaches and Technologies*, 7(1): 1–16.

Sussman, L. (2008). Disclosure, leaks, and slips: Issues and strategies for prohibiting employee communication. *Business Horizons*, 51(4): 331–339.

Sutanto, J., Phang, C. W., Tan, C. H. and Lu, X. (2011). Dr. Jekyll *vis-à-vis* Mr. Hyde: Personality variation between virtual and real world. *Information & Management*, 48(1): 19–26.

Symons, J. and Stenzel, C. (2007). Virtually borderless: An examination of culture in virtual teaming. *Journal of General Management*, 32(3): 1–17.

Tavana, M. and Kennedy, D. T. (2006). N-site: A distributed consensus building and negotiation support system. *International Journal of Information Technology & Decision Making*, 5(1): 123–154.

Thamhain, H. J. (2011). Critical success factors for managing technology-intensive teams in the global enterprise. *EMJ – Engineering. Management Journal*, 23(3): 30–36.

Thomas, D. and Bostrom, R. (2008). Building trust and cooperation through technology adaptation in virtual teams: Empirical field evidence. *Information Systems Management*, 25(1): 45–56.

Thomas, D. M. and Bostrom, R. P. (2010). Team leader strategies for enabling collaboration technology adaptation: team technology knowledge to improve globally distributed systems development work. *European Journal of Information Systems*, 19(2): 223–237.

Thomas, K. W. (1992). Conflict and negotiation processes in organizations. *Handbook of Industrial and Organizational Psychology*, 3: 652–717.

Thomas, R. J., Bellin, J., Jules, C. and Lynton, N. (2012). Global leadership teams: diagnosing three essential qualities. *Strategy & Leadership*, 40(3): 25–29.

Thomsen, J., Kunz, J. C. and Levitt, R. E. (2007). Designing quality into project organizations through computational organizational simulation. *Journal of Organizational Computing and Electronic Commerce*, 17(1): 1–27.

Timmerman, C. E. and Scott, C. R. (2006). Virtually working: Communicative and structural predictors of media use and key outcomes in virtual work teams. A previous version of this work was presented as a top 3 paper in the organizational communication division at the International Communication Association Annual Conference, New Orleans, LA (May 2004). *Communication Monographs*, 73(1): 108–136.

Tiwana, A. and Bush, A. (2001). A social exchange architecture for distributed web communities. *Journal of Knowledge Management*, 5(3): 242–249.

Townsend, A. M., DeMarie, S. M. and Hendrickson, A. R. (1998). Virtual teams: Technology and the workplace of the future. *The Academy of Management Executive*, 12(3): 17–29.

Trzcielinski, S. and Wypych-Zoltowska, M. (2008). Toward the measure of virtual teams effectiveness. *Human Factors and Ergonomics in Manufacturing & Service Industries*, 18(5): 501–514.

Tuffley, D. (2009). Leadership of integrated teams in virtual environments. In *Handbook of research on socio-technical design and social networking systems*. Massey University (Albany), Auckland, New Zealand.

Turban, E., Liang, T.-P. and Wu, S. P. (2011). A framework for adopting collaboration 2.0 tools for virtual group decision making. *Group Decision and Negotiation*, 20(2): 137–154.

Turel, O. and Zhang, Y. J. (2011). Should I e-collaborate with this group?

A multilevel model of usage intentions. *Information & Management*, 48(1): 62–68.

Tyran, K. L., Tyran, C. K., and Shepherd, M. (2003). Exploring emerging leadership in virtual teams. In *Virtual teams that work: Creating conditions for virtual team effectiveness*, 183–195. Jossey Bass.

Uflacker, M. and Zeier, A. (2011). A semantic network approach to analyzing virtual team interactions in the early stages of conceptual design. *Future Generation Computer Systems*, 27(1): 88–99.

Verburg, R. M., Bosch-Sijtsema, P. and Vartiainen, M. (2013). Getting it done: Critical success factors for project managers in virtual work settings. *International Journal of Project Management*, 31(1): 68–79.

Vlaar, P. W., van Fenema, P. C. and Tiwari, V. (2008). Co-creating understanding and value in distributed work: How members of onsite and offshore vendor teams give, make, demand, and break sense. *MIS Quarterly*, 32(2): 227–255.

Wageman, R. (1995). Interdependence and group effectiveness. *Administrative Science Quarterly*, 145–180.

Wakefield, R. L., Leidner, D. E., and Garrison, G. (2008). Research note: A model of conflict, leadership and performance in virtual teams, *Information Systems Research*, 19(4): 434–455.

Wallerstein, I. (1974). The rise and future demise of the world capitalist system: concepts for comparative analysis. *Comparative Studies in Society and History*, 16(4): 387–415.

Walsh, J. P. and Ungson, G. R. (1991). Organizational memory. *Academy of Management Review*, 16(1): 57–91.

Walther, J. B. and Bunz, U. (2005). The rules of virtual groups: Trust, liking, and performance in computer-mediated communication. *Journal of Communication*, 55(4): 828–846.

Wang, C.-W., Chen, A. S.-Y. and Lin, Y.-C. (2011). Exploring the creativity performance of virtual teams from the perspectives of leadership and creative personality. *Chiao Da Management Review*, 31(1): 135–168.

Wang, C.-W., Fan, K.-T., Hsieh, C.-T. and Menefee, M. L. (2009). Impact of motivating language on team creative performance. *Journal of Computer Information Systems*, 50(1): 133–140.

Warkentin, M. and Beranek, P. M. (1999). Training to improve virtual team communication. *Information Systems Journal*, 9(4): 271–289.

Warkentin, M. E., Sayeed, L. and Hightower, R. (1997). Virtual teams versus face-to-face teams: An exploratory study of a web-based conference system. *Decision Sciences*, 28(4): 975–996.

Watson-Manheim, M. B., Chudoba, K. M. and Crowston, K. (2012). Perceived discontinuities and constructed continuities in virtual work. *Information Systems Journal*, 22(1): 29–52.

Webster, J. and Wong, W. (2008). Comparing traditional and virtual group forms: identity, communication and trust in naturally occurring project teams. *The International Journal of Human Resource Management*, 19(1): 41–62.

Wegner, D. M. (1987). Transactive memory: A contemporary analysis of the group mind. In *Theories of Group Behavior*, 185–208. Springer.

Wegner, D. M., Giuliano, T. and Hertel, P. T. (1985). Cognitive interdependence in close relationships. In *Compatible and Incompatible Relationships*, 253–276. Springer.

Weinstein, O. (2011). L'organisation des entreprises dans une économie mondialisée. *Cahiers Français*, 365(1): 70–75.

Wikipedia (2012a). Information systems. Available at: http://en.wikipedia.org/wiki/Informationsystems. (Accessed 14 March 2016.)

Wikipedia (2012b). Information technology infrastructure. Available at: http://en.wikipedia.org/wiki/Information_technology_ infrastructure. (Accessed 14 March 2016.)

Wikipedia (2012c). Organizational structure. Available at: https://en.wikipedia.org/wiki/Organizationalstructure. (Accessed 14 March 2016.)

Wilson, J., Crisp, C. B. and Mortensen, M. (2013). Extending construal level theory to distributed groups: Understanding the effects of virtuality. *Organization Science*, 24(2): 629–644.

Wilson, J. M., Straus, S. G. and McEvily, B. (2006). All in due time: The development of trust in computer-mediated and face-to-face teams. *Organizational Behavior and Human Decision Processes*, 99(1): 16–33.

Wilson, S. (2003). Forming virtual teams. *Quality Progress*, 36(6): 36–41.

Winkler, V. A. and Bouncken, R. B. (2011). How does cultural diversity in global innovation teams affect the innovation process? *EMJ – Engineering Management Journal*, 23(4): 24–35.

Wong, S.-S. and Burton, R. M. (2000). Virtual teams: what are their characteristics, and impact on team performance? *Computational & Mathematical Organization Theory*, 6(4): 339–360.

Workman, M. (2005). Virtual team culture and the amplification of team boundary permeability on performance. *Human Resource Development Quarterly*, 16(4): 435–458.

Xue, Y., Sankar, C. and Mbarika, V. W. (2004). Information technology outsourcing and virtual team. *Journal of Computer Information Systems*, 45(2): 9–16.

Yates, K. and Beech, R. (2006). Six crucial steps to effective global communication. *Strategic Communication Management*, 10(5): 26–29.

Yoo, Y. and Alavi, M. (2004). Emergent leadership in virtual teams: what do emergent leaders do? *Information and Organization*, 14(1): 27–58.

Zaccaro, S. J. and Bader, P. (2003). E-leadership and the challenges of leading e-teams: Minimizing the bad and maximizing the good. *Organizational Dynamics*, 31(4): 377–387.

Zakaria, N., Amelinckx, A. and Wilemon, D. (2004). Working together apart? Building a knowledge-sharing culture for global virtual teams. *Creativity and Innovation Management*, 13(1): 15–29.

Zander, L., Mockaitis, A. I. and Butler, C. L. (2012). Leading global teams. *Journal of World Business*, 47(4): 592–603.

Zhang, P., Li, N. and Sun, H. (2006). Affective quality and cognitive absorption: Extending technology acceptance research. In *System Sciences, 2006. HICSS'06. Proceedings of the 39th Annual Hawaii International Conference on*, Vol 8: 207a. IEEE.

Zhang, S. and Fjermestad, J. (2006). Bridging the gap between traditional leadership theories and virtual team leadership. *International Journal of Technology, Policy and Management*, 6(3): 274–291.

Zhang, S., Tremaine, M., Egan, R., Milewski, A., O'Sullivan, P. and Fjermestad, J. (2009). Occurrence and effects of leader delegation in virtual software teams. *International Journal of e-Collaboration (IJeC)*, 5(1): 47–68.

Zhang, S., Tremaine, M., Milewski, A. E., Fjermestad, J. and O'Sullivan, P. (2012). Leader delegation in global software teams: occurrence and effects, *Electronic Markets*, 22(1): 37–48.

Zhuge, H. (2003). Workflow and agent-based cognitive flow management for distributed team cooperation. *Information & Management*, 40(5): 419–429.

Zigurs, I. (2003). Leadership in virtual teams: Oxymoron or opportunity? *Organizational Dynamics*, 31(4): 339–351.

Zivick, J. (2012). Mapping global virtual team leadership actions to organizational roles. *The Business Review, Cambridge*, 19(2): 18–25.

Zolin, R., Hinds, P. J., Fruchter, R. and Levitt, R. E. (2004). Interpersonal trust in cross-functional, geographically distributed work: A longitudinal study. *Information and Organization*, 14(1): 1–26.

Index

and collaboration 139–41
definition of 137
workflow systems *see* workflow
   systems
workflow systems 67, 138–9, 141, 166,
   230–31
working from home 8, 82, 243
work-life balance 19, 21, 123, 174, 205,
   230–32, 245

world-system 15, 23
Wypych-Zoltowska, M. 18

Xue, Y. 134

Yoong, P. 59

Zander, L. 162
Zhuge, H. 139